£9·45

PLATONISM AND POETRY IN THE TWELFTH CENTURY

The Literary Influence of the School of Chartres

Platonism
and
Poetry
in the Twelfth Century

THE LITERARY INFLUENCE OF
THE SCHOOL OF CHARTRES

Winthrop Wetherbee

PRINCETON, NEW JERSEY
PRINCETON UNIVERSITY PRESS
1972

Publication of this book
has been aided by a grant from
the Louis A. Robb Fund
of Princeton University Press

This book has been composed
in Linotype Electra, with Caslon display
Printed in the United States of America by
Princeton University Press
Princeton, New Jersey

For Paul Piehler

CONTENTS

vii

CONTENTS

ACKNOWLEDGMENTS

I would like to acknowledge the kindness of the University Library, Cambridge, and the Trustees of the British Museum in allowing me to quote from unpublished material in their possession, and of the Clarendon Press, Oxford, in permitting me to borrow the text and translation of the lyric "Dant ad veris honorem" from Peter Dronke, *Medieval Latin and the Rise of European Love-Lyric.* I am also grateful to the Fordham University Press for permission to reprint portions of my article "The Function of Poetry in the *De planctu naturae* of Alain de Lille," which originally appeared in *Traditio* 25 (1969), and to the Pontifical Institute of Medieval Studies, Toronto, for a similar kindness in regard to my article "The Literal and the Allegorical: Jean de Meun and the *De planctu naturae,*" which was published in *Medieval Studies* 33 (1971).

My research for this book has been aided by a Kent Graduate Fellowship awarded by the Danforth Foundation, and by a grant from the College of Arts and Sciences of Cornell University. Leisure to complete and revise it has been provided by a fellowship awarded by the American Council of Learned Societies. The project first took shape as a doctoral dissertation under the direction of Professor Phillip Damon, to whom I am grateful for much sound advice. I have gladly incorporated a number of valuable suggestions made by Professors Theodore Silverstein and John V. Fleming, who read my work for the Press. I have found an unfailing source of provocative dialogue and generous information in my medievalist colleagues at Cornell, John Freccero, Robert E. Kaske, Giuseppe Mazzotta, Joseph S. Wittig, and especially Thomas D. Hill. I am very grateful also for the conversation and encouragement of William R. H. Alexander, Neil H. Hertz, Phillip L. Marcus, Frank D. McConnell, and Richard S. Peterson. Such friends and colleagues, and my beloved Andrea, have helped to make the writing of this book a great pleasure.

WINTHROP WETHERBEE

Seville
March 1971

PREFACE

It will be obvious how much this study owes to previous scholarship, particularly in regard to twelfth-century intellectual history. A secondary purpose of my work, in fact, is to show the relevance to literary study of the work of scholars concerned with twelfth-century philosophy, theology, and biblical study. There is a tendency to treat medieval literary theory as static, its laws irrevocably fixed by St. Augustine or by the *Rhetorica ad Herennium*, but its evolution was gradual, and can not be separated from developments in these other fields. Aside from the standard works of Chenu and de Lubac, my principal *auctores* have been Marie-Thérèse d'Alverny, Roger Baron, Tullio Gregory, Edouard Jeauneau, Theodore Silverstein, and Jerome Taylor. I regret not having become familiar earlier with Robert Javelet's important volumes on the *imago Dei* in twelfth-century thought; in particular his analyses of the roles of cosmological and physical doctrines in Victorine and Cistercian authors would have enriched greatly the comparisons I suggest between the Chartrians and other schools of thought in the period.

In dealing with the position of poetry in the twelfth century I have often been guided by Huizinga's pioneering study of Alain de Lille. His insights into the relations of poetry and philosophy remain fresh and important after forty years, and my few specific citations are not an adequate reflection of his contribution to this study. I have also found particularly suggestive Richard McKeon's analysis of the ambiguous status of poetry in twelfth-century thought, and Silverstein's demonstration of how, in the work of Bernardus Silvestris, poetry supplements philosophy and presents its insights in a subtler, more oblique and less controversial form than rational argumentation can attain. The precedent of Peter Dronke's bold interpretations of the medieval lyric has encouraged me to follow out my own intuitions as to the meaning of the complex imagery of the Chartrian poets. The particular focus of this study has enabled me to make only limited use of the writings of C. S. Lewis and D. W. Robertson, but despite basic disagreements

xi

my reading of medieval poetry has been fundamentally affected by both. To have thought through one's quarrels with these critics is to realize the extent of their contribution to our understanding of medieval allegory.

One note of clarification seems necessary, regarding the frequent mention in the following pages of the School of Chartres, "Chartrian" ideas and "Chartrian" poetry. It must be understood that the Chartrian label is largely a matter of convenience, and refers to a body of ideas and the scholars and poets who developed them, as well as to an institution precisely located in place and time. Most of the major figures with whom I deal had close ties with the actual cathedral school at Chartres, where Bernard lectured and where Thierry's "Heptateuch" came to define the program of studies; but as R. W. Southern has recently shown, the evidence linking Guillaume de Conches, John of Salisbury, Bernardus Silvestris, and Gilbert de la Porrée with the School has been somewhat overworked, and many hypotheses about the role of Chartres in the humanist movement of the twelfth century have unjustly assumed the status of dogma. In any case, as I hope will be sufficiently clear, my main concern is with a continuity of intellectual interests, and with the development of certain ideas and motifs in philosophy and poetry.

PLATONISM AND POETRY IN THE TWELFTH CENTURY

The Literary Influence of the School of Chartres

1108-09.   Adelhard of Bath, *De eodem et diverso*
1114-26.   Bernard, teacher of Guillaume de Conches and Gilbert de la Porrée, teaching at Chartres
1115-50.   Thierry (brother of Bernard?) active in the schools
1119-25.   Peter Abelard, *Introductio ad theologiam, Theologia christiana*
1120-54.   Guillaume de Conches active in the schools
1130.   Hugh of St. Victor, *Didascalicon*
1138-41.   John of Salisbury a student under Guillaume de Conches
1142.   *Metamorphosis Goliae episcopi*
1147.   Bernardus Silvestris, *De mundi universitate (Cosmographia)*, dedicated to Thierry
1150-60.   *Roman d'Eneas*
1159.   John of Salisbury, *Metalogicon*
1160-70.   Alain de Lille, *De planctu naturae*
1165-70.   Chrétien de Troyes, *Erec et Enide*
1175.   Matthew of Vendome, *Ars versificatoria*
1182.   Alain de Lille, *Anticlaudianus*
1184.   Jean de Hanville, *Architrenius*
1185-87.   Andreas Capellanus, *De amore*
1240.   Henri d'Andeli, *Li Bataille des vii ars*

INTRODUCTION

The purposes of this book are three: to characterize the work of an important group of twelfth-century poets; to explain the intellectual background against which their work must be read and the conception of poetry on which it is based; and to suggest their place in the literary history of the twelfth century, the period when medieval poetry came into its own. The dominant figures in this group are the philosophical allegorists Bernardus Silvestris, Alain de Lille, and Jean de Hanville, and the unifying element in their work is their common engagement with the Platonism of the School of Chartres.

That the Chartrian poets are "important" has been recognized for a long time, but their importance has been variously explained. It was a century ago that Hauréau compared Bernardus Silvestris to Dante, and claimed to see in Alain de Lille "le plus fecond et le plus brillant de tous les mystiques de ce temps." Since Hauréau wrote the meaning and the merits of these poets have been much debated. Much has been made of their role in promulgating "naturalist" views and so preparing the way for the arch-naturalist Jean de Meun; this is the theme of a famous essay by Faral, and has been elaborated with varying degrees of distortion by subsequent critics. But no less an authority than Étienne Gilson has argued the essential orthodoxy of the allegory of Bernardus Silvestris, R. H. Green has reassessed the poems of Alain de Lille to the same end, and the standard of Paul and Augustine has been planted in the rich earth of the *Roman de la Rose* itself by D. W. Robertson and his followers. Eugenio Garin and Cesare Vasoli have responded to Gilson and Green by pointing out the difficulty of classifying such complex syntheses as those of Bernardus and Alain on the basis of their orthodoxy or heterodoxy, and have reopened in a more tentative way the old question of naturalistic elements.

The School of Chartres itself has been the subject of a similar debate but here, at least, a reasonably balanced judgment can now be made. Our knowledge of twelfth-century Platonism has greatly increased in recent years, making it possible to see the thought of

3

Chartres as less isolated and less subversive than it had once appeared, and to recognize the definite limits within which a prevailing traditionalism allowed it to develop. Though the Chartrians plainly exercised a new freedom in their cosmological speculations and their reliance on secular *auctores*, and incurred a certain amount of criticism from traditionalists, their methods and insights were also exploited in twelfth-century spirituality, and subsumed by an "anagogical" view of nature derived from the pseudo-Dionysius and John Scotus Eriugena. Both the real differences which existed between Chartrian Platonism and the more mystical thought of their contemporaries—between what I call "rationalism" and "symbolism"—and the synthesis which was effected between the two points of view are important for an understanding of the poetry inspired by Chartrian thought.

The great originality of the Chartrians consisted in their emphasis on the rational and scientific as against traditional authority. At the same time they were continually engaged with syncretistic and "sapiential" conceptions in which intuition played a major role. Where this intuitive element was not reduced to a version of the anagogical, symbolist point of view, it tended to express itself in what may most simply be called poetry. Chartrian thought, it can be said, begins and ends in a kind of poetry: poetic intuition is finally the only means of linking philosophy and theology, pagan *auctores* and Christian doctrine, *sapientia* and *eloquentia*. The Chartrian ideal of a "cohaerentia artium," a perfect marriage of Philology and Mercury, is ultimately a poetic metaphor, a figure no more capable of objective realization than Cardinal Newman's omniscient Man of Philosophic Habit.

In the symbolist view, poetry in this sense is displaced by an avowed mysticism, for it looks to a reality which is beyond conceptualization in even the purest Platonic terms. It is the difference between seeing in nature as a whole the copy of an ideal world, analogous to, and so metaphorically accessible in terms of, our own world, and seeing in nature only a cluster of individual natures, any of which can be fully understood only as it is seen to

4

embody the divine. Poetry is the highest possible expression of the rationalist view, completing its hard-won insights into the *musica mundana*; but to the symbolist view, whose objects are real only in a sense that transcends human insight, poetry of this Platonic sort is finally irrelevant. The rationalist's allegory begins with the discovery and, as it were, the personification of natural forces and processes; the symbolist's, on the level of the bestiary or lapidary, in a poetry which already defies analysis.

As we will see, the opposition between rationalism and symbolism is by no means absolute: Hugh of St. Victor, probably the single most influential "symbolist," was deeply versed in the rationalist cosmological tradition, and incorporated a number of typically Chartrian insights into the system of his *De Sacramentis*. Conversely, we find the philosopher Gundissalinus drawing on Hugh's analysis of divine revelation in expounding the heterodox Arabic doctrine of the "three worlds." The clear opposition between Hugh and Guillaume de Conches did not prevent a mid-twelfth-century compiler from trying to combine the *Didascalicon* and the *De philosophia mundi*, and similar fusions of Chartrian and Victorine thought were attempted by the Cistercian Garnier de Rochefort and the Porretan theologian Alain de Lille. For the two views have in common a deep concern with the ascent of the mind to the vision of truth, "per creaturas ad creatorem." This is the great theme of the poets of the Chartrian tradition, and in the *De mundi universitate* and *Anticlaudianus* rationalism and symbolism function together far more effectively than in the more scientific theology of the period.

This is of course a complex subject and will be treated in detail below. More easily explained and of equal importance for later literature are the fortunes of the School of Chartres itself. An antiphilosophical movement seems to have developed in the schools of northern France toward the mid-century, centered among the Cistercians but visible also at St. Victor, and its effect was to discredit the study of the *artes* as a worthy accompaniment to serious religious thought. During the general decline of liberal studies in the

5

next few decades, the study of the *auctores* was carried on chiefly at such centers as Tours and Orleans, where *grammatici* paid lip-service to the ideal of the omniscient philosopher but were mainly interested in their own special varieties of belles-lettres. In the history of humanism it was, as Bolgar says, a period of selective assimilation, following naturally on the great advances of the earlier years of the century. There was also a tendency to take the *auctores* less seriously, and to value modern culture more highly in comparison. The *artes poeticae* appeared, challenging students to essay the *ornatus difficilis* for themselves, and setting modern examples of style side by side with *flores* from the classical poets. Latin as well as vernacular poetry used modern forms for classical themes, suggesting a new familiarity. In all of this the tradition of Chartres had its influence: Bernardus Silvestris turned the essence of Chartrian thought into poetry in his much-imitated *De mundi universitate*; the apparatus of learning which Guillaume de Conches had applied to the *integumenta* of the *Timaeus* survived to point a moral in the glosses of Arnulf of Orleans on Ovid and Lucan; Jean de Hanville lectured at Rouen on the inseparability of universal learning from great poetry, and was felt by many to have attained this lofty ideal in his *Architrenius*.

Indeed it was as a result of its relegation to the sphere of mere literature that Chartrian thought found its noblest and most influential expression in the series of philosophical allegories which is the principal concern of this study. With the cosmology of Plato's *Timaeus* and the theory of macrocosm and microcosm as a framework, these poems explore the significance of the cosmos as a motive force and source of meaning in human existence, centering on the ordering power of nature and natural philosophy as means to stability and moral guidance. They exploit the freedom of reference discovered by Guillaume de Conches in the *integumenta*, the philosophical myths and metaphors of the *Timaeus*, and emulate the richly suggestive diction and imagery of Martianus Capella and Boethius, as well as the more mystical Neoplatonism of the pseudo-Dionysian tradition, and so serve to crystallize a number of major traditions in twelfth-century thought.

As I shall try to show, however, it is essential to recognize in the work of these poets not simply a poeticizing of, but a development from previous thought; for as J.A.W. Bennett observes, each poet "continues the exploration both of what may be said in terms of poetry, and of the manner of saying it, beyond the point to which the exploration has been carried before." This extension and refinement typify the relations of poets within the tradition, as well as their common relation to the Platonisms current in their day. It is evident in their changing response to the cosmic model which provides the framework for their allegories. All the Chartrian poets were deeply aware of the sense in which their cosmology, and the rhetorical *ornatus* with which the *auctores* had adorned it, stood for a perfection of consciousness, an integration with the *musica mundana*, which man has lost, and toward which he yearns in his art and speculation. This insight gives continuity to the attempts of these poets to adapt their allegory to other and more complicated aspects of human experience than the philosophical relationships which are their *donnée*. In the poems of Bernardus and Alain, Chartrian humanism becomes itself a theme for poetry, and the quest for knowledge is shown to be less important than the act of self-definition implicit in it. In the *Architrenius* of Jean de Hanville, and in the *Roman de la Rose* as augmented by Jean de Meun, the framework of society interposes itself between man and nature, and the old Platonist assumptions about the guiding power of cosmic order are subjected to the test of worldly experience. The ascent to spiritual vision becomes a less immediate concern than the need to recover from the *descensus ad inferos*, the immersion of the spirit in the chaos and duplicity of earthly life. As worldly standards of *largitas* and *curialitas* are set in coexistence with traditional moral values, and with the scholarly "comprehensio eorum quae sunt" declared by Thierry of Chartres to be the mark of the wise man, ambiguities inevitably arise, and often seem to reflect the deliberate intention of the author. This conflict of ideal and worldly values finds its allegorical counterpart in a tension between formal and realistic elements of personification and detail which gradually leads to the total transformation of the old allegorical patterns, and

7

finally, in the work of such late medieval poets as Chaucer, to their fragmentation. But these late developments are beyond the scope of the present study.

Nearly half of this book is devoted to the intellectual milieu of Chartrian poetry. I have tried to show the function of poetic imagination in the thought of Chartres, which was particularly concerned with the implications of analogy, and sought constantly to devise an epistemology adequate to its sense of the implications of formal order, in the universe and in the mind. This poetic element in philosophical speculation was closely bound up with a new willingness to recognize deep significance in the writings of the *auctores*, and reveals a conception of the capacities of human reason and imagination which was outgrowing the restrictive assumptions of earlier monastic *accessus ad auctores* and pedagogical writings. Literary theory and practice were intimately related in the twelfth century, and a new appreciation of the vision and techniques of the ancient authors inspired *moderni* to expand the range of their own art and address problems not readily definable in terms of conventional wisdom. As background to discussing the exploitation of ancient forms and themes by the poets of the Chartrian tradition, I have devoted a chapter to the allegories of Boethius and Martianus Capella, and the commentaries of Guillaume de Conches and Bernardus Silvestris upon them. Both Boethius and Martianus dramatize the experience of the philosopher, and they were, with Plato, the most influential exponents of the theme which, as formulated in the commentaries of Bernardus, became virtually the archetypal pattern of Chartrian allegory: the theme of what may be called intellectual pilgrimage, the experience of the spirit in its attempts to rise above its earthly situation through an understanding of *naturalia* and attain a vision of truth. This theme, common to Bernardus, Alain de Lille, and Jean de Hanville, was recognized by them as a unifying concern of the great *auctores* from Plato to Boethius, and was, of course, so regarded by Dante.

In a brief chapter on the poetry of the schools I have tried to give a representative survey of the adaptation of the themes and motifs of the Chartrians and their *auctores* to the uses of various

John has this vision △ it is static - does not involve a pilgrimage, moment.

minor poetic genres. In addition to illustrating the more general shifts from cosmology to psychology, and philosophy to poetry, which mark the course of the Chartrian tradition from the mid-twelfth century, these poems dramatize and elaborate problems encountered by the Chartrians. The *Metamorphosis Goliae,* written shortly after the death of Abelard, is perhaps the most striking document we have regarding the uncertain situation of humanism in the face of the authoritarian reaction mentioned above. It is also a paradigmatic illustration of the uneasy relationship between mythology and cosmology in the Chartrian reading of classical poetry, the difficulty of reconciling violence and adultery among the gods with their roles as symbols of cosmic and psychological order. This general theme, exploited for a variety of purposes in erotic and satirical verse, is explored at length by the Chartrian allegorists, and provides a link between their epic themes and those of later twelfth-century poetry in general.

The chapters which follow are devoted to the major works of Bernardus and Alain, and to a general and very tentative survey of relations between the Chartrians and vernacular poets. The allegories of Bernardus and Alain may be seen as complementary. Bernardus' account of the creation in his *De mundi universitate* says all that can be said about the human condition in strictly "natural" terms, and his cosmogony serves finally to define, by the limitations it reveals, the need for a new dispensation. In his *De planctu naturae* and *Anticlaudianus* Alain develops the relation of the new dispensation to the old in a series of rich sexual and cosmic metaphors which provide innumerable points of comparison. His synthesis of mystical and cosmological Platonism may be seen as a poetic counterpart to the system of the *De sacramentis* of Hugh of St. Victor. Both Bernardus and Alain, in their development of imagery capable of linking allusively the orders of nature and grace, and in their elaboration of the "epic" aspects of their theme, reveal striking affinities with the early romancers, notably Chrétien de Troyes and the anonymous author of the *Eneas.*

A final chapter deals with two works in which Chartrian allegory is tested by the facts of life in the world. The *Architrenius*, by Jean

9

de Hanville, is both the least known and the most controversial of major Chartrian allegories. It seems deliberately to reject Alain's assertion of the need for redemption, and the total transformation of man's natural state, and seeks instead a purely natural norm by which human life may be rectified. The *Architrenius* is the earliest attempt to incorporate significant amounts of realistic detail into what remains basically a cosmological allegory. The bulk of the poem is a ramble through scenes illustrative of the vices of the age, but it begins and ends as a quest for the meaning of Nature. Its structure, and its mixture of the realistic and the abstract, give the work a strong resemblance to the *Roman de la Rose*, and like the *Roman* it raises questions which it cannot answer. In the very process of redirecting the Chartrian tradition and bringing its influence to bear on social themes, Jean de Hanville signals the beginning of the end of the tradition in its recognizable form. His search for a rational alternative to the Christian Platonist view of man is undertaken in a spirit more strictly humanistic than that of Bernardus or Alain, but he lacked both their philosophical understanding and their powers of synthesis, and his assertion of the standard of Moderation as the answer to the problems raised by his poem is deeply unsatisfying. The *Architrenius* is finally most significant in its anticipation of the concern with the relations of authority and experience, institution and practice, which characterizes the poetry of the later middle ages.

From the work of Jean de Hanville it is only a step to that of Jean de Meun, whose use of Chartrian materials seems to be carefully confined to the delineation of problems, and who does not attempt to vindicate the view of life which his allegory portrays. His elusive and ironic point of view toward his human *personae* looks forward beyond the middle ages, and the real affinity of the *Roman* is with the great satires of the Renaissance humanists.

CHAPTER ONE

TWELFTH-CENTURY PLATONISM AND THE PURSUIT OF WISDOM

1. The Twelfth-Century Renaissance

In his *Dialogus super auctores*, composed in the early twelfth century, Conrad of Hirsau warns his students about reading Ovid.[1] The *Fasti* and the *Ex Ponto*, he says, contain tolerable matter, but the *Metamorphoses* present problems. At times Ovid seems to have deviated into sense in the poem: the "quisquis fuit ille deorum" of the opening cosmogony, like the Athenian altar "to the unknown God" of *Acts* 17, suggests a dim awareness of a deity who is one and supreme. But the work as a whole is idolatrous. It tells of men transformed into beasts and stones and birds, and so denies that rationality which proves man to be made in God's image.

Toward the end of the twelfth century Arnulf of Orleans, introducing his commentary on the *Metamorphoses*, gives a different account of the poem.[2] Far from making light of the power of reason, he says, Ovid has attempted "so to describe mutability that we may understand by it not simply those changes which take place around us, altering material things for good or ill, but those also which take place inwardly, in the soul." By these means, Arnulf tells us, Ovid seeks "to recall us from error to a recognition of the true creator."

To explain this spiritual theme, and the correspondence of internal change with cosmic mutability on which it depends, Arnulf describes the two basic movements of the soul: an irrational tendency which imitates the wanderings of the planets, and a rational countermovement like that of the stable firmament; for the firmament governs the planets just as the rational principle should gov-

---

[1] Conrad of Hirsau, *Dialogus super auctores*, ed. R.B.C. Huygens (Brussels, 1955), p. 51.

[2] Fausto Ghisalberti, "Arnolfo d'Orléans, un cultore di Ovidio nel secolo XII," *Memorie del Reale Istituto Lombardo* 24 (1932), p. 181.

ern the irrational and sensual. This tension in the soul accounts for a broad opposition between spiritual and earthly tendencies of will which the *Metamorphoses* depict through fable. In showing transformations from one state of being to another, Ovid stresses continually "the stability of heavenly things and the changeableness of things on earth." And so, Arnulf concludes, the poem is of great value in providing an "erudicio divinorum habita ex mutacione temporalium."

In principle at least, Conrad and the tradition of monastic study which he represents cannot allow Ovid's masterpiece a higher status than that of a handy collection of stories and a model of Latin style.[3] Arnulf is clearly more willing to assess the poem on what he takes to be its own terms. He respects the poet's intuitions and brings a broad range of learning to the task of extracting his deeper meaning. He clearly sees the *utilitas* of the *Metamorphoses* as involving much more than its value as a compendium, or a source of exemplary lessons in moral conduct, the highest function that Conrad will allow any pagan author.

But the very different approaches of the two commentators are determined by historical factors as well as differences of intention. Arnulf's interpretation reflects important intellectual developments which had taken place between Conrad's time and his own.

[3] On classical poetry in the monastic schools prior to the twelfth century, see Jean Leclercq, *The Love of Letters and the Desire for God*, tr. Catherine Misrahi (New York, 1961), pp. 139-84; R. R. Bolgar, *The Classical Heritage and Its Beneficiaries* (Cambridge, 1954), pp. 183-201. Though Ovid was, of course, well known in the early middle ages, such documentary evidence as exists suggests a relative lack of interest in the *Metamorphoses*. The one pre-twelfth-century commentary known to me which deals with Ovid's philosophy does so partly on the assumption that Ovid was a crypto-Christian; see C. Meiser, "Ueber einen Commentar zu den Metamorphosen des Ovid," *Sitzungsberichte der kgl. Bayerischen Akademie der Wissenschaften* (1885), pp. 49-52; Bernhard Bischoff, "Living with the Satirists," in *Classical Influences on European Culture. A.D. 500-1500*, ed. R. R. Bolgar (Cambridge, 1971), pp. 83-84.

On the evolution of the twelfth-century appreciation of Ovid see Franco Munari, *Ovid im Mittelalter* (Zurich and Stuttgart, 1960), pp. 9-14, 22-29; and especially Salvatore Battaglia, "La tradizione di Ovidio nel Medioevo," *Filologia romanza* 6 (1959), pp. 185-91.

His assumption that Ovid's fables are the figural embodiment of philosophical insights, his ready recourse to the structure of the universe for an illustration of the principles of Ovid's psychology, and the close association he suggests between the perception of cosmic order and the "cognitio veri creatoris," all show him responsive to the influence of the "twelfth-century renaissance," with its rediscovery of man and the natural world.[4] An important feature of this rediscovery was a new humanism, a new conception of the value to be derived from the study of the ancient *auctores*; and it was typified by a firm trust in the quasi-poetic cosmology of Plato's *Timaeus* as a source of insight into the meaning of man's cosmic relations. The capacious intellectual framework within which Arnulf places his author and the rich thematic implications, moral and psychological, of the poetic *erudicio* which he finds in the *Metamorphoses*, are of the essence of twelfth-century humanism, and they are the critical counterpart to a new seriousness of spirit and breadth of scope which the poets of the schools, writing in emulation of the *auctores*, had begun to exhibit a generation or so before Arnulf wrote.

It is with these developments and their implications for medieval poetry in general that this book is primarily concerned, and the purpose of this chapter is to sketch the intellectual history of the shift in attitude which I have illustrated by comparing Conrad and Arnulf. I will try to show how the cosmology to which Arnulf alludes was developed in twelfth-century thought, and how it came to hold a special significance for the interpretation of poetry, even such subtle and elusive poetry as Ovid's. We will see, in this and the following chapter, how mythical and psychological analyses of human life were related to this Platonic model, and how, in the

[4] See M. D. Chenu, *La théologie au douzième siècle* (Paris, 1957), pp. 19-51. A selection from this indispensable guide to twelfth-century thought is available in English as *Nature, Man and Society in the Twelfth Century*, tr. Jerome Taylor and L. K. Little (Chicago, 1968); discussion cited, pp. 1-48.

Another application of Burckhardt's famous definition of the Renaissance to the twelfth century is the conclusion to Étienne Gilson, *Heloise and Abelard*, tr. L. K. Shook (Ann Arbor, 1960), pp. 124-44.

course of the century, there emerged a new recognition of the nature and value of imaginative literature as a source of knowledge about God and man.

It goes without saying that these events of literary history are part of a broader movement. The widening of intellectual horizons in the twelfth century was made possible in the first place by social changes.[5] The settling of the Normans in England and Sicily, the flourishing of French feudalism, the expansion of the governmental structure of the Church, all contributed to the demand for lawyers and statesmen, clear thinkers and effective writers, so that facilities for training such men assumed a new importance. This in turn gave rise to a new emphasis on the study of the classical authors, who had never lost their place in education as models of correctness and eloquence. The conquest of Sicily and the reconquest of Spain brought the Latin world into contact with Greek and Arab science and philosophy, an encounter which did much to stimulate the twelfth century's concern with cosmology and metaphysics.

The "renaissance" thus effected was by no means cohesive, and its influence was far from universal: literary studies, under the pressure of practical necessity, declined all too easily to the level of the *ars dictaminis,* whose students, with a few noble exceptions, paid lip-service to the high principles of ancient rhetoric while devoting themselves to letter-writing.[6] The influence of the pioneering transmitters of Greek and Arab lore was slow and haphazard, due perhaps to their wandering in search of new texts and intellectual adventures, and revealed itself as much in a widespread fascination with astrology and divination as in the development of a rational view of nature.[7] But it is plain enough that the early

[5] C. H. Haskins, *The Renaissance of the Twelfth Century* (Cambridge, Mass., 1927), pp. 3-27; Hans Liebeschütz, *Medieval Humanism in the Life and Writings of John of Salisbury* (London, 1951), pp. 84-90; R. W. Southern, *The Making of the Middle Ages* (New Haven, 1953), pp. 170-218.

[6] See L. J. Paetow, *The Arts Course in Medieval Universities,* University of Illinois Studies 3, No. 7 (1910), pp. 3-34, and the introduction to his edition of *La Bataille des vii ars,* by Henri d'Andeli (Berkeley, 1914), pp. 13-31; also G. M. Paré et al., *La Renaissance du douzième siècle. Les écoles et l'enseignement* (Paris and Ottawa, 1933), pp. 27-29.

[7] Liebeschütz, *Medieval Humanism,* pp. 76-78.

twelfth century saw the emergence of a stable and largely self-sufficient intellectual culture. Social stability and increasing commerce provided new leisure for the pursuit of knowledge and channels for its diffusion; the libraries and curricula of the schools expanded; disputation and scholarship became a way of life. The union of *eloquentia* and *scientia,* the arts of expression and the sciences of the *quadrivium,* became a commonplace in educational thought, and their pursuit was increasingly accepted as valuable in itself, rather than simply as a preparation for traditional religious studies. This last point demands special emphasis, for the concession of a certain intrinsic value to learning and philosophy prepared the way, as we will see, for the elevation of poetry to a similar dignity.

The development of a richer and more humane conception of secular learning and a serious interest in the order and meaning of the natural world is paralleled by certain features of twelfth-century spiritual thought. The relations between the human psyche and its macrocosmic environment were a theme for mystical vision and spiritual exercise as well as scientific investigation, and thinkers so diverse as Guillaume de St. Thierry, Hildegarde of Bingen, and Adelhard of Bath show a common concern to curb human *curiositas,* the aimless love of earthly multiplicity, by posing an alternative, structured vision accessible through intuition of a reality underlying the *visibilia* of nature.[8] For the contemplative, a mystical awareness of cosmic symbolism could perform a function strikingly analogous to that of "scientific" Platonism in the speculation of the philosophers. Otto Von Simson, tracing the development of Gothic architecture at St.-Denis and Chartres, has shown how Platonist cosmology and Neoplatonist mysticism conspired with Augustinian musical and mathematical theory to produce an architecture in which cosmic and anagogical vision were synthesized in the form of the sanctuary itself.[9]

This capacity for synthesis is a great achievement of the twelfth

---

[8] This aspect of twelfth-century psychology is documented by Edgar de Bruyne, *Études d'esthétique médiévale* (Bruges, 1946) II, 130-45.

[9] *The Gothic Cathedral,* 2nd edn. (New York, 1962), pp. 21-58.

century, a manifestation of that "mentalité symbolique" whose intellectual history has been written by M. D. Chenu.[10] Noting the growing importance of figurative expression, metaphor and symbol, in the articulation of religious ideas, Chenu sees it as reflecting a pervasive sense of "the mysterious kinship between the physical world and the realm of the sacred." Natural objects are increasingly regarded as expressive of a higher presence operative in and through them, and the response takes forms so diverse as the debate over universals, a new interest in medicine and astrology, and exploratory ventures into the psychology of love. The universe is seen in terms of the cosmic eroticism of hermetic tradition, or the emanationism of the pseudo-Dionysius; man is the center of creation, the hub of the intellectualized cosmos of scientific Platonism, or he is an alien, all but lost in the dense symbolic undergrowth of Arthurian romance.

All these views reflect in some degree a cooperation of imaginative thought and expression with religious vision. They point to a higher world accessible, as Chenu remarks,[11] by a "transposition," a metaphorical reading of the sensible world. "Such symbolic transposition," he goes on, "was the admirable means of penetrating the mysterious material density of things—natural objects or historical personages, biblical or profane—and of getting 'through the shell, to the savory kernel of truth.' Poetry was in the service of wisdom —of philosophical or theological wisdom."

Chenu is speaking broadly here; by "poetry" he means only the recourse to allegory in a general sense, and so he uses the terms "symbol" and "metaphor" almost interchangeably. But in the twelfth century, as Chenu also observes,[12] there was a new tendency to distinguish between these two modes of *figura*, and they came to serve two more or less distinct approaches to the relations between the sensible world and transcendent reality. The relationship between these two approaches, which I have found it convenient to label the "rationalist" and the "symbolic," will be a major concern of this chapter.

[10] *La théologie*, pp. 159-90 (Taylor-Little, pp. 99-145).
[11] *Ibid.*, p. 160 (Taylor-Little, p. 100).
[12] *Ibid.*, pp. 175-78 (Taylor-Little, pp. 123-28).

Metaphor was a fundamental tool of those rationalist philosophers who sought knowledge of God from the study of the structure of the universe and the complex laws, causes, and analogies by which it is linked with the human mind. Symbolism, on the other hand, lent itself to an "anagogical," an open-ended, and ultimately mystical view, closely related to the traditions of biblical exegesis, but tending increasingly to embrace the natural world as well, under the influence of a renewed interest in the cosmic sacramentalism of the pseudo-Dionysius and John Scotus Eriugena. In this view *naturalia* were of value to the extent that they could be seen as directly reflective of God.

The symbolist and rationalist points of view were closely interrelated, and appear at times to be virtually indistinguishable, but it is important to recognize that they were by no means simply complementary. Indeed the differences between them provided the occasion for an ongoing debate which affected every area of twelfth-century thought. The relation of biblical to secular studies underwent profound changes during the century: the Liberal Arts assumed a new importance in the exegesis of sacred texts,[13] while the modes of symbolic interpretation traditionally associated with Scripture were extended to extrabiblical history and the natural world.[14] The development of a theology devoted to seeking the truth of Scripture through the employment of the Arts and the study of nature stimulated serious debate over the extent to which dialectic and secular learning might be allowed to encroach upon the traditional province of exegesis, and the authority of Plato be permitted to coexist with that of Augustine.[15]

A striking instance of the impact of new ideas is the development

[13] See C. Spicq, *Esquisse d'une histoire de l'exégèse latine au moyen âge* (Paris, 1943), pp. 66-83; Beryl Smalley, *The Study of the Bible in the Middle Ages*, 2nd edn. (Oxford, 1952), pp. 76-106; but cp. Henri de Lubac, *Exégèse médiévale* (Paris, 1959-64) i.i, pp. 43-118, where the continuity of twelfth-century practice with traditional biblical study is asserted.

[14] See Chenu, *La théologie*, pp. 159-72 (Taylor-Little, pp. 99-119); de Lubac, *Exégèse* ii.i, pp. 9-14.

[15] On the "Platonisms" of the twelfth century see Chenu, *La théologie*, pp. 108-41 (Taylor-Little, pp. 49-98); Spicq, *Esquisse*, pp. 77-78; de Lubac, *Exégèse* i.i, pp. 79-88, 110-18.

which has been called "the elimination of time," the displacement of the continually evolving plan of salvation by the self-contained structure of the natural universe as a framework for the analysis and dramatization of spiritual experience.[16] The sort of symbolic thinking I have mentioned as typical of the century is the product of a concern with the nature of spiritual reality, its relation to the visible creation, the *opus Sapientiae*, and the psychological process involved in its apprehension; what is often hard to detect is a clear concern with the temporal orientation of the soul in relation to the Last Things. Eschatology in its traditional forms is challenged in twelfth-century thought by an "anagogy" strongly influenced by, and tending always to verge into Neoplatonism,[17] and it is clear that this development is connected with the age's pervasive interest in cosmology. It reflects, of course, only a shift of emphasis, rather than a deliberate substitution, and its radical implications are to a great extent neutralized in the great theological syntheses of a Hugh of St. Victor or an Alain de Lille, where cosmology and history are presented as complementary manifestations of God's wisdom. But these thinkers too are keenly sensitive to new modes of thought and expression, and indeed, as I shall try to show, a comparison of Hugh with Alain may serve as an index to the effect of these developments in the course of the century. They stand at opposite ends of a period of debate and experimentation which saw the rise and decline of a great movement of humanistic and scientific thought, a movement of which the signs are visible everywhere in Europe, but which has traditionally been most closely identified with the cathedral school at Chartres.

It was apparently at Chartres, during the School's relatively brief flowering, that the scientific and humanist strains of twelfth-cen-

[16] See de Lubac, *Exégèse* ii.i, pp. 340-41, 418-35; Yves M. J. Congar, "Le sens de l'économie' salutaire dans la 'Théologie' de S. Thomas d'Aquin," in *Festgabe Joseph Lortz* (Baden-Baden, 1957) ii, 73-75. On the twelfth century's awareness and continual revaluation of history and its relation to religious and philosophical thought see Chenu, *La théologie*, pp. 62-77 (Taylor-Little, pp. 162-73).

[17] See Chenu, *La théologie*, pp. 129-35, 174-78 (Taylor-Little, pp. 79-88, 123-28); de Lubac, *Exégèse* i.ii, pp. 640-42.

tury thought received their fullest expression in a curriculum and a philosophy which, solidly grounded in the study of classical authors, sought to embrace the "summa totius philosophiae." This humanist enterprise was uniquely and profoundly important for the subsequent development of medieval poetry, and it is with the fortunes of "Chartrian" ideas, in the twelfth century and after, that this study is mainly concerned. But the special qualities of Chartrian thought and the reasons for its great influence on poetry and poetics will appear more clearly when the work of the School is compared with the more spiritual program of St. Victor as exemplified by Hugh, the most influential of the great Victorine masters. At both schools from an early date the convergence of new currents stimulated a concern for unified and clearly defined educational programs, and the contrast and occasional conflict between them will help us to define important questions about the relation of tradition to progress in the twelfth century. The contrast of Chartrian rationalism with the ultimately traditionalist position of Hugh also serves to explain the gradual discrediting of Chartrian thought and the redirection of the School's influence into the channels of literary study and poetic expression. A survey of these developments will bring us to our main subject, the influence of Chartrian thought on medieval poetry.

2. The School of Chartres

Such topics as the nature and structure of the universe and its relation to the will of God, the value of classical learning, and the relation of ancient philosophy to Christian doctrine were not wholly unfamiliar when they emerged in the twelfth century as the great concerns of Chartrian thought. During the two centuries and more which separate the flowering of Chartres from the great but controversial systematizing of John Scotus Eriugena and the humanist encyclopedism of Remigius of Auxerre there had been grammarians less reluctant than Conrad of Hirsau to concede a humane value to pagan literature.[18] A number of scholars, notably Bovo of

[18] Education from the Carolingian period to the twelfth century is sur-

Corvey and Adalbold of Utrecht, had striven to define the relation of Plato and Boethius to the Augustinian mainstream of Christian thought.[19] Indeed by the end of the eleventh century interest in secular studies had become sufficiently intense to provoke the polemical reaction of Peter Damian, Manegold of Lautenbach, and others, whose condemnations embraced all the ancients from Plato and Pythagoras to the mad and wanton poets.[20]

The great accomplishment of the Chartrians in the next century was the drawing together of the diverse strands of earlier medieval humanism into a coherent program, and the exercise of a new originality and boldness in developing them. A convenient introduction to their work is the *De eodem et diverso* of Adelhard of Bath, composed in the early years of the twelfth century. It is unlikely that Adelhard was ever directly associated with Chartres,[21] but the *De eodem* anticipates in important ways the nature and ideals of Chartrian thought. It is set in the form of a dialogue, in which *Philocosmia*, the love of worldly things, challenges Philosophy for the affections of man, matching wealth, power, rank, fame, and pleasure against the Liberal Arts, and mocking reason and study as

---

veyed by Emile Lesne, *Histoire de la propriété ecclésiastique en France* v (Lille, 1940); see also Bolgar, *The Classical Heritage*, pp. 140-201. On pre-twelfth-century Chartrian humanism see Loran Mackinney, *Bishop Fulbert and Education at the School of Chartres* (Notre Dame, Indiana, 1958), pp. 12-47; A. Clerval, *Les écoles de Chartres au moyen âge* (Chartres, 1895), pp. 30-142.

[19] Platonism was expressed chiefly in commentaries on the *De consolatione philosophiae* of Boethius. See Pierre Courcelle, "Étude critique sur les commentaires de la Consolation de Boèce," *Archives d'histoire doctrinale et littéraire du moyen âge* 12 (1939), pp. 12-76; also his *La consolation de philosophie dans la tradition littéraire* (Paris, 1967), pp. 29-66, 275-99. Commentaries of Bovo and Adalbold, ed. Huygens, "Mittelalterliche Kommentare zum 'O qui perpetua,'" *Sacris erudiri* 6 (1954), pp. 375-98, 404-26. See also Tullio Gregory, *Platonismo medievale: studi e ricerche* (Rome, 1958), pp. 1-15.

[20] See Gregory, *Platonismo medievale*, pp. 17-30; Eugenio Garin, *Studi sul platonismo medievale* (Florence, 1958), pp. 23-33; Courcelle, *La consolation*, p. 301.

[21] See Franz Bliemetzrieder, *Adelhard von Bath* (Munich, 1935), pp. 196-201. Bliemetzrieder dates the *De eodem* c. 1108/9 (pp. 23-27, 89-90).

blind and foolish. Philosophy replies with an account of the human condition which sets the lofty tone of the discourse which follows:[22]

> The creator of things, supremely good, drawing all creatures into his own likeness, so far as their nature allows, has endowed the soul with that mental power which the Greeks call *Nous*. This power she freely enjoys while in her pure condition, untroubled by disturbance from without. She examines not only things in themselves but their causes as well, and the principles of their causes, and from things present has knowledge of the distant future. She understands what she is herself, what the mind is by which she knows, and what the power of reason by which she seeks to know. Once bound by the earthly and vile fetters of the body she loses no small portion of her understanding; but this elemental dross cannot wholly obliterate its splendor. . .

The reminiscences of Plato's *Timaeus*, Boethius' *De consolatione*, Anchises' discourse on the soul in the Vergilian Elysium, define what will come to be the essential context, cosmic and psychological, of Chartrian thought, and introduce a number of its major themes. The cosmos, says Adelhard, is the measure of man's mind and spirit; to know the causes of things is to know one's self,[23] and the way to such knowledge lies through the cultivation of the Seven Liberal Arts. Through these the soul may learn "her duty to her creator, and that of the rest of creation to her."[24] They are her solace, imprisoned by the flesh and its passions, and they are empowered to set her on the path which leads to her true home; for

---

[22] "Des Adelard von Bath Traktat De eodem et diuerso," ed. Hans Willner, *Beiträge zur Geschichte der Philosophie des Mittelalters* 4 (1903), No. 1, pp. 9.33-10.9. All references to the *De eodem* are to page and line in Willner.

[23] *De eodem et diuerso*, p. 14.15-22.

[24] *Ibid.*, pp. 16.30-17.7: "His igitur anima in corporis carcere uinculis oppressa unum inter uniuersa remedium est, quo eadem se sibi reddit domumque reducit: doctrinae uidelicet huius philosophiae artesque, quas uocant, liberales. . . . Has igitur, quotienscumque a uero decidit, si respicit, a casu resurgit. *Habet enim in istis, quid ipsa auctori, quid sibi cetera debeant, rerumque communitates et differentias absolute distinctas.*"

they teach her to participate in the harmony, to gauge the proportions and dimensions of her cosmic environment, and to intuit its archetypal pattern, and in the process enable her to realize her intrinsic dignity and its divine origin. The noble principles here enunciated by Adelhard were basic to the program of Chartres, and his rendering of them in the manner of Boethius and Martianus Capella anticipates more ambitious variations on the same models by the Chartrian poets, Bernardus Silvestris and Alain de Lille.

Adelhard was a pioneer in many respects, an ardent apologist for the disciplines of the *quadrivium* and a tireless seeker of new and better *auctores*.[25] At Chartres there were no such manifestoes until a generation after the writing of the *De eodem*, and the new learning was only gradually assimilated into a more traditional curriculum. It is from the *Metalogicon* of John of Salisbury, written to justify the study of the Arts and *auctores* against the opportunistic logicians of a later day, that we learn of the early stirring of the School's humanist tendencies, and of the work of Bernard, the first of the great twelfth-century *magistri* associated with Chartres. None of Bernard's works survive, but the evidence of John's secondhand account has led scholars to imagine him as a scholar-saint, whose effectiveness as a teacher was "almost magical."[26] The whole range of Chartrian speculation is adumbrated in his attempt to reconcile Platonic idealism with what was understood to be Aristotle's empiricist denial of universals. Following Boethius, who had made a similar attempt, Bernard describes the relation of God's perfect being to created existence in terms of two kinds of form: the true ideal, which, though created, is eternal in the mind of God, and the *forma nativa*, which issues from the ideal but has its existence *in materia*.[27] John of Salisbury expresses skepticism about the pos-

[25] *Ibid.*, p. 32.27-29: "Quod enim Gallica studia nesciunt, transalpina reserabunt; quod apud Latinos non addisces, Graecia facunda docebit."

[26] Bolgar, *Classical Heritage*, p. 175.

[27] *Metalogicon* 4.35 (ed. C.C.J. Webb, Oxford, 1909, pp. 205-06). Cp. Boethius, *De Trinitate* 2 (in *The Theological Tractates and the Consolation of Philosophy*, ed. H. F. Stewart and E. K. Rand, Cambridge, Mass., 1918, pp. 8-12).

sibility of reconciling two men who disagreed "quamdiu in vita licuit," and we may perhaps understand in his famous reference to Bernard as "perfectissimus inter Platonicos seculi nostri" the implication that Bernard had been too deeply committed to realism to understand the full force of the challenge posed by Aristotle.[28] Successful or not, however, Bernard's attempt provided the basis for many Chartrian essays in metaphysics.[29] It reveals, moreover, a concern to harmonize authorities, a sense that knowledge is finally one, which emerges in a simpler form in his teaching, and which remained a Chartrian ideal.

In the famous chapter of the *Metalogicon* which describes Bernard's way of teaching grammar we are shown a rudimentary version of that rigorous scrutiny of the texts of the *auctores* which seems to have been the characteristic activity of the School in its great days.[30] We learn that his treatment of a classical text involved not only the excerpting of illustrations of syntax and rhetoric, and the analysis of *cauillationes sophismatum*, moral problems, and paradoxes, but the demonstration of how the work could be related to other branches of learning. It is uncertain how far Bernard led his students in exploring these other disciplines; much in John's account only serves to remind us of the earlier monastic schools, where systematic instruction was far less important than the ability to adapt the *auctores* to the capacity of a given student, and where the system of the Arts, even when it could be found

[28] *Metalogicon* 4.35 (Webb, p. 205). John is unusually precise in his use of epithets (cp. Abelard who, in his *Introductio ad theologiam* refers to both Cicero and Boethius as "maximus philosophorum latinorum"), but his reference to Bernard is nonetheless hard to interpret. Étienne Gilson, "Le platonisme de Bernard de Chartres," *Revue néoscolastique* 25 (1923), pp. 5-19, suggests that John's characterization of Bernard and his apparent skepticism about the work undertaken by his followers are really a reflection of John's own distrust of realism; by "Platonist" he means simply one who adheres to a doctrine of ideas. See also *Metalogicon* 2.17-19 and Liebeschütz, *Medieval Humanism*, pp. 75-76.

[29] Gilson, "Le platonisme de Bernard," pp. 14-19; Marie-Thérèse d'Alverny, *Alain de Lille: Textes inédits* (Paris, 1965), pp. 163-80.

[30] *Metalogicon* 1.24 (Webb, pp. 55-59).

entire, was a secondary consideration. Bernard himself, John tells us, was concerned in drawing on higher learning to keep his students active and alert, rather than force them to leap from *singulis* to *universa*, and he worried lest they founder in pedantry and lose sight of an objective which was essentially ethical. Nonetheless the description of his methods is prefaced by a vivid description of the riches of classical literature which reflects the concerns of the Chartres of John's own day:[31]

> [The ancient authors], when they had taken up the raw material of history, argument, fable, or whatever, would refine it through *diacresis*, which we might call "illustration" or "imagery," with such abundant learning, such graceful style and adornment, that the finished work would somehow appear an image of all the Arts. All the hosts of Grammar and Poetry pour forth, and take over the whole surface of the matter which is being expounded. Across this field, as it may be called, Logic, bearing the devices of dialectic, casts the golden darts of her reasoning. And Rhetoric, clad in the *topoi* of persuasion and the bright trappings of eloquence, shines with the brilliance of silver. *Mathematica* is borne along in the four-wheeled chariot of her *quadrivium*, and, following in the path of these others, intermingles her manifold variety of devices and charms.[32] Physics, having delved into the secrets of nature, brings forth from her abundant supply the complex splendor of her own ornamentation. . .

The notion that a perfect work of literature is "an image of all the arts" is a characteristic Chartrian idea, but we must not be misled by the rich imagery of this passage. Though John makes Bernard employ the manner of his own Chartrian mentors, the ideal he presents is one which, even at Chartres, meant different things to different people. With Bernard, John regarded moral instruction

[31] *Ibid.*, 1.24 (Webb, pp. 54-55).
[32] *Mathematica* is used here in its general sense as embracing the four sciences of the *quadrivium*; cp. Hugh, *Didascalicon* 2.6 (ed. C. H. Buttimer, Washington, 1939, pp. 29-30).

24

as the greatest benefit of literary study; the passage just quoted is climaxed by the introduction of *Ethica*, "the noblest part of philosophy."[33] He recognized the value of the Arts in developing breadth and acuteness of mind, and once, at least, in a beautiful passage toward the close of the *Metalogicon*, he was moved to extol the power of philosophy, working with Grace, to discern the mysterious *virgo fontana*, the source of existence.[34] But his own ideal, as Liebeschütz has shown, was Cicero's model orator, whose broad learning is oriented wholly toward ethical and political practice.[35]

John stands midway between the intellectualized humanism of the Chartres of his day and a long-standing tradition of Christian humanism; and the deviation of Thierry, Guillaume de Conches, and Bernardus Silvestris from the norm he represents may be seen as paralleling their divergence from the scholastic traditions maintained at St. Victor. The breadth of his learning and the social bearing of his ideals distinguish John from the monastic *grammatici* of an earlier age, but he was at one with them in seeing classical literature as primarily ethical rather than philosophical in value. He seems to have had a deep respect for their assumption that any classic possessed an ethical *utilitas* which, though it might not appear in the literal meaning, or even the conscious intention, of the author, could always be detected by analysis of style and tone, or "reverently expounded" by *moralisatio*.[36] He realized as well that whatever intellectual sophistication one brought to the task of exposition only enhanced the finesse of moral discrimination with which it could be performed. Thus when he suggests that in grammatical studies one must learn "aliqua ignorare," to reject that which is of no significance, he is not cautioning the inexperienced student but challenging the skill of the *grammaticus* himself.[37] And his appreci-

[33] *Metalogicon* 1.24 (Webb, p. 55): "Illa autem que ceteris philosophie partibus preminet, Ethicam dico, sine qua nec philosophi substitit nomen."
[34] *Ibid.*, 4.37 (Webb, p. 208).   [35] *Medieval Humanism*, pp. 63-94.
[36] See E. A. Quain, "The Medieval Accessus ad auctores," *Traditio* 3 (1945), pp. 215-33; Leclercq, *The Love of Letters*, pp. 144-50; and the *accessus* published by R.B.C. Huygens, "Accessus ad auctores," *Latomus* 12 (1953), pp. 296-311, 460-86.
[37] *Metalogicon* 1.24 (Webb, p. 57): "Unde inter uirtutes gramatici mer-

ation of the taste and moral sensitivity with which Bernard had expounded the *auctores* is surely the basis of the deep affinity which he seems to have felt for this master of his own masters.

The Chartrian masters who followed Bernard shared John's appreciation of the value of literary style, but they introduced a significant shift of emphasis. The secular wisdom itself which their reading of the *auctores* revealed, rather than any practical application of it, was their main concern. A common motif in their works is the marriage of Philology and Mercury, wisdom and eloquence, used by Martianus Capella to represent the divine harmony and cosmic scope of the Liberal Arts.[38] John, too, often employs this image to illustrate the necessary basis of social intercourse in the *Metalogicon*,[39] but for the Chartrian masters it was almost a sacred theme, implying the mind's power to attain truth through universal knowledge. Thus Thierry of Chartres, defining the principles of his *Heptateuchon*, a huge compendium of texts relative to the seven Arts which was the basis of the School's curriculum in his day, uses Martianus' allegory to express the Chartrian ideal:[40]

> For we have brought together no mere discoveries of our own, but those of men renowned for their learning in the several arts, and in the hope of producing a noble tribe of philosophers we have joined *trivium* and *quadrivium* in marriage. For so the

---

ito reputatum est ab antiquis, aliqua ignorare." Cp. *Policraticus* 7.2 (ed. Webb, Oxford, 1909, II, 98-99). Comparable to John's "savoir ignorer" but closer to the typical Chartrian view is the doctrine of Fulgentius, *Mitologiae* 3.10 (*Opera*, ed. R. Helm, Leipzig, 1898, p. 78): "Aliut est enim aput grammaticos aliena agnoscere, aliut sua efficere; aput rethores uero aliud est profusa et libero cursu effrenata loquacitas, aliud constricta ueritatisque indagandae curiosa nexilitas . . . uocis ergo pulchritudo delectans interna artis secreta uirtutem etiam misticam uerborum attingit."

[38] On this motif see Gabriel Nuchelmans, "Philologie et son mariage avec Mercure jusqu'à la fin du xiie siècle," *Latomus* 16 (1957), pp. 84-100; M.-T. d'Alverny, "La Sagesse et ses sept filles," in *Mélanges F. Grat* (Paris, 1946) I, 245-78.

[39] The best illustration is *Metalogicon* 1.1 (Webb, p. 8).

[40] *Prologus in Eptateuchon*, ed. Edouard Jeauneau, *Medieval Studies* 16 (1954), 174. In defining *sapientia* Thierry follows Boethius, *De institutione arithmetica* 1.1.

poets of both Greece and Rome declare Philology and Mercury to have been united, amid the rejoicing of Apollo and the Muses, by solemn epithalamic rites, and through the intermediary agency of these seven Arts, as though without these the union could not have been achieved.

Our accomplishment is not without merit: for since the two principal tools of the philosopher are the understanding and that which gives it expression; and since the *quadrivium* illumines the understanding, while the *trivium* supplies it with an elegant, rational, and varied means of expression, it is manifest that our "Seven Books of the Arts" constitute a single unique means to philosophical understanding. Philosophy, moreover, is the love of wisdom, and wisdom is the coherent understanding of the true nature of existence, which can hardly be attained save by one who seeks it with love. No man is wise, therefore, save the philosopher.

For Thierry the Arts are a "synod" called together "ad cultum humanitatis," a phrase which is difficult to interpret, despite its fine ring. For John the Arts are a means "ad cultum virtutis," and "liberal" in that they free man from preoccupations irrelevant to the pursuit of wisdom,[41] but Thierry implies something more. In his view the Arts lead to a transcendent "philosophy" closer to that described by Hugh of St. Victor in the *Didascalicon*. Hugh defines that philosophy of which the Arts are the elements as "the love of that Wisdom which . . . is the living Mind and the sole primordial Idea or Pattern of things."[42] The Arts help to realize human values,

[41] *Metalogicon* 1.23 (Webb, p. 53): "Ceterum operationem *cultumque uirtutis* scientia naturaliter precedit, neque enim uirtus currit in incertum. . . ."; *ibid.* 1.12 (Webb, p. 31): ". . . et sepissime [artes liberales] liberant a curis his, quarum participium sapientia non admittit."

[42] *Didascalicon* 1.2, 2.1 (Buttimer, pp. 6-7, 23); cp. Boethius, *In Porphyrium dialogi* 1.3 (*Patrologia latina*, ed. J.-P. Migne, Paris, 1844-64, 64.10). As Jerome Taylor has shown (tr. *The Didascalicon of Hugh of St. Victor*, New York, 1961, pp. 33-34), Hugh uses "philosophy" in a special sense which includes all religious as well as secular knowledge, though he also employs the conventional division of philosophy into *mechanica* (tech-

for Hugh, insofar as they restore in man his original likeness to God, by creating in his mind the image of the divine wisdom. All the Arts are necessary to this task, since they "so hang together and so depend upon one another in their ideas that if only one of the arts be lacking, all the rest cannot make a man a philosopher."[43]

But the Chartrian vision is finally *sui generis*. It combines something like John of Salisbury's devotion to the *auctores* with an intuition like Hugh's of the transcendent value of philosophy, but without the ethical and political orientation of the one or the other's Augustinian concern to emphasize the contingency of all knowledge on the truth of Scripture and the effects of Grace. It shows a remarkable freedom in relation to traditional authority, and what Häring has aptly characterized as "a pronounced tendency, not to disregard the teaching of the past, but to integrate Christian and non-Christian thoughts and to propose them in a largely new and more scientific form."[44]

3. "Ipsius Veritatis Arcanum": The *Timaeus* at Chartres

Chartrian thought begins and ends in the study of the *auctores*. The respect traditionally accorded to the Fathers was largely transferred to the *philosophi* who comprised the School's curriculum. We can hardly understand the great significance which Thierry's *Heptateuch* had for the Chartrians; the existence of a complete "Book of the Arts," with one or more ancient authors presiding over every discipline, really seemed to bring within the reach of mere *moderni* a vast body of wisdom hitherto inaccessible. Thus Thierry's introduction of Aristotle's *Analytica* and *Sophistici elenchi* into the schools of France was duly recorded in his epitaph, side by side with his own achievements in philosophy, and John of

---

nology), *practica* (ethics), and *theorica* (the Arts, the sum of the Arts). On *theorica* see n. 144 below.

[43] *Didascalicon* 3.4 (Buttimer, p. 55).

[44] N. M. Häring, "The Creation and Creator of the World according to Thierry of Chartres and Clarenbaldus of Arras," *Archives d'histoire* 22 (1955), p. 180.

Salisbury remembered him as "artium studiosissimus investigator."[45] A number of reminiscences in the writings of the famous scholars who were his students proclaim the success of his mating of *sapientia* and *eloquentia*.[46] In the words of his epitaph,[47]

> Though her form had hitherto been veiled, Philosophy revealed herself openly to this man, and permitted herself to be beheld. Having bestowed herself in marriage upon so worthy a husband, she bore sons renowned the world over. Hence springs a progeny blest in both parents; living doctrines give rise to an endless lineage.

The stature assumed by the *auctores* in the School's program had a curious effect on the attitude of the Chartrians toward original thought. Thierry declared with pride that the *Heptateuch*, unlike the compendia of Varro and Martianus, contained "no mere discoveries of our own"; and Guillaume de Conches, the most prolific of the Chartrian scholars, devoted himself mainly to commenting on the texts of the *auctores*, restricting the content of his own systematic works to what might serve "ad philosophorum lectionem."[48]

The greatest of the *auctores* was Plato, whose *Timaeus* was revered as the "flower of all philosophy." It is impossible to exaggerate the importance of the Timaean cosmos as a model for Chartrian thought. Not only was it the framework for original speculation, but all serious literature, indeed all knowledge, was assumed to imply a Platonic cosmological setting without which

[45] *Metalogicon* 1.5 (Webb, p. 16).

[46] Bernardus Silvestris dedicated his *De mundi universitate* to Thierry, and Hermann of Carinthia his translation of the *Planisphere* of Ptolemy; see André Vernet, "Une épitaphe inédite de Thierry de Chartres," in *Recueil de Travaux offert à M. Clovis Brunel* (Paris, 1955) II, 661-62. See also the letter prefixed by Clarembald of Arras to Thierry's *De sex dierum operibus* (ed. Häring, "Creation and Creator," pp. 183-84), which refers to Thierry as "totius Europae philosophorum praecipuus."

[47] Epitaph of Thierry, lines 29-34 (ed. Vernet, "Une épitaphe inédite," p. 670).

[48] Cited from Guillaume's *Dragmaticon* by Edouard Jeauneau, ed. *Glosae super Platonem* by Guillaume de Conches (Paris, 1965), p. 11.

it could not be fully understood.[49] In addition to Calcidius' commentary, the allegory of Martianus' *De nuptiis*, Macrobius' commentary on the *Somnium Scipionis*, the philosophical treatises of Apuleius, and such anonymous works as the Hermetic *Asclepius* were valued largely for the insights they provided into the meaning of Plato's cosmology. Boethius' magnificent cosmic prayer, the "O Qui perpetua," was a brilliant summary of the cosmology of the *Timaeus*, and largely for this reason was one of the texts most frequently glossed throughout the medieval period.[50] Thierry's major work is an attempt to reconcile Plato's cosmogony with the opening verses of *Genesis*, and Guillaume de Conches labored for much of his career over a full-length commentary on the *Timaeus* itself.

All of the speculation inspired by the *Timaeus* depended on certain assumptions present in some form in the text itself. Three of these were fundamental:[51] that the visible universe is a unified whole, a "cosmos"; that it is the copy of an ideal exemplar; and that its creation was the expression of the goodness of its creator. The ideal exemplar, *archetypus mundi*, was identified by the Chartrians with the divine wisdom, while the abiding goodness of the creator was seen as expressed by Plato's World Soul, which thus assumed a providential as well as an organizational function. God the Creator had a double role: He had performed the initial act of creating matter (an evasion of the apparent dualism of the *Timaeus* which was justified in part by certain hints in the commentary of

---

[49] See the anonymous *De mundi constitutione* (PL 90.902A): "Plato cuius auctoritas preponderat et quem maxime Macrobius imitatur," and a gloss from Munich, Clm. 331, f. 2v, cited by Jeauneau, ed. *Glosae super Platonem*, p. 24: "Secundum Timaeum Platonis, id est secundum ipsius veritatis et naturae arcanum." As Jeauneau notes, this echoes Macrobius, *Commentarii in Somnium Scipionis* 1.6.23: "secundum Platonem, id est secundum ipsius veritatis arcanum." The twelfth-century commentator's insertion of the words "et naturae" would seem to emphasize the spiritual connotations of the Platonic *veritas*.

[50] See notes 19 and 20 above.

[51] See the lucid discussion of Raymond Klibansky, "The School of Chartres," in Marshall Clagett et al., *Twelfth-Century Europe and the Foundations of Modern Society* (Madison, 1961), pp. 7-9.

Calcidius),[52] and He was present as the operative force in the formation of the universe.[53]

On the basis of these dogmata it was possible to regard God as both wholly transcendent and accessible to reason through the visible universe. Augustine had noted that the ineffability of Plato's "author," and the contrast of his absolute being with the existence even of the "gods" to whom he delegates his power, are strikingly suggestive of the Mosaic "I am that I am."[54] But to make the cosmic exemplar and the World Soul attributes of God was to bring Him into intimate contact with his handiwork; and so it was possible to engage in virtually unlimited scientific investigation, as Klibansky observes, "without the sense that reason and faith were in conflict or even unrelated to each other."[55] The great value of the *Timaeus*, says Guillaume de Conches in the *accessus* to his commentary, is that "when divine power and wisdom and goodness are beheld in the creation of things, we fear one so powerful, worship one so wise and love one so benevolent."[56] These three aspects of God, whether defined as *opifex*, *archetypus*, and *anima* or as Efficient, Formal, and Final Cause, were the source of all creation, and even conservatives like John of Salisbury discerned in them a manifest expression of the Trinity.[57]

In much of this speculation the Chartrians were in accord with

[52] On twelfth-century treatments of this problem see Theodore Silverstein, "The Fabulous Cosmogony of Bernardus Silvestris," *Modern Philology* (46) (1948-49), 98-104; as Silverstein shows, Calcidius' reference to the Pythagorean *singularitas* and *duitas* as comparable to *deus* and *silva* was appropriated by Thierry as a metaphorical reference to the origin of all things in God. See Calcidius, *Commentarius in Timaeum Platonis* 295 (ed. J. H. Waszink, London and Leiden, 1962, p. 297); Thierry, *De sex dierum operibus* (Häring, "Creation and Creator," pp. 194-95).

[53] Guillaume de Conches, *Glosae super Platonem*, pp. 98-99; Thierry, *De sex dierum operibus* (Häring, "Creation and Creator," pp. 184-85).

[54] *De civitate Dei* 9.10.   [55] *Twelfth-Century Europe*, p. 7.

[56] *Glosae super Platonem*, p. 60. For other occurrences of the formula in the twelfth century see Robert Javelet, "Image de Dieu et nature au xiie siècle," in *La filosofia della natura nel Medioevo: Atti del Terzo Congresso Internazionale di Filosofia Medievale*, 1964 (Milan, 1966), p. 290.

[57] *Policraticus* 7.5 (Webb, II, 108).

contemporary orthodoxy. The identification of the cosmic exemplar with the divine Wisdom of the Trinity had the sanction of patristic tradition, and the separation of the creation of matter "in forma confusionis" from its formation into the ordered universe, though much debated, was defended by Hugh of St. Victor, who was otherwise strongly opposed to his contemporaries' preoccupation with cosmology.[58] The crucial point on which the Chartrians diverged from tradition, and that on which their boldest essays in "natural theology" depended, was their treatment of the World Soul. By an easy extension of the syncretic process which identified the divine Wisdom with the Platonic archetype,[59] it was possible to equate the World Soul with the Holy Spirit, considered as a bond between the universe and the divine Wisdom expressive of God's love. This position was adopted by Thierry and, in his early writings, Guillaume de Conches. But there was much controversy over its implications, for it seemed to many to suggest too radical a separation among the Persons of the Trinity, and to apply indifferently to the whole creation what was intended to apply to man alone. A more acceptable theory, vividly set forth in the opening chapters of Hugh's *Didascalicon*, treated the *anima mundi* as representing the human soul, which, being both sensible and rational, comprehends both the visible and the invisible, and thus "contains" the universe within itself.[60] Guillaume de Conches met severe criticisms, even outright attacks on his position, and so came to reject the precise identification of *anima mundi* with *spiritus sanctus*.[61]

[58] Silverstein, "Fabulous Cosmogony," pp. 98-104. On Hugh's attitude toward cosmological speculation see the excellent discussion of Taylor, tr. *Didascalicon*, pp. 19-28.

[59] Guillaume de Conches, *Glosae super Platonem*, pp. 99, 113, 125-26, 284; Silverstein, "Fabulous Cosmogony," pp. 107-12.

[60] *Didascalicon* 1.1-4 (Buttimer, pp. 4-11).

[61] On Guillaume's rejection of his early view see Gregory, *Platonismo medievale*, pp. 100-34, and *Anima mundi: la filosofia di Guglielmo di Conches e la Scuola di Chartres* (Florence, 1955), pp. 154-74. That the glosses on Boethius as well as those on the *Timaeus* were revised in response to criticism is suggested by Peter Dronke, "L'amor che move il sole e l'altre stelle," *Studi medievali* 6 (1965), pp. 410-13, on the basis of London, B.M. Royal

32

Thus in his later commentaries, and in most cosmological treatises of the period, the World Soul is a principle of uncertain character, possibly the Holy Spirit or a special manifestation thereof, possibly a separate, inferior intermediary between God and the cosmos. In any case it continued to be seen as a link between the sensible and the archetypal world, and as an expression of God's love. It retained a profound importance, for it confirmed the most basic of the Chartrian assumptions about the integrity and significance of cosmic order. Without the World Soul's informing presence, says the anonymous author of the *De mundi constitutione*, "mundus non potest totum vocari."[62] And an anonymous disciple of Guillaume de Conches, defining the World Soul as "ille creatoris amor eternus," asserts that just as we tell by a man's breathing the state of his mind, "ita per huius amoris visionem pervenitur ad mentis divine cognitionem."[63]

Whatever its relation to God, the World Soul was practically autonomous within the universe, and as a result the physical workings of the universe and the sciences through which they were explored assumed a certain autonomy of their own. Thus Thierry, in his *De sex dierum operibus*, interprets the biblical account of creation exclusively "secundum physicam."[64] Once God has performed the initial act of creating the elements and imbuing them with seminal virtues, they themselves become the agents of subsequent creation, fire becoming "quasi artifex et efficiens causa," earth the material cause, and air and water mediating between them. Over the whole process, bestowing form and serving as a *connexio* with God, presides that power which Moses called "spiritus domini," Plato

---

15.B.III. But as Dronke notes, this version cannot with certainty be assigned to Guillaume, though it incorporates virtually all of his commentary, and certain details have suggested to me the possibility of interpolation (and perhaps emendation) by a disciple. See below, n. 104. For another theory regarding Guillaume's supposed second redaction, see below, n. 105.

[62] *De mundi constitutione* (PL 90.910).

[63] Quoted by Gregory, *Platonismo medievale*, p. 126, from Paris, B.N. lat. 8624, f. 17r.

[64] Häring, "Creation and Creator," p. 184.

"anima mundi," and Vergil simply "spiritus," and which Christians recognize as the "spiritus sanctus."[65]

The Chartrians' intense interest in the World Soul, and the large, vague terms in which they conceived its activity, had important consequences for the poetic allegories produced under the influence of Chartrian thought. The World Soul belongs neither to philosophy nor theology, but exists as a sort of *tertium quid* between the two. And it is on just such a middle ground that Bernardus Silvestris and Alain de Lille located the activity of such figures as *Natura* and *Genius*. As Gregory has shown,[66] the attempt to explain the World Soul led directly to the development of the idea of a more or less autonomous "Nature," operative in cosmic and human life and ensuring moral as well as physical stability. The work of this power and its meaning, the scope and limits of its influence, are a major theme of "Chartrian" poetry of many kinds.

For the moment we may note the role of the World Soul in linking the cosmos to the human concerns of Chartrian thought. As the creation culminated in man, so the system of the Chartrians "part d'une cosmologie pour aboutir à une anthropologie,"[67] and both the integrity of the cosmic order in itself and its providential relation to the divine Wisdom were fundamental to the Chartrian view of man as microcosm. As the *Timaeus*, even in its fragmented medieval form, illustrates in fascinating detail, man's physical constitution corresponds to that of the universe: he is composed of the same elements and subject to the same physical laws. The human soul differs from the *anima mundi* only in its liability to confusion by the fallible senses. By nature, and in men before the Fall, it possessed the World Soul's perfect comprehension of the divine Wisdom, and like the World Soul it has vital cosmic affinities. It brings to bear on the human condition those influences, providential and *ex necessitate*, which govern temporal life, and which, as Guillaume de Conches explains with reference to Plato's

[65] *Ibid.*, pp. 193-94.
[66] *Platonismo medievale*, pp. 135-50.
[67] Philippe Delhaye, *Le Microcosmos de Godefroy de St.-Victor* (Lille, 1951), p. 148.

34

notion of the soul's preexistence among the stars, "a Deo fiunt, sed per effectum stellarum."[68] To know nature was thus to know man, and on the basis of their correspondence the twelfth-century cosmologist could shift his emphasis easily from natural to moral law. To discern and adhere to the laws of nature is the basis of rational conduct; "natural justice," the theme of the *Timaeus*, is the foundation of "positive justice," moral and political order. As an anonymous gloss on the *Timaeus* explains, Socrates, finding no state governed by positive justice, designed his own, ordering it "secundum dispositionem quem consideraverat in macrocosmo et microcosmo."[69]

The richer and darker implications of these themes were not fully elaborated in Chartrian thought, and it was left to the poets, Bernardus Silvestris and Alain de Lille, to dramatize the situation of the human psyche amid the complexities of its nature. Indeed the confident rotundity of the Platonic notions just cited is somewhat deceptive; for as Silverstein has noted, it is a difficulty of the Chartrian system that it fails to bridge the gap between different levels of reality. The Chartrians' conception of the harmony between the natural and the divine depended on a series of progressively higher abstractions, in the course of which the visible world came to seem less and less substantial. The analysis of *visibilia* in terms of the Four Causes did not preserve them from this; the clash and fusion of the elements in Thierry's *De sex dierum operibus* are largely a matter of mathematics. Edgar de Bruyne, considering the aesthetic implications of Chartrian thought, makes essentially the same point in suggesting that the Chartrians reduced all perception to the second of the three *gradus contemplationis*.[70] Concerned neither with the superficial nor with the symbolic and

[68] Charles Jourdain, ed. "Des commentaires inédits de Guillaume de Conches et de Nicholas Triveth sur la Consolation de la Philosophie de Boèce," *Notices et extraits des manuscrits de la Bibliothèque Impériale* 20 (1862), pt. 2, p. 78.

[69] Quoted by Gregory, *Platonismo medievale*, p. 61, from Oxford, Bodleian Digby 23, f. 54. Cp. Guillaume de Conches, *Glosae super Platonem*, pp. 58-59.

[70] *Études* II, 278-79.

anagogical aspects of the visible universe, they saw it instead as the work of a perfect artist who had "ordered all things in measure and number and weight," a wholly rational sphere within which one could observe countless analogies between ideal and actual, physical and psychological nature, between the divine order and that which, ideally at least, exists in human life.

What the *Timaeus* gave to the Chartrians, then, and what they in turn transmitted to the poets of the later twelfth century, was a structure, a model of reality which could be "read" allegorically as a means to philosophical understanding. There is obviously a strong imaginative element in speculation of this sort; the *Timaeus* is itself a poetic vision, and its terms, particularly the World Soul, lent themselves readily to adaptation in poetic allegory. There is in fact a markedly poetic tendency in the thought of the Chartrians, and their canon of *auctores*, in which Boethius, Martianus Capella, and the pseudo-Apuleius were treated with equal seriousness as heirs of Plato, could only further this tendency. In the later twelfth century this led poets and commentators to dwell with special emphasis on the *experience* of the philosophizing mind, the quality of its intuitions and the stages of its journey toward truth, and to devote less effort to defining the goal of the journey. Thus it is necessary to examine the ways in which the Chartrians themselves came to terms with the poetic element in the works of their *auctores*, and the special mode of philosophical-literary analysis which they evolved to deal with it.

4. *Integumentum*: The Figural Significance of the *Auctores*

One effect of the Chartrians' reading of the universe was to attribute to natural law an authority which, at least from the methodological standpoint, was not unlike that exercised by Christian doctrine in the interpretation of Scripture,[71] and it is not surprising to

[71] The comparison cannot be pushed too far, and one will seek in vain for a clear medieval formulation of it, but it presents itself again and again in twelfth-century literature. See de Bruyne, *Études* II, 328-34, who concludes: "Lorsque les poètes, en effet, s'inspirent de l'Écriture et même simplement

find that process of abstraction which characterized the Chartrian approach to *visibilia* applied to the texts of the *auctores*. The assimilation of secular writings to Christian contexts, as in the equation of Plato's personifications and mythical figures with the persons of the Trinity, was justified by the conviction that Plato and other ancient philosophers and poets had expressed their deepest wisdom mysteriously, shrouding it in veils of imaginative detail which might consist of mere invented personifications and cryptic etymologies, or involve the use of an extended myth or *fabula*. The relation of such fictions to their underlying truths was like that of the visible world to the divinely ordained cosmic order, and could be discerned by the same rational means, once the presence of such *involucra* was recognized.[72]

In all of this the Chartrians acknowledged the authority of Macrobius who, in a much-quoted passage of his commentary on the *Somnium Scipionis*, had dwelt on the analogy between nature and literature. Those who use fables for serious purposes do so, he suggests,[73]

because they realize that a frank, open exposition of herself is distasteful to Nature, who, just as she has withheld an understanding of herself from the uncouth senses of men by envel-

---

de la Nature, *puisque dans la structure des faits historiques et physiques Dieu a inscrit la figure de réalités surnaturelles et mystérieuses*, ne faut-il pas supposer que dans toutes les oeuvres, il y a au moins un germe de signification allégorique, toutes en définitive parlant de *choses* dont la structure, voulue par Dieu, se réfère à l'*Invisible*?" (Emphases are de Bruyne's.) Attempts to establish a doctrinal harmony between Platonist cosmology and Christian doctrine are discussed by Jeauneau, "Macrobe, source du platonisme chartrain," *Studi medievali* 1 (1960), pp. 12-16. See also the survey of "Christian Humanism" in D. W. Robertson, *A Preface to Chaucer* (Princeton, 1962), pp. 337-65.

[72] This general point of view is analyzed by de Bruyne, *Études* II, 255-301, 368-70.

[73] *Commentarii in Somnium Scipionis* 1.2.17-18 (ed. James Willis, Leipzig, 1963, p. 7; tr. W. H. Stahl, New York, 1952, pp. 86-87). I have given my own rendering of the final clause. With the central image of the passage cp. the poem printed by F.J.E. Raby, *Secular Latin Poetry*, 2nd edn. (Oxford, 1957) II, 22-23.

oping herself in variegated garments, has also desired to have her secrets handled by more prudent individuals through fabulous narratives. Accordingly, her sacred rites are veiled in mysterious representations so that she may not have to show herself even to initiates. Only eminent men of superior intelligence gain a revelation of her truths; the others must be drawn to venerate her by the agency of those *figurae* which protect her secrets from debasement.

He declares that a certain respect for sacred things has always led true philosophers to employ fables and myths when they would discuss the inner realities of the sensible world or the powers which govern it. But when they wish to speak of God or of the divine Wisdom they cannot without impiety use such means, and rely instead upon *similitudines* and *exempla*, as when Plato describes the Good indirectly by comparing it to the sun.[74]

Macrobius does not pursue this distinction between the functions of *involucrum* and similitude, and it tended to be neglected in twelfth-century interpretation. The term *involucrum*, together with the more specific *integumentum*, was applied to all texts from which a hidden significance, moral, cosmological or spiritual, could be extracted.[75]

Probably the earliest and certainly one of the most striking exploitations of the concept of *involucra* as an element in ancient literature occurs in the *Introductio ad theologiam* and *Theologia christiana* of Abelard, works which make a powerful case for the study of the *auctores*, and in particular the *Timaeus*. Abelard speaks of Plato as a sort of gentile prophet: recalling Valerius Maximus' account of the bees spreading honey on the infant philosopher's lips as he slept, he finds it fitting to see the incident as a miracle and to suppose "that God conferred this presaging token upon him through whom He was to reveal so effectively the hidden

[74] *Commentarii* 1.2.15 (Willis, p. 7).
[75] Chenu, "Involucrum: le mythe selon les théologiens médiévaux," *Archives d'histoire* 22 (1955), pp. 75-79; Jeauneau, "L'usage de la notion d'integumentum à travers les gloses de Guillaume de Conches," *Archives d'histoire* 24 (1957), pp. 36-43; de Lubac, *Exégèse* II.ii, pp. 186-97.

workings of His divinity."[76] This glorification of Plato is only one aspect of what amounts to a major theme of the two treatises, the scope of divine revelation, which Abelard evidently considers as having extended to the gentiles as well as the Jews. On a number of critical points pagan and Christian authorities are placed side by side; even such mysteries as the Trinity, says Abelard, "Divine providence saw fit to manifest to the Jews through their prophets and to the gentiles through their philosophers."[77] This common inspiration seems at times to extend to their modes of expression: Plato's notion of the World Soul is a way of approaching the Holy Spirit "per pulcherrimam involucri figuram," a use of metaphor well known to both philosopher and prophet and indeed to "Veritas ipsa," whose promise of the Kingdom was delivered under the "involucro parabolarum suarum."[78] And Abelard quotes Augustine on the beneficial effect of the work required to uncover such hidden wisdom. In effect he sets Plato on an equal plane with the Old Testament, and his conviction of the divine inspiration of his author leads him to subject the *Timaeus* to a kind of exegesis normally reserved for Scripture. He finds it easy to imagine, "si fas esset," a prophecy of universal salvation through the Crucifixion in the Demiurge's construction of the circles of Same and Different, which meet in the form of an "X" and cooperate to define the sphere within which the World Soul comprehends the universe.[79] Elsewhere he explicitly compares such passages with the prophecy of Caiaphas, which was inspired by the Holy Spirit though he did not know it.[80]

The chronological relation of Abelard's treatises to the early work of Guillaume de Conches and Thierry is uncertain, but they plainly reflect the major concerns of Chartres.[81] Abelard is concerned, as

[76] *Introductio ad theologiam* 1.20 (PL 178.1029).

[77] *Ibid.*, 1.12 (PL 178.998).

[78] *Ibid.* 1.20 (PL 178.1023); *Theologia christiana* 1 (PL 178.1154-55).

[79] *Theologia christiana* 2 (PL 178.1172). Cp. *Timaeus* 36B-C.

[80] *Introductio* 1.20, 21 (PL 178.1128, 1132).

[81] Surprisingly little has been done on the question of Abelard's relations with the Chartrians. See Liebeschütz, "Kosmologische Motive in der Bildungswelt der Frühscholastik," *Vorträge der Bibliothek Warburg 1923–24*

are the Chartrians, to stress the correspondence of his "philoso-phorum testimonia" with Christianity, and historians have taken for granted the essential continuity of his position with theirs. But this continuity seems to me questionable. When Abelard attributes a typological meaning to an image in the *Timaeus*, and claims for the work the authority of prophecy, he does so incidentally and without undertaking a systematic analysis. Nowhere in his work is the general relationship between inspiration, on the one hand, and poetic technique and philosophical intuition on the other, made clear. He seems to vacillate between the positions of Macro-bius and Augustine, now accepting as genuinely spiritual the motives and meanings of his authors, now relegating them to the level of mere "literature."[82] The result is a mode of interpretation very dif-ferent from that practiced by the Chartrians.

Guillaume de Conches, whose glosses on Plato provide a useful comparison, concurs with Abelard in seeing Plato's images as veil-ing deep truths, and he even distinguishes *verba, litera,* and *summa integumenti* in a way that suggests exegetical practice.[83] But Guil-laume never credits this mode of expression with the typological

---

(1926), pp. 114-20. For a useful discussion of the limited role of "natural philosophy" in Abelard's thought see Jean Jolivet, "Éléments du concept de nature chez Abélard," *Filosofia della natura* (cited above, n. 56), pp. 297-304. As Jolivet notes, Abelard was primarily concerned with language and differed fundamentally from Thierry and Guillaume in having no serious interest in physics.

[82] As de Lubac observes (*Exégèse* II.ii, p. 186), Abelard's free application of Macrobius' doctrine has its limits. He notes (p. 208) that when Abelard compares the figural language of the Bible with that of the *auctores* he uses the parables as his sole instance of the former, thus in effect asserting only a similarity of technique, rather than inspiration. At one moment he will place the Sibylline prophecy of Vergil's fourth eclogue higher in authority than the prophecies of the Old Testament (*Introductio*, Prol., PL 178.-1008B; *Exégèse* II.ii, p. 255), while at other times his views are in perfect conformity with Augustine and with his more orthodox contemporaries. (*Exégèse* II.ii, pp. 137-40, 152-53, 216.)

[83] *Verba* and *sensus* (*sententia*, "content") are explicitly opposed in the prologue to the *Glosae super Platonem*, p. 57. For the presentation in order of *verba, summa integumenti* and *continuatio literae* see, e.g., *Glosae*, pp. 93-94 (Ericthonius), 150 (World Soul), 167 (shaping of the World Soul).

reference of biblical symbolism as Abelard does. He treats it rather as a poetic shorthand for conveying complex philosophical doctrines. When he says that Plato, to show the workings of the divine, expresses himself by " 'probationibus incongruis' quantum ad verba, 'sed necessariis' quantum ad sensum mysticum," he adopts as his frame of reference nothing more mystical than the order of the universe itself.[84] And while Abelard often refers directly to Scripture or the Fathers for his interpretations, Guillaume turns almost invariably to the Arts. That philosophy is always subordinate to Scripture in authority is a point Guillaume emphasizes carefully. After a naturalistic interpretation of the creation of Eve, the scriptural account of which he feels cannot be taken *ad litteram*, he asks, in a way which seems to anticipate criticism, "in what way do we go against Scripture if we explain *how* that was done which is there said to have been done?"[85]

The difference between the two scholars' methods of preserving the "orthodoxy" of their sources may be shown by a comparison of Abelard's treatment of the formation of the World Soul, with Guillaume's explanation of the statement that the Demiurge "fashioned souls equal in number with the stars, and distributed them, each soul to its several star," an assertion which seems to imply the preexistence of the soul. Guillaume acknowledges that God is continually creating new souls, and that many have accused Plato of speaking heretically here. "However," he says, "if one considers not simply Plato's words, but their sense, he will discover not only

[84] *Glosae super Platonem*, p. 202, on *Timaeus* 40E. Cp. the various meanings assigned to *mysticus, mystice*, etc., by Hugh of St. Victor, discussed in Roger Baron, *Science et sagesse chez Hugues de St. Victor* (Paris, 1957), pp. 167-68, and *Didascalicon* 2.18 (Buttimer, p. 37).

[85] *De philosophia mundi* 1.23 (PL 172.56). This passage was in fact one of those singled out for criticism by Guillaume de St. Thierry in his *De erroribus Guillelmi de Conchis* (PL 180.340). As the passage indicates, Guillaume did not hesitate to bring science to bear on Scripture, and even to substitute it for the literal sense of a given text ("irridet historiam divinae auctoritatis" says Guillaume de St. Thierry). For other instances see Jeauneau, "Notes sur l'École de Chartres," *Studi medievali* 5 (1964), pp. 847-51. But this, like Thierry's use of the *Timaeus* to explain *Genesis*, is very different from Abelard's intuitions, an essay in *physica* rather than syncretism.

nothing heretical, but the most profound philosophy sheltered in the integuments of the words." And Guillaume, lover of Plato that he is, as he remarks, goes on to explain that the assignment of souls to stars is meant "causally, not locally," as a metaphor for the stars' influence on temperament, well-being, and length of life.[86]

Moreover, when Guillaume does introduce Christian doctrine it is more often for purposes of correction than of confirmation, and he is willing to reject the authority of his source at any point where it diverges from what he recognizes as orthodox. Later in the section of the *Timaeus* just quoted, Plato speaks of the soul as enduring the life-cycle until such time as it is sufficiently purified to return to its birthplace. Guillaume justifies his author against the misinterpretation of Origen, who had read the passage as a proclamation of universal salvation, by explaining that Plato is not speaking of all souls, but only of those which are sufficiently pure.[87] But when in the course of glossing Macrobius he is faced with a reference to Plato's Er, uttering the doctrine that the guilty are ultimately freed from torment, and with Macrobius' confirming assertion that "of course every soul must return to its original abode," he acknowledges that here Plato is clearly heretical, and echoes, almost ruefully, Vergil's imaginary rejoinder to the accusations of Fulgentius: "Si in aliquo non errassem, achademicus [i.e., paganus] non fui."[88]

The precise relation of the *integumentum*, Guillaume's usual term for the figural element in the *auctores*, to the broader range of figural *involucra* which includes Scriptural allegory seems never to have attained any generally accepted formulation.[89] It is clear,

---

[86] *Glosae super Platonem*, pp. 211-15; cp. *Timaeus* 41D. See Jeauneau, "L'usage de la notion d'integumentum," pp. 53-55.

[87] *Glosae super Platonem*, pp. 219-20.

[88] See Jeauneau, "Macrobe, source du platonisme chartrain," pp. 20-22; Macrobius, *Commentarii* 2.17.13-14 (Willis, p. 153). Following Jeauneau, I assume that Guillaume's words recall Fulgentius' *Virgiliana continentia* (*Opera*, p. 103).

[89] It seems plain enough that the term *allegoria* was generally associated with Scripture, *integumentum* with pagan texts, though Abelard's usage shows that the terminology was by no means precise. (See also Jeauneau,

however, that no simple equation can be made between the techniques and assumptions underlying the Chartrians' analyses of pagan texts and those which govern scriptural exegesis. Abelard cites Augustine and Gregory in support of his procedure, but Guillaume, even when setting the World Soul and the Holy Spirit in intimate relation, demands only that his reader be enough of a philosopher to understand him, and to see the *integumentum* as a means whereby all the Arts may be brought to bear on serious speculation. And he never allows the *summa integumenti,* the higher wisdom figured by the words of the text, to diverge from what may be construed as the conscious intention of the author.

The differences between Guillaume and Abelard are even more interesting in view of what they have in common. Abelard's reading of Plato obviously reflects his well-known concern to vindicate the capacities of human reason; its boldness and its implications for theology were clearly recognized by his contemporaries. And Guillaume's view of the *integumentum,* though less obviously radical in its implications, is equally so in its affirmation of the integrity of the philosopher's vision, and the constant presence in his writing of an underlying *sensus mysticus.* The subjectivity and the intuitive approach of Abelard were vastly influential; he was a gadfly to twelfth-century thinkers, and his effect on the attitude of later poets and commentators toward the *integumentum* may be compared to the way in which the Chartrian view of the Platonic cosmology was complicated by Hermetic and Arabic doctrines, and by the influence of the medical writers. But the nature and implications of the *integumentum* as a poetic and interpretative device were most decisively established by Guillaume. His more rationalistic approach, and his emphasis on the author's own design as the primary basis for assessing the figurative meaning of his language and im-

"Notes sur l'École de Chartres," p. 850; de Lubac, *Exégèse* ii.ii, pp. 189-200.) The distinction is clearly made in a commentary, apparently by Bernardus Silvestris, discussed and quoted by Jeauneau, "Notes," p. 856, and in ch. 2, pp. 112-13 below. Here *integumentum* and *allegoria* are declared to be wholly distinct forms of *involucrum,* one proper to *fabulae,* the other to sacred history.

agery, brought philosophy and literary criticism into a new and intimate relationship.

As Jeauneau remarks, "grammaire et philosophie font, à Chartres, très bon ménage."[90] Thierry declared of grammar that "expositionem omnium auctorum sibi debitam profitetur," and Guillaume was recalled by his pupil John of Salisbury as "grammaticus post Bernardum carnotensem opulentissimus."[91] The method of his *Glosae super Platonem* consists in a delicate balancing of philology and philosophy which gives the work a coherence unprecedented in medieval compilations of its kind. In his prologue he complains of the imbalances in the work of former commentators. The *glossatores*, proceeding word by word, have possessed too little learning, and so have tended to be "in levibus superflui, in gravibus vero obscurissimi," while the more philosophical *commentatores* have occupied themselves with Plato's *sententia* to the total neglect of the letter. Guillaume intends to steer a middle course, "aliorum superflua recidentes, pretermissa addentes, obscura elucidentes, male dicta removentes, bene dicta imitantes."[92] Though he draws continually on Servius, Macrobius, Remigius, and the mythographic tradition, as well as Calcidius and perhaps other commentators on the *Timaeus*, his synthesis is his own achievement. Guillaume, in the spirit of Thierry's *Heptateuchon*, takes seriously the challenge issued by Philosophy and the Muses to Fulgentius, who had been shown a vision of the Liberal Arts and assured that if he followed their precepts with care they would transform him "from a mortal to a celestial being" and gain him a place among the stars, "not as Nero, by mere poetical flattery, but as Plato, through an understanding of mystery."[93]

The element most nearly common to all forms of *integumentum* is myth,[94] and the most common interpretative device is moraliza-

---

[90] Ed. *Glosae super Platonem*, p. 19.

[91] *Metalogicon* 1.5 (Webb, p. 16).   [92] *Glosae super Platonem*, p. 57.

[93] *Mitologiae* 1, Prol. (*Opera*, pp. 14-15).

[94] See Chenu, "Involucrum," pp. 75-79; *La théologie*, pp. 122-24, 164-66 (Taylor-Little, pp. 70-71, 106-08); de Lubac, *Exégèse* II.ii, pp. 195-208; Jeauneau, ed. *Glosae super Platonem*, pp. 19-20.

tion. As in all mythographical compendia, the interpretations are often forced, but the more sophisticated the *integumentum* the more this enforced significance gives way to a genuine continuity. Plato himself had pointed out the naturalistic origin of much ancient myth and its development by philosophers (who saw deeper themselves and knew that behind the gods was a single deity) as a concession to the brutishness of their fellow men: "and they called the planets gods, and made the four elements attributes of these, called the earth's natural power of putting forth seed Ceres. . . . But they shielded the truth with names and images lest these powers be devalued."[95]

The simplest *integumenta* are etymologies of proper names from mythology, and in interpreting these Guillaume draws freely on the mythographers.[96] On a higher level whole myths are translated intact into cosmological or moral terms. Guillaume's astrological interpretation of the myth of the soul's sojourn among the stars has been mentioned; and the Egyptian priest of Critias' introductory discourse offers an analysis of the story of Phaethon which Guillaume embellishes.[97] The births of Rhea and Phorcys are adapted to the themes of the *Timaeus*: Rhea represents primordial matter and is the wife of Saturn because time and material existence are inseparable; Phorcys is the *archetypus mundus*, and he and Rhea, with Saturn, are children of heaven and earth because these represent the fiery and earthly elements, without which no conjunction of form and matter is possible.[98]

But the use of *integumenta* goes beyond myth in the ordinary sense; when Guillaume speaks of the "modum Platonis loquendi de philosophia per integumenta" he does not refer simply to the

[95] *Glosae super Platonem*, p. 201; cp. *Timaeus* 40D.

[96] See, e.g., *Glosae super Platonem*, pp. 86 (Athena), 93 (Vulcan), 94 (Erichthonius); for examples from the glosses on Boethius, where such etymological *integumenta* are equally common, see Jeauneau, "L'usage de la notion d'integumentum," pp. 39-41, and below, ch. 2, pp. 93-98.

[97] *Glosae super Platonem*, pp. 89-90; cp. *Timaeus* 22C. See also the glosses on Pan and Syrinx (p. 107) and Saturn (p. 91).

[98] *Glosae super Platonem*, p. 203, on *Timaeus* 40E.

interpolation of myth and allusive etymologies, but to the very language of philosophy.[99] Thus, he notes, Plato describes the composition and formation of the World Soul in elaborate scientific terms, yet "integumenta non deserens."[100] The World Soul is mixed in its composition "non essentia, sed possibilitate vivificendi et discernendi"; that it is said to be composed of Same and Different means that while as spirit it is indivisible, it is *dividua* in its influence on vegetable, animal, and spiritual existence.[101] The mathematical formulae which illustrate the formation of the World Soul are *integumenta* as well, for they illustrate its perfection, since nothing below God is so perfect as number.[102]

Every aspect of Plato's text, then, is figurative, and the insights it yields have a serious scientific value for Guillaume. But the process by which these insights are attained is also important: the ultimate object of cosmological study is the orientation of human life, and the kind of apprehension involved in the translating of *integumenta* can be a source of stability in itself.[103] Guillaume suggests this in a gloss on Plato's statement that "the god invented and gave us vision in order that we might observe the circuits of intelligence in the heaven and profit by them for the revolutions of our own thought":[104]

---

[99] Gloss on Boethius, *De consolatione* 3, metr. 11, quoted by Jeauneau, "L'usage de la notion d'integumentum," p. 53, from Troyes 1381, f. 68r.

[100] *Glosae super Platonem*, p. 153, on *Timaeus* 35B.

[101] *Ibid.*, pp. 150, 152, on *Timaeus* 35A.

[102] *Ibid.*, p. 154, on *Timaeus* 35B.

[103] The idea is latent in Macrobius' discussion, where the penetration of *involucra* is made a sort of initiation to the mysteries. It becomes a major theme of the *Aeneid* commentary of Bernardus Silvestris and the allegories of Bernardus and Alain de Lille.

Jeauneau compares the role of myth in Guillaume's writings to that of the "complex" in psychoanalysis ("L'usage de la notion d'integumentum," pp. 85-86), and Jacqueline Hatinguais speaks of his glosses on Boethius in similar terms ("Points de vue sur la volonté et le jugement dans l'oeuvre d'un humaniste chartrain," in *L'homme et son destin: Actes du Premier Congrès International de Philosophie Médiévale*, 1958, Paris and Louvain, 1960, p. 420). See also de Lubac, *Exégèse* II.ii, pp. 195-96.

[104] *Glosae super Platonem*, p. 254, on *Timaeus* 47B. Cp. the gloss on Boethius, *De consolatione* 1, pr. 4 printed by Jeauneau as a footnote to this

To this end, then, God gave men eyes: since man perceives two motions in the heavens and similar ones in himself, then by whatever means the divine *ratio* subordinates the erratic motion [i.e., of the planets] to the rational motion of the firmament, just so should he subjugate the erratic motion of the flesh to the rational movement of the spirit, which is the end of moral philosophy. Thus the eyes are of value in both kinds of philosophical activity.

The effect of such a conception is to make of the Timaean cosmology a single sustained *integumentum,* and to provide the necessary framework for Guillaume's *ad verbum* exegesis of Plato's text. The thoroughness of Guillaume's attempt to deal with the metaphorical intricacies of the *Timaeus* reveals a sense that no utterance of a true philosopher is trivial, that every detail is finally consonant with an underlying *sensus mysticus* which is far removed from the orientation of the traditional monastic *accessus,* and more disciplined than Abelard's handling of *involucra.* Guillaume addresses his author in a newly serious way, making unprecedented claims for the integrity of his work at all levels of intention. At his most ardent, if we may judge by the evidence of a late manuscript of his glosses on Boethius, he could contrast Aristotle, master of mere logical and dialectical word-play, with Plato, physicist and theologian, who had concerned himself not simply with words, but with *res,* substantial reality.[105] Guillaume's or not, the distinction

---

passage. In the Boethius commentary of London B.M. Royal 15.B.III, f. 19r, this gloss is elaborated in an interesting way, though the conventional religious language does not seem to me characteristic of Guillaume: "Iterum sunt quidam qui originem sumunt ab oriente, id est a deo patre, et uadunt per occidens, id est de necessariis carnis aliquantulum cogitantes, utuntur bonis temporalibus ad sustentanda corpora sua ut seruiantur deo et veniunt iterum in orientem unde exiere, scilicet quando adipiscuntur per sua merita eternam beatitudinem. Sunt etiam aliqui qui ab occidente exeunt, id est euasi sunt de una cura temporalium et uadunt per orientem. . . . Sed ibi non sistunt nec morantur, sed iterum tendunt in occidentem, id est reuertuntur ad curam temporalium et ad suam dampnacionem."

[105] Cited from Paris, B.N. lat. 6406, f. 9v, by Maurice de Gandillac, "Le platonisme au XIIᵉ et au XIIIᵉ siècles," in *Association Guillaume Budé, Con-*

suggests what many details in Chartrian writings would tend to confirm, that the Chartrian Platonic model was conceived as analogous, within the limits of poetic intuition and philosophical speculation, to the inner, sacramental structure of the world view of Christian tradition. The authority attributed to Plato's cosmology was the foundation on which the study of ancient literature was established. Vergil, Ovid, Boethius, Martianus Capella, all take on a new meaning when the role of *integumenta* in their writings is acknowledged; to their traditional moral authority is added a deep philosophical *significatio*, and they become an avenue to the "integra comprehensio veritatis eorum quae sunt."

With this approach to the great *auctores* as a starting point, I would like now to explore the analogy just suggested between the philosophical and sacramental world views by comparing Chartrian methods and assumptions with those of the "twelfth-century Augustine," Hugh of St. Victor. As in the case of Abelard and Guillaume de Conches, affinities as well as differences are involved, and we will observe the Chartrian and Victorine views of reality—the purest embodiments of what I have characterized above as the "rationalist" and "symbolist" views—combining to produce a third, hybrid view which is more a poetic figment than a philosophical or theological conception, a simplified and "mystified" Platonism with elements borrowed from the pseudo-Dionysius, Martianus Capella, and the pseudo-Apuleian *Asclepius*, among others. It is this hybrid system which is exploited to various ends in the great allegorical poems which are our chief concern.

---

grès de Tours et de Poitiers, 1953 (Paris, 1954), p. 273; cp. the references to Plato and Aristotle gathered by Chenu, *La théologie*, p. 109 (Taylor-Little, pp. 50-51). That the MS cited by de Gandillac embodies Guillaume's second redaction of the Boethius glosses is suggested by J. M. Parent, *La doctrine de la création dans l'École de Chartres* (Paris and Ottawa, 1938), p. 215, but this view is challenged by Courcelle, *La consolation*, p. 404. With the comparison cited cp. Hugh of St. Victor, *Didascalicon* 5.3 (Buttimer, p. 96): "philosophus solam nouit uocum significationem, sed excellentior ualde est rerum significatio quam uocum, quia *hanc usus instituit, illam natura dictauit.*" Hugh is of course referring to the *res* of Scripture as characterized in Augustine's *De doctrina christiana*, but his citing of *natura* gives a curious turn to the formula.

5. Hugh of St. Victor and the Chartrians

The work of Hugh of St. Victor may be compared with that of the Chartrians on two main grounds. Their application of the Arts and philosophical interpretation to the *integumenta* of their chosen texts and their vindication of the author's conscious intention are broadly analogous to the reforms introduced into biblical study by Hugh and his disciple Andrew. At the same time the cosmic scope of their analyses, and their concern to show the integrity of the author's conception in every detail, are strongly suggestive of the cosmic sacramentalism which entered twelfth-century thought with the revival of interest in John Scotus Eriugena and the pseudo-Dionysius, and of which Hugh was perhaps the most important exponent.

Beryl Smalley has argued forcibly that Hugh revealed virtually a new dimension of exegesis by his insistence on the grounding of the *lectio divina* in a comprehensive program of liberal studies.[106] How radical his innovations were in fact has been much discussed;[107] it is clear in any case that in his *Didascalicon* he emulated, and at the same time elaborated upon, the *De doctrina christiana* of Augustine.[108] The Arts, for Hugh, were essential to the full understanding of the letter of Scripture, the only means of ensuring a command of the text adequate to justify using it as a basis for doctrinal and theological interpretation and the unfolding of a *sensus allegoricus* for contemplation. In emphasizing the letter, and in his famous

---

[106] *The Study of the Bible*, pp. 85-106.

[107] Miss Smalley's view is directly opposed by de Lubac, *Exégèse* ii.i, pp. 289-91. He agrees that Hugh was an important and even controversial innovator, but insists that his innovations consisted chiefly in the systematizing of traditional practice, and entailed no rejection of allegorization (*Exégèse* i.i, pp. 45-56; ii.i, pp. 316-31, 419). His system entailed a separation of *lectio historica* from allegorical interpretation which had far-reaching and somewhat disruptive consequences, but these were not foreseen, let alone intended, by Hugh (*Exégèse* ii.i, pp. 418-35).

[108] The argument of Miss Smalley (*The Study of the Bible*, p. 86), who stresses Hugh's desire to restore the Augustinian program, and that of Taylor (tr. *Didascalicon*, pp. 28-32), who is at pains to note differences between the *Didascalicon* and the *De doctrina christiana*, are really complementary.

exhortation "Omnia disce," he stood opposed to the growing tendency of his day, when the many opportunities open to *litterati* encouraged a hasty and superficial training in which Scripture, if studied at all, was read by way of glosses from which a sketchy knowledge of allegorical and historical meanings could be gained quickly. Traditional in this respect, his attitude is at the same time very like that attributed by John of Salisbury to the Chartrian masters who, versed in all the Arts themselves, were scornful of those who sought fame through a mastery of logic to the neglect of other studies, and especially of the opportunistic "Cornificiani," who rejected the Arts in all but name, and pursued a bastard *quadrivium* geared to preferment or simple self-preservation.[109]

Again, in his emphasis on the letter Hugh suggests the Chartrians' sensitivity to the interaction of *sapientia* and *eloquentia*. His concern to bring out the full meaning of the letter led him to give special attention to the author's intent. If he was not, perhaps, so unique as Miss Smalley suggests, he was certainly uniquely explicit in his insistence that the letter of Scripture includes every meaning, figurative, ironic or allusive, as well as that which the syntactical arrangement of words conveys, which the author may have sought knowingly to express. Thus he could consider the letter as worthy of exegesis in its own right. "All Scripture, if expounded according to its own proper meaning, will gain in clarity," he says in the prologue to his homilies on *Ecclesiastes*, cited by Miss Smalley as evidence of his view;[110] and he goes on to stress the "true reasons and plain persuasion" employed by the Preacher, rather than any mystical element. His discussion of the historical or literal sense of Scripture in a wonderful chapter of the *Didascalicon* includes a warm reminiscence of his own careful training in mathematics, astronomy, music, and the *trivium*, followed by a justification which might have served Guillaume de Conches as a statement of the principles of his *glosae*:[111]

---

[109] *Metalogicon* 1.4, 5 (Webb, pp. 12-16).

[110] PL 175.113. See Smalley, *The Study of the Bible*, p. 100; de Lubac, *Exégèse* ii.i, pp. 433-34.

[111] *Didascalicon* 6.3 (Buttimer, p. 115; tr. Taylor, p. 137). Hugh's view of

Some things are to be known for their own sakes, but others, although for their own sakes they do not seem worthy of our labor, nevertheless, because without them the former class of things cannot be known with complete clarity, must by no means be carelessly skipped. Learn everything; you will see afterwards that nothing is superfluous. A skimpy knowledge is not a pleasing thing.

What sharply distinguishes Hugh from the Chartrians is his attitude toward secular literature. The great legacy of the *auctores* in his eyes is the *artes* themselves, a lucid, precise "theorica philosophia" which presents itself as a set of finely honed tools for the analysis of the letter of Scripture. The Arts in this pure form are wholly divorced from any application to secular literature, for the very *auctores* whose preeminence as theoreticians he acknowledges were incapable of employing them in a consistently effective way.[112] Secular literature is murky and deceptive by its very nature, based on a view of man and the universe which has no central coordinating principle. Its material is the *opus conditionis*, the universe as created, rather than the *opus restaurationis*, the universe seen in the light of the Incarnation.[113] Without the central fact of the Incarna-

---

the function of the Arts is compared with other twelfth-century views, in particular that of Guillaume de Conches, by Taylor, tr. *Didascalicon*, pp. 12-19; see also Baron, *Science et sagesse*, pp. 92-96, 151-54.

[112] See Taylor, tr. *Didascalicon*, pp. 20-22, where, however, Hugh's disdain for pagan authors is exaggerated. See *Didascalicon* 3.14 (Buttimer, pp. 64-66; tr. Taylor, pp. 97-99), based primarily on Jerome, *Epist.* 52, where instances of the love of wisdom among the ancients are admiringly catalogued; also Baron, *Science et sagesse*, pp. 93-96. Taylor's remarks apply chiefly to Platonist cosmological writings current in the twelfth century, some of which seemed to threaten the authority of Scripture; see Taylor, tr. *Didascalicon*, pp. 19-20.

[113] On the two *opera* see Taylor, tr. *Didascalicon*, pp. 34-35; 172-73, notes 166-68. Again, his characterization of Hugh's attitude toward *theologia mundana* seems too harsh; cp. Baron, *Science et sagesse*, pp. 149-66. Baron stresses the sense in which the two *opera* form a hierarchy, the one leading to the other as the Arts lead to the study of Scripture. He quotes (p. 162) the *De arca Noe morali* 1.6 (PL 176.672D): "electi de operibus conditionis per opera restaurationis ad conditionis et restaurationis auctorem ascendunt."

tion, the relative importance of things is unclear and the search for wisdom goes astray. Hugh's position is well stated in the introduction to his commentary on the *Celestial Hierarchy* of the pseudo-Dionysius:[114]

> For two *simulacra* were presented to man, whereby he might discern things invisible: one was the work of nature, the other of grace. . . . And God was revealed in both, but He was not made intelligible in both, since although the spectacle of the natural world tells us something about Him who made it, it cannot reward contemplation with illumination. The homofaction of the Savior was the medicine which brought light to the blind. . . . For first He bestowed illumination and then explanation. Nature, on the other hand, demonstrates but cannot illuminate, and the world offers visible evidence of its Creator but does not infuse men's hearts with any understanding of Truth. Through the *simulacra* of nature the Creator was only reflected; but in the *simulacra* of grace the presence of the godhead was revealed.

Hugh goes on to distinguish *theologia divina*, which sees all things in the light of the Incarnation, from *theologia mundana*, which is finally incapable of expressing truth since it has no instance of grace to guide it, no standard of humility, and hence is at the mercy of pride in its own learning.

In the homilies on *Ecclesiastes* the vanity of cosmological speculation is a recurring theme, and its applicability to the thought of the Chartrians is obvious. To seek knowledge of God in the chaos of *visibilia* is to ignore the true source of illumination within.[115] Though the philosopher should gain complete knowledge of nature, "yet wisdom is beyond all these things, nor can that be discovered anywhere in all the universe by which all the universe was

[114] *Expositio in Hierarchiam Coelestem* 1.1 (PL 175.926C). On the meaning of the passage and its relation to the two theologies discussed above see Baron, *Études sur Hugues de St.-Victor* (Paris, 1963), pp. 139-49, and the references given in the preceding note.

[115] *In Ecclesiasten Homilia* 5 (PL 175.156).

made."[116] The homilies are pervaded by a Pascalian sense of the vastness of the divine plan, and a deep distrust of the vanity of human intellect in presuming to comprehend it.

The distinction between worldly and divine theology once firmly established, Hugh is prepared to allow that theology may augment its consideration of the effects of the Incarnation with the study of natural objects, "ut in illis eruditionem conformaret."[117] Like Guillaume de Conches he finds the divine expressed in the universe, and even signs of the Trinity.[118] Many passages in his writings, considered outside of the larger context of his thought as a whole, seem to be close in spirit to the ideas of the Chartrians. Thus when he discusses the several *sensus* of Scripture and asserts that tropology involves *res* rather than mere *verba* he adds this explanation:[119]

> For in [the meaning of "things"] lies natural justice, out of which the discipline of our own morals, that is, positive justice, arises. By contemplating what God has made we realize what we ourselves ought to do. Every nature tells of God; every nature teaches man; every nature reproduces its essential form, and nothing in the universe is infecund.

It is precisely the dependence of "positive" on "natural" justice that provides the rationale for the glosses of Guillaume de Conches on Plato,[120] and accounts for the role of *Natura* in the allegories of Bernardus Silvestris and Alain de Lille. Elsewhere in the *Didascalicon* Hugh devotes a chapter to the various meanings of the term "nature" and the work is pervaded, as Taylor has shown, by the language and imagery of Platonist cosmological writings.[121]

In relation to passages like these, the distinction between *con-*

---

[116] *In Eccl. Hom.* 10 (PL 175.177B).

[117] *In Hier. Coel.* 1.1 (PL 175.927A).

[118] See Taylor, tr. *Didascalicon*, pp. 34-35, and *De tribus diebus* (PL 176.811-38, printed as Book Seven of the *Didascalicon*).

[119] *Didascalicon* 6.5 (Buttimer, p. 123; tr. Taylor, p. 145).

[120] See above, n. 68, and Gregory, *Platonismo medievale*, pp. 59-73.

[121] *Didascalicon* 1.10 (Buttimer, pp. 17-18). See Taylor, tr. *Didascalicon*, pp. 19-28; Silverstein, "Fabulous Cosmogony," pp. 104-05.

ditio and *restauratio* becomes crucial. For *restauratio* means pre-
cisely the recovery of man's original communion with the divine
Wisdom, and this involves the perception of nature not simply as
a harmonious work of the divine artificer, but as illumined and
transformed for man by the psychological effect of the Incarnation.
To attain true wisdom is to discover its image in one's own mind,
says Hugh,[122] and he reduces the Platonic archetype and World
Soul to metaphors for the scope and the divinity of the human
soul.[123] This "sapiential" view of the Incarnation is omnipresent in
Hugh's thought.[124] It is a nature illumined and transformed that
provides the basis for the "positive justice" attained through tropol-
ogy,[125] and the source of its meaning is not in the affinity of the
microcosm and macrocosm, but in that of the soul with God.

What is important for our purposes is the effect of this sapiential
view of knowledge on Hugh's conception of figural expression. Not
surprisingly he is adamant in excluding all mere "literature,"[126] and
especially poetry, from the realm of useful knowledge. Poetry is a
mere appendage which "touches in a scattered and confused fash-
ion on topics lifted out of the Arts," but which is at an even further
remove from order and truth than secular philosophy.[127] This
topic leads Hugh to some harsh remarks about these pseudo-philos-
ophers who see poetry as possessing a profundity worthy of exposi-
tion. As Taylor points out, his criticisms correspond almost point

[122] See *Didascalicon* 1.1-3, and esp. 2.1 (Buttimer, pp. 4-10, 23).

[123] See Taylor, tr. *Didascalicon*, pp. 23-27, and the apt formulation of
Baron, "La situation de l'homme d'après Hugues de St.-Victor," in *L'Homme
et son destin* (cited above, n. 103), p. 436: "Dans la perspective des *opera
conditionis*, la situation de l'homme est fonction de la situation de l'univers;
quand s'achèvent les *opera restaurationis*, la situation de l'univers est fonction
de la situation de l'homme."

[124] On the history of these conceptions see Taylor, tr. *Didascalicon*, pp.
164-65, n. 42; 175-78, notes 1-5; 186-87, n. 42; also Baron, *Science et sagesse*,
pp. 151-66, 171-79.

[125] See *Didascalicon* 5.3 (quoted above, n. 105), where *natura* is introduced
in a context clearly allegorical.

[126] On the special meaning for Hugh of the forms *litteratus*, *litteratura*,
which could bear implications of pride and spiritual blindness, see de Lubac,
Exégèse II.i, pp. 291-94.

[127] *Didascalicon* 3.4 (Buttimer, p. 54).

for point with the practices of the Chartrians when he speaks of those[128]

> whom today we commonly call "philosophers," and who are always taking some small matter and dragging it out through long verbal detours, obscuring a simple meaning in confused discourses—who, lumping even dissimilar things together, make, as it were, a single "picture" from a multitude of "colors" and forms.

To become learned in the Arts themselves only to abandon them in favor of this entanglement with their mere by-products is madness, and on this grounds Hugh commends the study of the Arts in theory rather than by way of the *auctores*.

Whether or not Hugh has the Chartrians in mind here, his remarks plainly exclude recourse to *integumenta* as a way of justifying the study of the *auctores*. The analysis of biblical symbolism as conceived by Hugh begins, like the interpretation of the *integumentum*, on the literal level, and draws on the Arts and philosophy in its initial stages. But in pursuing it, he says, we must pass "through the word to a concept, through the concept to a thing, through the thing to its idea, and through its idea arrive at truth."[129] Whereas the analysis of an *integumentum* would elaborate the concept behind the word rationally and poetically, as an expression of natural law and harmony, the symbolist passes from abstraction to a new realization of the "thing" on a level at which its significance becomes mystical, and is divorced from any significant relation to the natural order or the pattern of meaning imposed by the human author. The next step is the merging of the "thing" with its idea or *ousia*,[130] in which it is seen as it exists in the mind of God. Philosophy is left behind. Dialectic and the sciences may be useful, even essential up to a point, but where the student of the *auctores* is forced into poetry to express his intuition of the suprarational *fons*

[128] *Ibid.*, 3.4 (Buttimer, p. 54; tr. Taylor, p. 88). But it is worth noting that Hugh caps his denunciation of literary frivolity with a charming quotation from Vergil's *Eclogues*.

[129] *Ibid.*, 5.3 (Buttimer, p. 96; tr. Taylor, p. 122).

[130] On *ousiae* see *ibid.*, 1.6 (Buttimer, p. 13; tr. Taylor, pp. 14, 186, n. 42).

of the process he has defined, the symbolist abandons all human resources in response to illumination.

The wisdom concealed by *integumenta* is restricted by the inspiration of the human artist, and unless one accepts Abelard's view of the *auctor* as prophet, his significance can never transcend the intrinsic significance of the *opus conditionis*, literal and nonsymbolic. It was on just this point, the degree to which the cosmic order itself manifests the divine Wisdom, that Hugh and the Chartrians were opposed. The necessity of preserving the authority of Scripture led Hugh to stress the distinction between the two *opera* with a new firmness, and to go beyond Augustine in elaborating the implications of this distinction. As Chenu points out,[131] Augustine had not found it necessary to distinguish literary *figurae* from symbolic *translatio*. But once made, the distinction amounted to a denial of the transcendental implications of philosophy, and drew its resources into the service of the *lectio divina*.

However, despite the clear and traditional purpose of Hugh's pedagogical writings, his crucial distinction between *theologia mundana*, with its "inferior wisdom,"[132] and the divine theology founded in Scripture and illumined by Christ becomes harder to maintain when set in relation to other themes of his theology. Hugh was deeply interested in the problem of revelation, and especially in the relations of cosmology and history as constituting, respectively, the vehicle and the process of divine providence. The two are embraced together in the *De Sacramentis*, where the term *sacramentum* and the historical Incarnation are defined with such breadth as to complicate somewhat the relations of creation and restoration. There were, says Hugh, natural sacraments, as well as those of the written law and those of grace.[133] The Incarnation is

[131] *La théologie*, p. 187 (Taylor-Little, p. 141). At the same time, as Baron shows (*Science et sagesse*, pp. 113-21), Hugh is not wholly consistent in excluding mere metaphor and other literary figures from the sphere of *allegoria* as it pertains to Scripture.

[132] *De Sacramentis christianae fidei*, Prol., 6 (PL 176.185): ". . . omnes artes naturales divinae scientiae famulantur; et *inferior sapientia* recte ordinata ad superiorem conducit." See above, n. 113.

[133] See *De Sacramentis* 1.11 (PL 176.343-48); cp. 1.8.11 (PL 176.312-13),

"retroactive" in its effect, and its efficacious sacramental tokens have existed *ab initio*.[134] And this large view of revelation is accompanied, both in the *De Sacramentis* and in the commentary on the pseudo-Dionysian *Celestial Hierarchy*, by a rich sense of what Baron calls the "osmosis" which brings into relation the different levels and structures of religious Platonism.[135]

In all of this Hugh reveals the powerful influence of the treatises of the pseudo-Dionysius, and the *Celestial Hierarchy* in particular, where the manifestations of the *opus restaurationis* are, as it were, carried outside the limits of Scripture and become a sacramental vision of the universe itself. The universe of the pseudo-Dionysian writings is a hierarchy of more or less imperfect emanations of God, "theophanies" which not only express His goodness but reveal His immanent presence. As the *Celestial Hierarchy* declares, God's immanence is as "a unifying power" which "fills us and directs our minds to the unity of the shepherding Father."[136]

The theory of symbolism of the pseudo-Dionysius depends, like Hugh's conception of the *opus restaurationis*, on the fact of the Incarnation, and the reillumination of the soul thereby, but the Neoplatonist language makes it difficult to establish a precise demarcation of the effect of grace from the general condition of man in a God-informed universe. Christ is "the light of the Father," which "becomes manifold and issues forth," pervading the created world under "a variety of sacred veils."[137] One such veil is the hier-

---

De arca Noe mystica, c. 5 (PL 176.689AB). On Hugh's treatment of the imparting of the divine Wisdom see Taylor, tr. *Didascalicon*, p. 176, n. 2.

[134] See Baron, *Études*, pp. 148-49; *De Sacramentis* 1.9.8, 1.11.1 (PL 176.328, 343B), and *In Hier. Coel.* 1.1 (PL 175.927A): "Theologia vero divina opera restaurationis elegit secundum humanitatem Jesu, *et sacramenta eius quae ab initio sunt.*"

[135] See Baron, *Science et sagesse*, pp. 173-79.

[136] Pseudo-Dionysius, *Celestial Hierarchy* 1 (tr. John Scotus Eriugena, PL 122.1037C): "Sed et omnis Patre moto manifestationis luminum processio, in nos optime et large proveniens, iterum *ut unifica virtus* restituens *nos replet et convertit ad congregantis Patris unitatem.*"

[137] *Celestial Hierarchy* 1 (Pl 122.1038C): "et pulchre *multiplicatur* [paternum lumen] *et provenit.* . . . Etenim neque possible est aliter nobis lucere divinum lumen, nisi *varietate sacrorum velaminum* circumvelatum." On the

archy of the Church, modeled on the celestial hierarchy of intelligences who dwell in constant apprehension of God. Another is Scripture, which uses images of all sorts to express God, and so provides an example of how we may view a third, which is the natural world. "Nothing that exists is entirely deprived of participation in good, for as the truth of our eloquent Scriptures declares, 'all things are most beautiful.' "[138] The pseudo-Dionysian symbolism is thus in its pure form considerably more radical than Hugh's version of it; it makes the separation of symbolic from rational meaning into a positive virtue, presenting all natures as open to the direct influence of the divine so that, as Chenu remarks, metaphysical schemata become impossible.[139]

It would seem that Hugh was not fully aware of the dangers of these views for one versed only in the Augustinian tradition. Their effect was to stimulate him to highly complex investigations of the various modes of revelation, but at the same time to flaw deeply his system as a whole. To a great extent Hugh's concern with the range and nature of sacramental manifestations of salvation and his concern with the historical procession of these sacraments are two separate things. The purpose of the De Sacramentis is to show how history and the natural order are "geared" to one another,[140] and thereby to demonstrate the necessary interrelation of the temporal and cosmic modes of revelation, historia and allegoria. But the more the two subjects are pursued, the more Neoplatonism and historicism seem to contradict one another. As de Lubac says,[141] the result of Hugh's systematizing is a "grande parenthèse"; history and allegory assume new and highly technical meanings, but are rendered wholly separate. Thus, paradoxically, the effect of Hugh's program was at odds with his original intention: having sought to revivify

implications of the pseudo-Dionysian view of the Incarnation, see Chenu, La théologie, pp. 289-99.

[138] Celestial Hierarchy 2 (PL 122.1042B): ". . . nihil eorum quae sunt esse universaliter boni participatione privatum. Siquidem ut eloquiorum veritas ait, omnia bona valde."

[139] La théologie, pp. 129-31, 174-78 (Taylor-Little, pp. 79-83, 123-28).

[140] The image is Chenu's, La théologie, p. 67.

[141] Exégèse ii.i, p. 420.

the traditional, integrated study of Scripture by establishing its main pursuits on the soundest intellectual foundations, he instead provided the rationale for new and newly "scientific" disciplines which were pursued in growing isolation from one another. And in the surge of interest in the pseudo-Dionysian writings which marked the years following his death in 1141, his emphasis on the historical view of revelation was more or less ignored. A synthesis of historical and cosmic perspectives which has deep affinities with Hugh's was attained by Alain de Lille in his *Anticlaudianus*, but his main legacy to the later twelfth century was his version of the pseudo-Dionysian theory of symbolism.

In his commentary on the *Celestial Hierarchy* Hugh defines a "symbol" as "a coaptation of visible forms to demonstrate something invisible."[142] As we have seen, Hugh's conception of this process is rigorous and mystical. It is an illumination whereby "the eye of the mind" sees natural objects as transfigured,[143] the culmination of the process of intellectual and spiritual understanding for which the program of the *Didascalicon* provides the basis, and which preserves the distinction between "worldly" and "divine" theology made in the preface to the commentary. Thus Hugh goes on in the same preface to define the parts of philosophy as *physica*, *mathematica*, and *theologia*, the last of which "contemplates invisible substances, and the invisible natures of invisible substances."[144] But he then distinguishes theology based on nature alone from the

---

[142] *In Hier. Coel.* 2 (PL 175.941B; cp. 960D): "Symbolum est collatio formarum visibilium ad invisibilium demonstrationem." On the implications of the definition see Chenu, *La théologie*, pp. 162, 184-87 (Taylor-Little, pp. 103, 137-41).

[143] See *Celestial Hierarchy* 3 (PL 122.1045C): "Oportet itaque, ut aestimo, purgandos quidem puros perfici omnino, et omni liberari dissimilitudinis confusione: illuminandos vero repleri divini luminis, ad contemplativam habitudinem et virtutem in castissimis mentis oculis renovandos . . ."

[144] *In Hier. Coel.* 1.1 (PL 175.927-28): "theoricae tres partes sunt . . . in quibus contemplatio veritatis, quasi quibusdam contemplationum gradibus ad summum conscendit. Prima enim, id est mathematica, speculatur visibiles rerum visibilium formas. Secunda autem, id est physica, scrutatur invisibiles rerum visibilium causas. Tertia vero sola, id est theologia, contemplatur invisibiles substantias et invisibilium substantiarum invisibiles naturas."

true theology of the pseudo-Dionysius, of which the "demonstrations" are not philosophical but are given "symbolically and anagogically," and are synonymous with illumination.[145]

However, in the middle and later years of the twelfth century, when an intense interest in natural science and the influence of the pseudo-Dionysius were both at work, symbolism and the habits of mind associated with it assumed a new aspect. In particular its "scientific" aspect was developed out of all relation to Hugh's conception. At first this amounted to no more than the use of treatises on flora and fauna, astronomical compendia, and other such materials to gain special knowledge which might enhance the allusive potentialities of a given image or object. Gradually, however, the distinction between symbolism and other modes of representation broke down, until the visible forms of which symbolism was the "coaptation" could be the simplest of metaphors, even simple names, or larger cosmic and psychological structures. Metaphor, analogy, scientific knowledge of form and structure, everything from rhetorical conventions to the most abstruse of genuine religious signs came to be seen as part of a common body of images disposed in conformity with the hierarchical paradigms of a cosmic sacramentalism. At the same time the hierarchical aspects of the pseudo-Dionysian system were coming to be an object of philosophical and psychological concern in themselves.

The effect of these two developments was to intellectualize the pseudo-Dionysian system and give it a character much more like that of the rationalist Platonism of Chartres than that of the spiritual discipline conceived by Hugh. Thus there arose the hybrid Platonism mentioned at the beginning of this section, a way of characterizing the relation of human understanding to truth which makes it almost impossible to distinguish clearly between intellectual and mystical experience. The stages of this development, which was of very great significance in the adaptation of Platonism to poetic allegory by Bernardus Silvestris and his followers, may be illustrated by a comparison of a passage from Hugh's *De unione*

---

[145] *Ibid.*, 2 (PL 175.941B): ". . . illuminationibus, id est demonstrationibus sacri eloquii symbolice et anagogice."

corporis et spiritus with passages from an early work of Alain de Lille and from a sermon of Garnier de Rochefort.

Commenting on *John* 3:6, "That which is born of the flesh is flesh, and that which is born of the spirit is spirit," Hugh discusses the means by which the two are reconciled:[146]

> Moses ascended onto the mountain and God descended onto the mountain. Had not Moses ascended and God descended they would never have come together. In all such [meetings] there are deep sacramental meanings. The flesh ascends, and the spirit descends. The spirit ascends and God descends. Where the flesh ascends it is higher than flesh; where the spirit descends it is lower than spirit. Similarly, when the spirit ascends it is higher than spirit, and when God descends He is lower than God. The flesh ascends through the senses, the spirit descends in a way perceptible by the senses. So too the spirit ascends in contemplation, and God descends in revelation. The vision of God [*theophania*] lies in revelation, understanding in contemplation, imagining in the activity of the senses, in sense itself the basis of sensory perception and the source of imagination.
>
> Behold the ladder of Jacob. It rested on the earth and the top of it reached the heavens. The earth is the flesh, the heavens God. Our minds ascend in contemplation from the depths to the most high: from flesh to spirit through the mediation of the senses and sensory perception; from spirit to God through the mediation of contemplation and revelation.

The argument seems straightforward enough in the context of Hugh's sapientially ordered view of spiritual experience, but it is a harbinger of new developments. The passage combines the pseudo-Dionysian tendency to move "anagogically" from one level of reality to another with a concern to define more or less scientifically the stages of the *scala caeli*. Very similar language is used in treatises devoted to the exposition of Arabic and hermetic doctrines which

[146] *De unione corporis et spiritus* (PL 177.285).

Hugh would have rejected,[147] and the schematizing of the experience described anticipates the major preoccupations of later twelfth-century symbolists.

During the quarter-century which separates Hugh's death from the early activity of Alain de Lille, theologians inspired by Gilbert de la Porrée were adapting the pseudo-Dionysian *anagogia* to the more philosophical Neoplatonism of Boethius, whose epistemology had provided the basis for the pioneering speculations of Bernard of Chartres.[148] The result was a way of analyzing the hierarchy of degrees of being which lent itself equally well to serious analysis of the Trinity and to bizarre, multi-leveled structures like that presented by Alain in a "sermon" on the hermetic "sphaera intelligibilis."[149] In this remarkable work, strewn with allusions to Martianus Capella, the *Asclepius*, Cicero, and Boethius, Alain undertakes to define the relation of temporal to eternal being in terms of four spheres: the sensible, the imaginable, the rational, and the intelligible. To these four correspond four modes of manifestation of the divine: sensible *ychones*, then *ychonie*, *ychome*, and finally the divine *ydee*.[150] After describing the "marriages" which these kinds of form undergo in their respective spheres, Alain proceeds to the human faculties to which they present themselves:[151]

[147] Dominicus Gundissalinus recalls the passage just quoted in his *De processione mundi* (ed. G. Bülow, *Beiträge zur Geschichte der Philosophie des Mittelalters* 24, 1925, No. 3, p. 53). Expounding the Arabic doctrine of the "three worlds" he speaks of that one which is "beyond the firmament, incorporeal and incorruptible": "In hunc autem mundum venimus contemplatione, illuminamur in eo veritatis cognitione et virtutis dilectione. *Ascendit enim mens humana, et descendit bonitas divina; et ista ascendit contemplatione, illa descendit revelatione.*"

[148] See Chenu, *La théologie*, pp. 133-35, 139-41, 178-87 (Taylor-Little, pp. 85-88, 94-98, 129-41); d'Alverny, *Alain de Lille: Textes inédits*, pp. 92-106, 166-80.

[149] Alain's text is the famous definition "Deus est spera intelligibilis cuius centrum ubique, circumferentia nusquam" (so given by d'Alverny, *Textes inédits*, p. 295). As Mlle. d'Alverny suggests (p. 164), a likely source is the hermetic *Liber* xxiv *philosophorum*.

[150] As Mlle. d'Alverny explains (p. 300), Alain simply appropriates four handy terms. *Ychome* may be his own invention.

[151] *Textes inédits*, pp. 302-03.

Through sense . . . the human soul enters the world, where, examining the lower orders of existence, sense beholds as if in a sort of book the spots, the taints of corruption which are, as it were, the letters. . . .

By imagination the human soul is borne into the abode of primordial matter, where she sees imaginatively forms which seem to weep at the disaster of their misshapen state, and beg for the support of a nobler kind of matter.

Through reason the soul ascends to the palace of the World Soul, where she beholds the vital spark, the inexhaustible fountain, the perpetual sun. . . .

Through intellection the soul is drawn up to the inner repository of the ideas, where she contemplates the eternal exemplars of created life, flourishing in the bloom of their eternity.

. . . Through sense and imagination the soul becomes man, through reason she becomes spirit, through intellection God. Through sense and imagination she exists outside of herself; through reason she passes within herself; by intellection she rises above herself.

In this passage, and in the work as a whole, a desire for symmetry has virtually extinguished any spark of psychological interest; there is imagination of a pedantic sort, but not the obvious devotional and sacramental concern of Hugh in the *De unione*. It is hardly surprising that several passages in the sermon correspond word for word with passages descriptive of the activity of Nature and Genius in the *De planctu naturae*.[152] For the balance here is definitely weighted on the side of a literary and philosophical, rather than a theological or mystical conception of mental experience.

Alain's sermon is clearly a literary exercise, a scholar-poet's address to an audience of connoisseurs, and thus Mlle. d'Alverny in editing it set it apart from Alain's more conventional essays in pastoral theology. But it is much harder to know how to deal with the sermons of Alain's contemporary, the latter-day Cistercian Garnier de Rochefort, whose Chartrian terminology and intellectual

[152] See below, ch. 5, n. 36.

approach to matters of devotion is as far removed from the vein of Bernard and Guillaume de St. Thierry as his treatment of symbolism from that of Hugh. In a sermon dedicated to John the Baptist, and concerned largely with relationships between different modes of perception,[153] Garnier draws a comparison between the "negative" and the symbolic mode of vision:[154]

When the mind is borne aloft by *theorica* . . . it ascends to the Most High by certain stages of contemplation. For it considers mathematically the visible forms of visible things, or, employing physics, the invisible causes of visible things; or it symbolically juxtaposes and adapts visible forms to demonstrate invisible things; or it contemplates invisible substances, and their invisible natures theologically.

Yet by all these means that eminent and supereminent order, the most blessed hierarchy of the Divine Father, is so far manifested in figurative symbols that at length the human mind, by an inspired consideration of the eloquent work of God, may even contemplate the innermost heavens anagogically; and thus it arises to behold perfection by two kinds of vision . . . : one, when the truth of things mysterious is shadowed forth by forms and figures and similitudes: this kind of vision is called in Greek "theophany," or divine apparition; the other, when the mind, rising and passing beyond itself, seeks to contemplate that most sacred heavenly Lordship openly and purely, as It exists in Itself, free of any integument: this kind of vision is called "anagogy."

The discussion of the sciences and the comparison of the two modes of vision which follows it are borrowed almost verbatim from two

[153] I cannot fully agree with de Lubac's summary of the sermon as dealing with the superiority of "theology" to "prophecy," the New Testament to the Old, "negative" to symbolic knowledge of God (*Exégèse* i.ii, p. 643). The ways of knowing seem continually to interrelate in Garnier's mind, and I see no such clear hierarchy as de Lubac suggests. He himself acknowledges that there is a certain amount of nonsense in Garnier's formulations.

[154] *Sermo* 25 (PL 205.730). The passage in its printed form is obviously corrupt.

quite separate sections of Hugh's commentary on the *Celestial Hierarchy*.[155] Garnier has fused the two by interpolating Hugh's definition of the symbol, which occurs in the second passage, into the hierarchy of the sciences in the first (where Hugh is talking only of secular studies, rather than the *lectio sacra*), and the result of his conflation is virtually to make rational analysis the necessary basis of illumination.[156] It is unlikely that he intended precisely this, but the hierarchical emphasis of the passage as a whole does nothing to clarify his purpose. In Alain's sermon we observed the intrusion of baldly rationalistic terms and formulations into an ostensibly devotional context. Garnier, dealing at once with philosophical and mystical notions, seems unable to distinguish between them.

Garnier's epistemological formulations show how far the symbolic view of reality could stray, both from its original association with scriptural exegesis and from the radically spiritual vision of the pseudo-Dionysius. In its scope and in its relation to authority, once established as a "scientific" approach to *naturalia*, it paralleled the rationalist view of the Chartrians. Both symbolist and rationalist sought to discern the true relation of nature to God, and both tended to deemphasize the historical sequence of creation, fall, and redemption in favor of a conception of providence in which continuity was the determining factor, and the historical Incarnation virtually indistinguishable from the general operation of the eternal on the temporal as the source of its being and of its illumination.

[155] The two passages are that quoted in n. 144 above, and the following (italics indicate phrases borrowed by Garnier): "Hierarchias dico manifestas nobis . . . ab ipsis, scilicet illuminationibus, id est demonstrationibus sacri eloquii symbolice et anagogice. *Symbolum est collatio formarum visibilium ad invisibilium demonstrationem.* Anagoge autem ascensio, sive elevatio mentis ad superna contemplanda. Notat autem hic *duplicem modum revelationis divinae quae theologorum et prophetarum mentibus infusa est* per visiones et demonstrationes, *quas Graeci theophanias appellant, id est divinas apparitiones.* . . . Ex his vero duobus generibus visionum, duo quoque descriptionum genera in sacro eloquio sunt formata. *Unum, quo formis, et figuris, et similitudinibus rerum occultarum veritas adumbratur. Alterum, quo nude et pure sicut est absque integumento exprimitur.*" (*In Hier. Coel.* 2, PL 175.941BC).
[156] See Chenu, "La décadence de l'allegorization," in *L'homme devant Dieu. Mélanges Henri de Lubac* (Paris, 1964) II, 133.

Thus, it is hardly surprising that as the century progressed each should have tended to appropriate the resources of the other.

6. From Philosophy to Poetry

On one level the mating of Chartrian rationalism and pseudo-Dionysian symbolism marks the termination of the intellectual developments with which this chapter has been concerned. It is true that the genuinely scientific side of Chartrian thought may be linked in many ways with the study of natural philosophy in the rising universities, and played a significant role in the work of encyclopedists like Vincent of Beauvais.[157] (Much that had been severely censured in the writings of Guillaume de Conches lived on, verbatim, in the depths of the *Speculum naturale*.) And of course the spiritual writings of Hugh of St. Victor inspired not only Garnier, but the great Victorine mystic Richard, and later Bonaventure. But for the particular twelfth-century forms of Chartrian and pseudo-Dionysian thought, particularly as contact between them increased, the shift from serious philosophy and theology to a sort of literary analogue of these was probably inevitable, the natural consequence of an attempt to pursue natural and metaphysical investigations with severely limited resources.

This tendency could only become more pronounced, in the case of the Chartrians, as they sought to articulate the insights of Platonism as it approaches the source of cosmic complexity in the unifying archetype, the *forma formarum*. Klibansky has indicated how tantalizing to the Chartrian mind must have been Calcidius' assurance that Plato's inaccessible *Parmenides*, a work which, the commentator declares, "welled forth from the fount of an utterly pure understanding of reality," had reconciled the unity and the plurality of forms.[158] Much of Thierry's trinitarian speculation can be

---

[157] See C. V. Langlois, *La conaissance de la nature et du monde* (Paris, 1927), pp. 157-63; W. J. Brandt, *The Shape of Medieval History* (New Haven, 1966), pp. 1-42.

[158] Klibansky, "Plato's Parmenides in the Middle Ages and Renaissance," *Medieval and Renaissance Studies* 1 (1941–43), pp. 282-83; Calcidius, *Commentarius*, 272 (Waszink, pp. 276-77).

viewed as an attempt to replace the lost dialogue,[159] but in fact the Chartrians never succeeded in reconciling physics and metaphysics, divine immanence and divine transcendence.[160] A barrier presented itself, the final *integumentum*, and poetry became the only possible means of expressing what lay beyond. Similarly, as we have seen, the systematizing of Hugh resulted in an imperfect, or in any case an imperfectly understood synthesis; and the cooperation he envisioned between science and spiritual insight resulted only in the reduction of both to the poetry and pseudo-science of Alain and Garnier. In both cases the reduction to poetry was the result of an apparent need to express what was inexpressible.

There were other reasons for the increasing use of literary forms and techniques to convey such intuitions. There was, as I have suggested, a certain traditionalist reaction to Chartrian thought in the middle and later years of the twelfth century. Generated largely by the Cistercians, this movement saw direct attacks on the writings of Guillaume de Conches (whose retirement from the schools may have been hastened by the *De erroribus Guillelmi de Conchis* of Guillaume de St. Thierry)[161] and Gilbert de la Porrée, to say nothing of the tragedy of Abelard. Its primary emphasis was on curbing the excesses of dialectic,[162] but it had the peripheral effect of creating a prejudice against secular studies in general.[163] So far as the study of the *auctores* is concerned, the prevailing attitude of twelfth-century religious was probably Hugh's: the study of the *auctores* is objectionable simply because it is irrelevant to salvation.

[159] The anonymous twelfth-century commentary cited by Klibansky has been shown to be Thierry's; see Häring, "A Commentary on Boethius *De Trinitate* by Thierry of Chartres (Anonymus Berolinensis)," *Archives d'histoire* 23 (1956), pp. 257-325.

[160] See Silverstein, "Fabulous Cosmogony," pp. 112-14.

[161] On the *De erroribus* and its effect see (in addition to the references given in n. 61 above) Garin, *Studi*, pp. 62-68; Jeauneau, "Notes sur l'École de Chartres," pp. 849-50.

[162] The best illustration is the *Contra quatuor labyrinthos franciae* of Gauthier de St. Victor (ed. P. Glorieux, *Archives d'histoire* 19, 1953, pp. 187-335), which attacks Gilbert, Guillaume de Conches, and Abelard.

[163] See Delhaye, *Le Microcosmos de Godefroy de St.-Victor*, pp. 13-49, and the works of Paetow cited above, n. 6.

Guillaume de St. Thierry grumbled at the preoccupation of Guil-
laume de Conches with *integumenta*, but seems to have had only
a vague sense of the term's meaning.[164] But it would seem that at
St. Victor, too, there arose doubts about the value of even so care-
fully qualified an intellectualism as Hugh's, since some time around
1180 the poet Godfrey was censured and possibly exiled from St.
Victor for writing a *Fons philosophiae* in the spirit of the *Didas-
calicon*.[165] It thus seems reasonable to suppose, with Silverstein, that
the recourse to the obliquities of poetry was at least partly a way
of evading heresy-hunters.[166]

Aside from such practicalities, it is important to recognize that
there were a number of strains in twelfth-century humanism and
scientific thought that could only with difficulty be categorized in
the Platonist scheme of things. I would like to touch briefly on
certain of these, though they have received too little scholarly at-
tention for their role to be described in detail, because they plainly
influenced the attitude of humanists and poets toward Chartrian
thought, and I will have occasion to mention them in connection
with the poems to be discussed below. There were many cosmologi-
cal and astrological treatises current in the century, grounded in
Arabic and hermetic doctrines as well as those of classical science,

[164] See notes 61 and 85 above. Sniping at Abelard, Guillaume de St.
Thierry says "Quod autem temporalitatis huius cursum [i.e., Abelard] vocat
involucrum Joannem Scotum sequitur, qui frequentius hoc inusitato vocabulo
usus, et ipse pro sua subtilitate de haeresi notatus est." (*Disputatio altera
adversus Abaelardum*, PL 180.322.) In fact, Eriugena does not seem to have
used the term, though it occurs in the *Clavis physicae* of Honorius Augus-
todunensis, which was instrumental in popularizing Eriugena's thought in
the twelfth century; see d'Alverny, "Le cosmos symbolique du douzième
siècle," *Archives d'histoire* 28 (1953), pp. 31-81.

[165] On Godfrey's career see Delhaye, *Le Microcosmos*, pp. 13-49; Phillip
Damon, "The Preconium Augustini of Godfrey of St. Victor," *Medieval
Studies* 22 (1960), 92-93. The *Fons philosophiae* is edited by Pierre Mi-
chaud-Quantin (Namur, 1956). Beryl Smalley observes, in explaining the
attitude of later Victorines toward the program of Hugh (*The Study of the
Bible*, p. 105): "The program . . . implied too high a tension between the
academic and the religious life. Hugh's ideal exegete was a combination of
Paris master and contemplative religious which only exceptional circum-
stances could produce."

[166] See Silverstein, "Fabulous Cosmogony," pp. 114-16.

of which traces are perceptible everywhere in Chartrian writings, but which, though they can hardly be said to explore the nature of things empirically, do not take wholly for granted the large Platonic generalities with which we have so far been mainly concerned. In a number of these compilations the interrelations of the various levels of cosmic life are linked to complex powers and subjected to the influence of *daimones* in ways which are scarcely hinted at in the *Timaeus*, but were probably suggested by Firmicus Maternus and translations of Ptolemy, as well as the richly allusive and widely influential *Asclepius* (a hermetic treatise falsely attributed to Apuleius), and were elaborated also in Arabic cosmological writings.[167] From the *Asclepius*, too, were derived the hints of a cosmic eroticism which occur in various treatises, which are brilliantly exploited by Bernardus Silvestris in his characterization of *Natura* in the *De mundi universitate*, and which, perhaps augmented by hints from Apuleius' discussion of *daimones* in the *De deo Socratis*, inspired the relationship of Nature and Genius in the *De planctu naturae* of Alain de Lille.[168] The speculation which these various sources

[167] Arabic astrology and its place in twelfth-century thought are outlined by T. O. Wedel, *The Medieval Attitude toward Astrology* (New Haven, 1920), pp. 49-63 (Yale Studies in English, No. 60); see also Silverstein, "Fabulous Cosmogony," pp. 96-97; Gregory, *Anima mundi*, pp. 218-35; Mirella Brini-Savorelli, "Un manuale di geomanzia presentato da Bernardo Silvestre da Tours (xii secolo): l'*Experimentarius*," *Rivista critica di storia della filosofia* 14 (1959), pp. 285-90.

The special status of the *Asclepius* in late antiquity is explained by Frances Yates, *Giordano Bruno and the Hermetic Tradition* (London, 1964), pp. 2-12. It is echoed in virtually every cosmological treatise of the twelfth century. As Silverstein notes (ed. "Liber Hermetis Mercurii Triplicis *de vi rerum principiis*," *Archives d'histoire* 22, 1955, p. 220), a particularly pregnant text was the account of the "outflowing" of divine life (*Asclepius* 3, in Apuleius, *De philosophia libri*, ed. Paul Thomas, Leipzig, 1908, p. 38). Very important also was the account of *daimones* in Apuleius' *De deo Socratis*; see, e.g., Gundissalinus, *De processione mundi* (ed. Bülow, pp. 44-45), where Apuleius' view of *daimones* is preferred to that of Augustine.

[168] A fine survey of cosmic eroticism, though its thesis is somewhat overstated, is Dronke's "L'amor che move il sole e l'altre stelle." His views have much in common with those of E. R. Curtius, *European Literature and the Latin Middle Ages*, tr. Willard Trask (New York, 1953), pp. 105-20. See Silverstein's comments on Curtius' account, "Fabulous Cosmogony," pp. 108-12.

inspired takes place, so to speak, within the boundaries of the *Timaeus*, but it does not always lend itself to the sort of domestication imposed, for example, by Guillaume de Conches on the astrology of Plato.

Closely parallel to the role of these heterodox cosmological writings was that played by the study of medicine, a concern of the school of Chartres from an early date.[169] Guided by such authorities as the *Premnon physicon* of Nemesius of Emessa and the various translations and adaptations of Constantinus Africanus,[170] it was possible to explore the elemental bases of man's physical existence, and the interrelations of the various aspects of his nature in ways which not only refined upon the *Timaeus*, but also at times abandoned the theoretical assumptions of Platonism to consider human nature empirically. Though the subject remains virtually unexplored, the influence of medical writings was clearly considerable. They inspired much original scientific investigation, and they must surely have contributed immeasurably to that awareness of the complexity of human nature which is so strikingly displayed in twelfth-century poetry. They provide a physiological counterpart, for example, to the moral-philosophical concern with the kinds and degrees of love, and especially with that "mixed" love, at once physical and elevating, humorously extolled by Andreas Capellanus, and explored with great and even tragic seriousness in lyric and philosophical poetry.[171]

[169] Scholarship to 1948 is summarized by Silverstein, "Fabulous Cosmogony," p. 97, n. 31. A survey of twelfth-century medical studies is given by Richard McKeon, "Medicine and Philosophy in the Eleventh and Twelfth Centuries: the Problem of Elements," *The Thomist* 24 (1961), 211-56. Medical works used by Guillaume de Conches are discussed by Gregory, *Anima mundi*, pp. 201-06; Silverstein, "Guillaume de Conches and Nemesius of Emessa: on the Sources of the 'New Science' of the Twelfth Century," in *Harry Austryn Wolfson Jubilee Volumes* (Jerusalem, 1965) II, 719-34. As Silverstein shows (pp. 721-23), Guillaume could use medical sources to correct and clarify the *Timaeus*, the anthropological portion of which he did not know.

[170] See McKeon, "Philosophy and Medicine," pp. 221-31.

[171] For a striking instance of the influence of medicine on poetry, see Dronke's discussion of the famous "Dum Dianae vitrea," *Medieval Latin*

Even harder to characterize, but of at least equal importance for the literature produced under Chartrian influence, is that spirit which von den Steinen has called "subjectivism,"[172] and of which the most striking early expression is the work of Abelard. I have suggested already how his intuitive approach to Plato testifies to a new faith in reason and imagination; it has important affinities also with the subjective element in Abelard's own *Planctus*, where the sufferings of Old Testament figures are endowed with a quasi-typological meaning by the poet himself, and in the *Historia calamitatum*, where a similar process is applied to his own experience. More generally, it corresponds to a growing concern with human experience as intrinsically meaningful which appears in later poetry and of which, at least for the author of the *Metamorphosis Goliae*, Abelard is the living symbol.

The diffusion of Chartrian influence among the centers of literary studies was a gradual process, but was well under way by the time of the School's rather abrupt decline in the third quarter of the century. In its early stages, at least, the formal aspects of the Chartrian curriculum, its view of the object of secular studies and of the hierarchy of knowledge through which the Arts were empowered to guide the aspiring mind, remained more or less intact. What eventually proved to be decisive changes took place at first within this established framework: a gradual deemphasis of the scientific in favor of the metaphorical implications of the Platonic cosmol-

---

and the Rise of European Love-Lyric (Oxford, 1965) I, 306-13. A likely link between the love poetry of the twelfth century and the kinds of scientific writing under discussion is the treatment of love in the second book of Apuleius' *De Platone* and in the *Asclepius*; see Silverstein, "Andreas, Plato and the Arabs," *Modern Philology* 47 (1949–50), 122-25. Also worth noting is the increasing concern with the role of the body reflected in the "gradualist" view of love discussed by Douglas Kelly, "Courtly Love in Perspective: The Hierarchy of Love in Andreas Capellanus," *Traditio* 24 (1968), 128-34.

[172] Wolfram von den Steinen, "Les sujets d'inspiration chez les poètes latins du XIIᵉ siècle, II: Abélard et le subjectivisme," *Cahiers de civilization médiévale* 9 (1966), pp. 363-73. See also the remarks of Dronke, *The Medieval Lyric* (London, 1968), pp. 53-55.

ogy; a complementary shift from rational analysis to poetic intui-
tion and elaboration; and more specifically, an emphasis on mythog-
raphy and the analysis of *integumenta*, not primarily as a means of
new insight into cosmological theory, but as a way of interpreting
a wider range of literature and bringing it into relation with the
traditional Chartrian curriculum.

Manifest in all of this is a new preoccupation with the role of
poetry in the expression of complex ideas, and with the complex-
ities of meaning attainable in poetic language. More and more such
interests were accompanied by a desire to exploit these resources
through imitation as well as study of the great *auctores*. Before
turning to consider twelfth-century poetry directly, it is necessary
to give some account of two authors who, from the strictly literary
standpoint, were easily the most influential figures in the early
stages of this poetic movement: Boethius and Martianus Capella.
I have already had occasion to mention these authors, who were
esteemed by the Chartrians as worthy successors of Plato; but in
the next chapter I would like to concentrate on their special role
as a link with the themes and materials of classical poetry, and in
defining the classical tradition as the twelfth century understood
it. Moreover, some sense of the literary quality of their work is
essential to an appreciation of the poetry of the Chartrian tradition.

Boethius' *De consolatione philosophiae* gave definitive expression
to the metaphorical implications of the cosmology of the *Timaeus*,
and placed special emphasis on the psychological experience of the
philosopher. The *De nuptiis* of Martianus, in addition to providing
a host of familiar motifs expressive of the cohesion and scope of
the Liberal Arts, was also the single most important point of ref-
erence for the interpretation of mythographical *integumenta*. These
special qualities are reflected in two unusually interesting commen-
taries, that of Guillaume de Conches on the *De consolatione* and
that of Bernardus Silvestris on the opening book of the *De nuptiis*.
To review their work is a highly appropriate way of marking the
transition from philosophical to literary study; for the whole range
of Chartrian thought, and its basic humanism, are summed up in
Guillaume's bold response to Boethius' incantatory use of cosmic

imagery, and the subtlety of his mythological allusions. Bernardus' handling of Martianus carries this originality still further, and imbues it with something of the subjectivity of Abelard. In him we may observe at once the first distinguished *litteratus* in the tradition of Chartres and the last of the Chartrian philosophers.

CHAPTER TWO

PHILOSOPHY AND EXPERIENCE: BOETHIUS, MARTIANUS CAPELLA, AND THEIR TWELFTH-CENTURY COMMENTATORS

1. Poetry and Argument in the *De consolatione philosophiae*

As Chenu has demonstrated, the twelfth century was in many respects an *aetas boethiana*,[1] and it is of course doing scant justice to the place of Boethius in the Chartrian program to isolate for special consideration the literary aspects of the *De consolatione*. For in their insistence upon a broad and humanistic curriculum, centered in theology but embracing all of philosophy and belles-lettres as well, the Chartrians sought to fulfill what seemed the ideal role defined by the *oeuvre* of Boethius, which included treatises on the specific arts of music, arithmetic, and logic, as well as profoundly influential theological writings, and, in the *De consolatione*, a unique synthesis of *eloquentia* and *sapientia*.[2] Of all the *auctores* it was Boethius who most nearly rivaled the authority of Plato. But the Chartrians seem to have recognized certain basic differences between the two authors. Boethius' purpose was more psychological than Plato's, his cosmology more simply a source of metaphor, and his use of mythological and other imagery more integrally bound up with his intention in writing. Thus the *De consolatione* provided a link between the abstract, philosophical

[1] *La théologie*, pp. 142-58. As Chenu notes (p. 142), Chartres was the great center of "Boethian" studies from an early date.

[2] See Courcelle, *La consolation*, pp. 67-72, 74-80, on manuscript illustrations showing Boethius as the patron of music, arithmetic, and theology; and Parent, *La doctrine de la création*, pp. 19, 60-62, 95-106, 111-12, on Boethius' role in the Chartrian program.

use of *integumenta*, which it exhibited in common with the *Timaeus*, and the role of such figures in poetry. In the following brief summary I will attempt to isolate the aspects of the *De consolatione* which account for the special nature of its influence.

A basic metaphor is introduced early in the opening book of the dialogue, in the song which Philosophy addresses to the downcast and resentful prisoner Boethius after expelling the harlot Muses of poetry from his cell.[3] Once, she says, his mind was free, and "ran along heavenly paths," seeking the causes of things, the secrets of nature. Now the weaknesses of his own nature have overwhelmed him. From this point forward, cosmic order, and the storms and clouds by which Fortune conceals it from the mind's eye, are recurring images for the powers of reason and passion in the prisoner's state of mind. Reproaching Philosophy for her indifference to his present grief, he reminds her of a time "cum mores nostros totiusque uitae rationem ad caelestis ordinis exempla formares,"[4] and he prays to the divine source of this order—"whoever thou art who makest fast the bonds of things"—that his trust in it may be restored.[5]

In the course of the first two books, Philosophy begins her cure by eliciting a reaffirmation of her disciple's confidence in providence, and by showing that the very loss he laments is in fact providential, enabling him to repudiate Fortune, and distinguish between true and abiding goods and those which are governed by material considerations. Again the point is reinforced by translation into cosmic terms: the relation of psychological to cosmic order is the theme of the concluding *metrum* of Book Two, in which Boethius' earthly desires are represented by the "pugnantia semina" of the universe. Just as appetite, by opposing reason, tears the robe of philosophy, so the elements, if they prevailed against the order of

---

[3] *De consolatione* 1, metr. 2, ed. Ludwig Bieler, *Corpus christianorum* (Turnhout, 1957), Vol. 94, 3-4. All quotations are from the text of Bieler. Translations are taken from the version of R. H. Green (Library of Liberal Arts, New York, 1962), adjusted occasionally to conform to Bieler's punctuation.

[4] *De consolatione* 1, pr. 4, p. 7.   [5] *Ibid.*, 1, metr. 5, pp. 11-12.

the universe, would destroy the *machina mundi*. The secret of cosmic, and ideally of mental stability is "the love which rules earth and sea, and commands the heavens."[6]

This rational love is closely bound up with knowledge, and when in Book Three the prisoner is granted a vision of cosmic order, the result is to raise the argument of the dialogue to a new plane. After a long analysis of worldly goods has convinced Boethius that happiness is only to be found in aligning one's will with that providence "quod fini iunxerit ortum,"[7] Philosophy prepares to ascend to a higher level of discourse by invoking the creator, after the manner of Plato in the *Timaeus*. Then follows the magnificent cosmic hymn which was the high point of the *De consolatione* for the Chartrians, and the subject of many commentaries throughout the middle ages. Doctrinally it is a brilliant summary of the cosmology of the *Timaeus*, but read in the context of the dialogue, it is also the fulfillment of the longing for an integrating vision expressed in the earlier *metra*, and brings the moral-philosophical and the psychological themes of the *De consolatione* into balance. It dramatizes the reattainment of mental stability, and implies the possibility of further enlightenment:[8]

> . . . tu cuncta superno
> Ducis ab exemplo, pulchrum pulcherrimus ipse
> Mundum mente gerens similique in imagine formans
> Perfectasque iubens perfectum absoluere partes.
> . . .
> Da pater augustam menti conscendere sedem,
> Da fontem lustrare boni, da luce reperta
> In te conspicuos animi defigere uisus.
> . . . Tu namque serenum,
> Tu requies tranquilla piis, te cernere finis,
> Principium, uector, dux, semita, terminus idem.

You fashion all things according to the eternal exemplar. You who are most beautiful produce the beautiful world from your divine

---

[6] *Ibid.*, 2, metr. 8, p. 36. (On this song see Dronke, "L'amor che move il sole e l'altre stelle," pp. 399-406.)

[7] *Ibid.*, 3, metr. 2, pp. 40-41.

[8] *Ibid.*, 3, metr. 9, lines 6-9, 22-28, pp. 50-51.

mind and, forming it in your image, you order the perfect parts in a perfect whole. . . . Grant, O Father, that my mind may rise to thy sacred throne. Let it see the fountain of good; let it find light, so that the clear light of my soul may fix itself in thee. . . . For thou art the serenity, the tranquil peace of virtuous men. The sight of thee is beginning and end; one guide, leader, path, and goal.

Before summarizing further it is worth stopping at this turning point in the dialogue to reflect briefly on the broad role of poetry in the movement of the *De consolatione*. As recent commentators have remarked,[9] the poetry, in which cosmological imagery is prominent, and the development of the moral argument in the *prosae* are not wholly congruent. The *metra* of the opening books stress the harmonious aspects of cosmic life, and convey the sense of an all-embracing *amor*, but are acutely sensitive also to disruptive forces, and seem at times to hint that man is somehow incapable of participating in the harmony of the universe. This creates a tension between the effect of the *metra* and that of the *prosae*, in which Philosophy's case for providence moves steadily forward, and this tension becomes increasingly important in the later books of the dialogue. As Dronke observes, Philosophy's vision is superimposed on that of Fortune,[10] and the intuition of harmony necessarily entails a recognition of the danger of dissolution. Rhythm is as important as reason in the development of Boethius' theme, and the dialectical movement of the *De consolatione* is not only in the dialogue of Philosophy with the prisoner, but in a larger dialogue between rational argumentation and poetry.[11]

The two strains come together in the great hymn, and in the

[9] See Dronke, "L'amor che move," pp. 403-04; Jean Györy, "Le cosmos, un songe," *Annales Universitatis Budapestensis: Sectio philologica* 4 (1963), pp. 92-94.

[10] "L'amor che move," p. 404.

[11] Philosophy seems to invite this interpretation in 3, pr. 12, p. 61, where she exhorts the prisoner to maintain the dialogue: " 'Accepisti,' inquit, 'in fabulis lacessentes caelum Gigantas; sed illos quoque, uti condignum fuit, benigna fortitudo disposuit. Sed uisne rationes ipsas inuicem collidamus? Forsitan ex huiusmodi conflictatione pulchra quaedam ueritatis scintilla dissiliat.' " The psychological aspect of this dialogue is emphasized by Luigi Alfonsi, "Storia interiore e storia cosmica nella 'Consolatio' boeziana," *Convivium* 23 (1955), 515.

remainder of Book Three its lofty idealism and imagery inform the prose argument itself, while the verse is relegated to the role of a moralizing chorus. Developing the theme of harmony between creator and creation, Philosophy teaches Boethius that the nexus between the two must be a mutual love.[12] To show their complementarity, she describes the "form of the divine substance," Parmenides' Being, "in body like a sphere, perfectly rounded on all sides."[13] Then, having, as she says, discovered all that reason can know of "the most important point of all," she ends Book Three with a poem on Orpheus and Eurydice.[14] This poem, which describes Orpheus' grief at the death of Eurydice, his descent into Hades, his successful appeal against fate, and his second loss of his love, brings poetry into play in a newly complicated way. It may be seen as a comment on the nature of the "cure" being effected by Philosophy, for it brings together in a single image the psychological and the intellectual aspects of the prisoner's situation. Conceived by Philosophy as an admonitory exemplum, it also gives eloquent expression to the very impulse it is intended to curb, the attachment to earthly things which is at the heart of the metaphor of imprisonment. It is also significant that the poem shows us poetry, inspired by love, suspending the working of necessity in the universe. Philosophy has attempted something very similar, for she has moved from persuasion and rational argument to an inspired use of poetry to bridge the gap between the situation of the dreamer and the divine harmony,[15] denying the reality of the dreamer's loss as

[12] *De consolatione* 3, pr. 12, p. 61: " 'Cum deus,' inquit, omnia bonitatis clauo gubernare iure credatur eademque omnia, sicuti docui, ad bonum naturali intentione festinent, num dubitari potest quin uoluntaria regantur seque ad disponentis nutum ueluti conuenientia contemperataque rectori sponte conuertant? 'Ita,' inquam, 'necesse est. . .' " C. S. Lewis points out that Philosophy goes on to explain God's governance in the language of the Book of Wisdom, causing the prisoner to remark on the pleasure given him by her choice of words; *The Discarded Image* (Cambridge, 1964), p. 79.

[13] *De consolatione* 3, pr. 12, p. 62.   [14] *Ibid.*, 3, metr. 12, pp. 63-64.

[15] A remark in the prologue to the glosses in B.M. Royal 15.B.III (see above, ch. 1, n. 61) seems to point to this aspect of the work: "Est autem alius modus tractandi, quia triplici genere probationis utitur, in principio ponendo argumenta rethorica deinde dyalectica, ad ultimum demonstra-

Orpheus seeks to deny the fact of the death of Eurydice. But poetry is a complex medium, and in doing justice to the complexity of the prisoner's situation it almost inevitably communicates emotions which are not reconcilable with reason. "Quis legem det amantibus?" asks Philosophy, and the moral which she addresses to all "who seek to raise your minds to sovereign day" seems to stress the difficulty, almost the impossibility of the task.

The poem on Orpheus is the first of three in which the pursuit of freedom and wisdom is dramatized in mythological terms. Early in Book Four Ulysses' sojourn on the island of Circe, who "has power over men's bodies, but cannot change their hearts,"[16] is contrasted with more insidious experiences which poison the mind. And when the prisoner has wrestled with the "Hydra-like" problem of fate and providence,[17] Book Four concludes with a poem which, after alluding to the sacrifice of Iphigenia and Ulysses' blinding of Polyphemus, centers appropriately on the labors of Hercules, concluding with his apotheosis and an exhortation to man to "overcome the earth" and claim the stars.[18] Again, the appeal of these poems is twofold, and emphasizes the sadness of the severing of earthly ties as well as the necessity and nobility of heroic sacrifice. The Homeric episodes alluded to all involve the loss of loved companions, and the sacrifice of Iphigenia is the harshest possible image, indeed a grim parody, of the renunciation of mortal affections, reminding us of the danger that in making such sacrifices one may only reap the wind. Thus these two poems have in common with that on Orpheus an undertone of suppressed feeling which is at odds with their ostensibly exemplary purpose.

---

tiones." Though Guillaume de Conches, in his prologue, asserts that the consolation given by Philosophy consists in a "rationabilis demonstratio" of the meanness of earthly joys, the term "demonstrationes" in the passage just quoted may perhaps be understood in the larger sense given it, for instance, in Hugh's definition of the symbol (see above, ch. 1, p. 59).

[16] *De consolatione* 4, metr. 3, pp. 72-73.

[17] *Ibid.*, 4, pr. 6, pp. 78-79: "Talis namque materia est ut una dubitatione succisa innumerabiles aliae uelut hydrae capita succrescant; nec ullus fuerit modus nisi quis eas uiuacissimo mentis igne coherceat."

[18] *Ibid.*, 4, metr. 7, pp. 87-88.

This undertone rests in unresolved coexistence with the major activity of Books Four and Five, the synthesis of the themes and imagery of the work as a whole and the exploration of its theological, as well as its moral implications. Providence is the dominant concern, and it confronts the prisoner with two great questions: what rationale governs the distribution of good and ill fortune; and what freedom man can exercise under the all-disposing and timeless knowledge of God. The first question is raised in the middle of Book Four, and to answer it, Philosophy makes a "new beginning,"[19] tracing all existence to its source in the divine mind and showing how all that comes to pass is part of a providential order. A series of analogies justifies her reasoning:[20]

> Therefore the changing course of Fate is to the simple stability of Providence as reasoning is to intellect, as that which is generated is to that which *is*, as time is to eternity, as a circle to its center. Fate moves the heavens and the stars, governs the elements in their mixture, and transforms them by mutual change; it renews all things that are born or die by the reproduction of similar offspring and seeds. This same power binds the actions and fortunes of men in an unbreakable chain of causes. . .

Against the prisoner's pragmatic objections Philosophy points out the limited power of man's earthly perception, and enjoins upon him the contemplation of the order of the heavens.[21]

But the prisoner is still unsatisfied. The famous passage of Book Five in which he questions the possibility of freedom is followed by a poem which summarizes all the ambiguities and doubts with which the cosmic metaphor has been associated in the earlier books. Recoiling from the effort of discussing such great questions, the prisoner argues against Philosophy in terms which seem to parody her own dialectical refutation of Fortune:[22]

[19] *Ibid.*, 4, pr. 6, p. 79.
[20] *Ibid.*, 4, pr. 6, pp. 80-81. Cp. the hierarchy of mental faculties described in 5, pr. 4 (quoted below, n. 23).
[21] *Ibid.*, 4, metr. 6, pp. 84-85.
[22] *Ibid.*, 5, metr. 3, lines 8-19, p. 94. Green's translation of the final

Sed mens caecis obruta membris	Sed quis nota scire laborat?
Nequit oppressi luminis igne	At si nescit, quid caeca petit?
Rerum tenues noscere nexus?	Quis enim quidquam nescius optet?
Sed cur tanto flagrat amore	Aut quis ualeat nescita sequi
Veri tectas reperire notas?	Quoue inueniat? quis reppertam
Scitne quod appetit anxia nosse?	Queat ignarus noscere formam?

Can the human mind, overcome by the body's blindness, not discern by its dim light the delicate connections between things? But why does the mind burn with such desire to discover the hidden aspects of truth? Does it know what it is so eager to know? Then why does it go on laboriously trying to discover what it already knows? And if it does not know, why does it blindly continue the search? For who would want something of which he is unaware, or run after something he does not know? How can such a thing be found, or, if found, how would it be recognized by someone ignorant of its form?

After thus venting his frustration at contradictions which seem to sunder the very bonds of cosmic order, the prisoner makes no further contribution to the dialogue. Philosophy proceeds to explain the relation of human freedom to divine foreknowledge, drawing an analogy between the hierarchy of human faculties and the comprehensiveness of God's understanding,[23] reiterating the analogy between temporal fate and eternal providence,[24] and drawing the classic humanist moral that man's erect carriage points the course his mind must pursue.[25] In all of this she remains securely within the metaphorical bounds of the *Timaeus*, and her discourse concludes almost abruptly with a highly compressed summary of the

---

twelve lines of this *metrum* seems to me to neglect the note of doubt which lingers beyond the lines I have quoted, and which Bieler emphasizes by placing a question mark, rather than a period, at the end of line 24.

[23] *Ibid.*, 5, pr. 4, p. 97: "Sensus enim figuram in subiecta materia constitutam, imaginatio uero solam sine materia iudicat figuram. Ratio uero hanc quoque transcendit speciemque ipsam quae singularibus inest uniuersali consideratione perpendit. Intelligentiae uero celsior oculus exsistit; supergressa namque uniuersitatis ambitum ipsam illam simplicem formam pura mentis acie contuetur."

[24] *Ibid.*, 5, pr. 6, pp. 101-02: "Hunc enim uitae immobilis praesentarium statum infinitus ille temporalium rerum motus imitatur. . ."

[25] *Ibid.*, 5, metr. 5, p. 100.

scope and attributes of the divine wisdom, and an exhortation to the prisoner to flee vice, cherish virtue, hope, and pray. She elicits from him no word of assent, and, for the first time, fails to cap her argument with poetry. Reason and intuition give way to faith.

It will be obvious that this summary has emphasized the darker side of the *De consolatione*, and largely ignored the ways in which it urges and points the way to a transcendent solution of the problems with which it deals. There is a strong Neoplatonic element in Boethius' thought,[26] and a definite quasi-mystical suggestion in the *De consolatione* that the bonds of nature in their very harmony are finally as confining to the human spirit as the bonds of vice and ignorance. But read as a work of imaginative literature, the dialogue seems to me more convincing as a dramatization of the psychological experience of the attempt, than as an exposition of the means of such transcendence. In any case its final effect is by no means simple. Like the philosophers of Chartres, and more directly, Philosophy employs poetry in expressing her deepest insights, and also in her most forceful appeals to the prisoner. And her use of myth to punctuate her argument has the effect of a double exposure of the course she urges. For her the heroic images she presents are models of decisive, liberating action, repudiations of fortune and the ties and fears of earthly life. For the prisoner, and for us, they are also images of the difficulty of such renunciation and transcendence. Boethius' use of dialogue, moreover, and his testing of the efficacy of Philosophy's lessons by their effect on the doubts and confusions of a mortal subject, make it difficult for the reader to acquiesce fully in even the most powerful affirmation of the Timaean vision.

These qualities did not escape the poets who made the *De consolatione* their model. It was largely through exploiting the contrast between the deep and often somber seriousness of Boethius and the optimism of the far more fanciful and abstract allegory of Martianus Capella that the Chartrian poets expressed their sense of the human condition.

[26] See Courcelle, *La consolation*, pp. 23-28, 161-76.

2. The *De nuptiis Philologiae et Mercurii*

The *De consolatione* is still read, but Martianus' *De nuptiis* is not. Motifs from the work can be found everywhere in medieval art and poetry, and Martianus is generally accepted as the source of the medieval classification of the Liberal Arts, but the elaborate *fabula* in which his educational ideals are set forth seems to have been ignored since the Renaissance.[27] Thus a rather unfair picture has been created by C. S. Lewis and certain other critics, who have written so engagingly about the failings of Martianus as a writer that they have tended to make him a proverbial figure for pretentiousness and pedantry;[28] the much larger group who have noted his influence on medieval poetry have tended to treat it as a sort of pedagogical convenience. In fact, however, it was Martianus' qualities of style and imagination at least as much as his didactic uses which interested the twelfth century; the first two books of the *De nuptiis*, which contain the allegory, were widely circulated as a separate work, and were the subject of many commentaries.[29] It was largely from Martianus that the Chartrian poets learned their subtly evocative use of mythology, and that carefully ambiguous "metaphysical" style which seems always to say more than can be extracted from it by rational analysis. Whether these were good influences in themselves is debatable, though it is certainly demonstrable that fine poetry came of them. Of more immediate concern to us is that in the process of assimilating and interpreting these aspects of Martianus' writing, twelfth-century poets and grammarians were provoked to ventures in literary creation and criticism which were equally influential in their day, and lasting in

[27] See Claudio Leonardi, "Nota introduttiva per un'indagine sulla fortuna di Marziano Capella nel Medioevo," *Bullettino dell' Istituto Storico Italiano per il Medioevo* 67 (1955), pp. 265-88; W. H. Stahl, "To a Better Understanding of Martianus Capella," *Speculum* 40 (1965), pp. 102-15.

[28] See, Lewis, *The Allegory of Love* (Oxford, 1936), pp. 78-90.

[29] See Stahl, "To a Better Understanding," pp. 102, n. 2; 106, n. 11. On Martianus' role in medieval iconography see above, ch. 1, n. 38; Emile Mâle, *Religious Art in France: XIII Century*, tr. Dora Nussey (London, 1913), pp. 75-94.

their effect. Again a brief summary may serve to bring out the pertinent features of the allegory.

The theme of the *De nuptiis* is stated in the opening prayer to Hymen, conceived as the cosmic power which, "constraining contentious particles with mysterious bonds, preserves union in discord by its divine embrace."[30] In a brief exchange the author then defends his preoccupation with such matters against the objections of his son for whom he undertakes to recount, "ni prolixitas perculerit," the *mythos* itself. This begins with a review of the evidence for monogamy among the gods, reiterating the theme of cosmic marriage mythologically. Mercury is then introduced, young, handsome, and in search of a wife. The search is difficult: *Sophia*, his first choice, is wedded to Eternity, and *Mantice*, spirit of prophecy, is devoted to Apollo. *Psyche*, the human soul, is his next object, and Martianus digresses to enumerate the rich gifts bestowed upon her by the gods:[31] these range from immortality, bestowed by Jupiter, and self-knowledge, from Urania, to Venus' gift of sensuality. Mercury has given the chariot of that eloquence for which he stands, which can traverse all knowledge. His hopes of winning Psyche are high until *Virtus* comes in tears to announce that her former intimate has been ensnared by Cupid. Mercury and Virtue then set out to seek the advice of Apollo.

"Eloquence, unenlightened by reason," says John of Salisbury, "is rash and blind." Martianus' Mercury, lacking the stability of knowledge and accompanied only by untutored virtue, is led, in his search for Apollo, through a wilderness of omen and augury, withered laurel, abandoned caves and groves. A fortunate encounter with *fama* leads them to Mount Parnassus where, entering Apollo's sacred grove, they are given a philosophical view of the order and destinies of things. They see first the endless train of *fortunae*, present, past, and future, of nations and rulers. A certain order can be discerned among events close in time, but at any remove, past or

[30] *De nuptiis Philologiae et Mercurii* 1.1, ed. A. Dick (Leipzig, 1925), p. 3. References to the *De nuptiis* will be to book and paragraph of the work itself and to page in Dick.

[31] *Ibid.*, 1.7, pp. 7-8.

future, their uncertainty becomes such that "uelut fumidae caliga-
tionis incredibilis haberetur aura." Through the maze of *fortunae*
may be discerned the higher order of the grove itself, its trees so
arranged as to resound in perfect harmony when struck by the
wind. As he becomes aware of this phenomenon, Mercury seems
to come to life, assumes his proper role as *eloquentia* and interprets
the grove for Virtue. The music of the grove, he explains, is also
that of the spheres, "nor is it surprising that the grove of Apollo
should conform to so wise a plan, since that same Delian god, as
the sun, also orders the heavenly spheres."[32]

Mercury and Virtue proceed to the abode of Apollo, who knows
their errand at once and greets them with a description of Philol-
ogy, *doctissima virgo*, whose insight into the nature of things con-
founds Jove himself.[33] As the protégée of *Sophia*, the "nurse" of
Mantice, and the instructress of *Psyche*, whom she strives endlessly
to make worthy of immortality, Philology combines the charms of
all Mercury's former loves. Such is her appeal that Virtue, hearing
her described, "aliquantulo de ingenito rigore descendens, etiam
corpore moueretur."

Before Philology may be approached the match must be ap-
proved by Jove, though this is assured by the fact that Mercury, as
the means by which the divine plan is articulated, is intimately
involved with all expressions of his will.[34] Accordingly, Virtue,
Apollo, and Mercury ascend to the heavens, while all creation joins
in expressions of joy. The Muses are joined in harmony with the
universe itself as they rise to their proper places among the spheres.
Apollo and Mercury are suddenly metamorphosized into their heav-
enly forms and simultaneously approach, *allegorice*, the palace of
Jove.[35] There Apollo argues in favor of the marriage and Jove and
Juno debate the matter, in an atmosphere scented with pedantic
bawdry. Jove fears that Mercury may be distracted by the joys of
marriage from the performance of celestial errands. Juno points out

[32] *Ibid.*, 1.11-12, p. 11.   [33] *Ibid.*, 1.22, p. 16.   [34] *Ibid.*, 1.25, p. 18.
[35] *Ibid.*, 1.30, p. 20: "atque ita metamorphosi supera pulchriores per
Geminos proprietate quadam signi familiaris inuecti augusto refulsere caelo
ac mox Tonantis palatium petiuerunt."

that Philology never rests, and indeed her far-ranging thoughts are continually summoning the very gods from their own beds, "quadam inaudita obsecratione," at all hours. Far from becoming lazy or weak-willed, Mercury will be inspired, "sustained in his flight by her, to seek to pass beyond the very limits of the universe."

At this point Pallas, divine wisdom, descends "de quodam purgatioris uibratiorisque luminis loco," and the case is referred to her. She frankly declares her preference that Philology remain, like herself, a virgin, and then symbolically dissociates herself from any propagation of knowledge by removing, with all the pride of "soliuaga uirginitas," her radiant crown of the seven arts, "ne feturarum copulis et causis interesset." But she acknowledges Mercury's deserts, and concludes with the warning that if a marriage is to take place Philology must first be accorded immortality by consent of all the gods in council.[36]

A council is decreed, and the assembling gods are described in a long catalogue which extends from the Olympians to such obscure figures as the "elementorum praesules" and "mentium cultores." Jove appears clad in robes representing the visible universe, and Juno in others inscribed with the phenomena of the atmosphere and upper air, and the two rulers contemplate a sphere, "set high among the stars," which is inscribed with "whatever universal nature can conceivably contain," and is so seen to be "the image and the idea of the universe."[37] Jove then appeals to the gods on Mercury's behalf, his appeal taking the form of a sort of hymn to eloquence, as the means whereby the mysterious order of the universe is expressed:[38]

> nam nostra ille fides, sermo, benignitas
> ac uerus Genius, fida recursio
> interpresque meae mentis ὁ νοῦς sacer.
> hic solus numerum promere caelitum,
> hic uibrata potest noscere sidera,
>
> . . .
>
> quaeque elementa liget dissona nexio,
> perque hunc ipse pater foedera sancio. . .

[36] *Ibid.*, 1.39-40, pp. 24-26. [37] *Ibid.*, 1.68, p. 32.
[38] *Ibid.*, 1.92, p. 39.

For he is our pledge, word, favoring aspect and very genius, faithful
reflection and interpreter of my mind, sacred intelligence. Only he
can expound the heavenly law of number, only he can know the
gleaming stars . . . and what union of discords binds the elements;
and through him I, the Father, make my covenant . . .

Such an eloquence, it is clear, needs only an understanding worthy
of itself to attain its fulfillment, and the first book ends with a
unanimous decision to immortalize Philology.

The eloquence presented by Martianus in the figure of Mercury
is clearly an almost mystical conception, a link between the divine
mind and human comprehension, and so, in conjunction with
knowledge, a means whereby the human soul may realize its situa-
tion and destiny. It is a visionary medium, and in its ideal form—
as characterized by Jove in the hymn just quoted—it reveals a
certain affinity between Martianus' Neoplatonism and the pseudo-
Dionysian notion of anagogy, the means whereby human percep-
tion transcends itself. And despite Martianus' thick veneer of liter-
ary embellishment we may see in the "immortalizing" influence of
Mercury and Philology something like the effect described by Hugh
of St. Victor in the opening book of the *Didascalicon*, the human
soul's recovery, through knowledge, of its likeness to the divine
Wisdom.

This transcendent aspect of *eloquentia* becomes clearer in Book
Two of the *De nuptiis*, which is largely taken up with the prepara-
tion of Philology for immortality. She is introduced in an anxious
state. Having read the stars she knows what is in store for her, and
a brief glimpse of Mercury (also the patron of the gymnasium)
"post unctionem palaestricam recurrentem" has served to quicken
her innate attraction to him.[39] But she is reluctant to forsake, as
she must, the *mythos*, the delights of poetry and the "historias
mortalium" which have solaced her vigil in the world. After an
extremely complicated set of auspices, involving her knowledge of
(at least) grammar, arithmetic, geometry, astronomy and music,
and evidently intended as a counterpart to Mercury's tortuous
search for Apollo, she is satisfied that all bodes well for the mar-

[39] *Ibid.*, 2.100, p. 42.

riage, and turns to thoughts of her new life. Her mother *Phronesis* (i.e., *Prudentia*, understanding) appears with bridal garments and ornaments, in which Philology appears the image of Pallas herself.[40]

In a burst of harmony the Muses enter, and each in turn offers Philology true understanding in place of mere earthly knowledge of her respective specialty. Urania begins in behalf of astronomy, Calliope and Clio oppose the music of the spheres and divine clarity to the deceptive nature of the earthly arts of expression, and Euterpe (perhaps to point up the limited nature of the transports which, in her earthly role, she inspires in the lyric poet) is made to proclaim the power of true philosophy to penetrate to the source of fate and destiny. Finally Thalia, Muse of elegy, glorifies the lovers and their power to render divine the earthly ties which unite them:[41]

nunc nunc beantur artes,
quas sic sacratis ambo
ut dent meare caelo,
reserent caducis astra
ac lucida usque ad aethram
pia subuolare uota.

per uos uigil decensque
nus mentis ima complet,
per uos probata lingua
fert glorias per aeuum.
uos disciplinas omnes
ac nos sacrate musas.

Now are the Arts blest, for together you so sanctify them that they grant access to heaven, open the stellar regions to mortal beings, and let faithful prayers ascend even to the bright ether. Through your observation and articulation, understanding fills the expanses of the mind. Through you well-tempered language attains eternal honor. Bestow your sacred power upon all the Arts, and upon us, the Muses.

But before these promises can be fulfilled the preparations for immortality must be completed. The Cardinal Virtues, and then Philosophy, attended by the Graces, appear, and at last *Athanasia*, immortality, descends amid a thundering of universal song. Her first act is to make Philology vomit forth the countless *volumina* of earthly knowledge she has absorbed. Of the huge pile of books thus created she consigns some, "whose letters seemed to be the likenesses of living creatures," to the depths of the temples of Egypt.

[40] *Ibid.*, 2.114, p. 48.   [41] *Ibid.*, 2.126, p. 56.

The Arts and Muses gather up appropriate portions of the rest, to be redistributed in the light of divine wisdom. *Athanasia* then accepts from her mother *Apotheosis*, and gives to Philology to drink, a certain "spherical and animate rotundity," by the effect of which she is made immortal.[42]

At last she ascends, borne by Labor and accompanied by the Muses, as well as by a noble youth who "was no son of the Venus of voluptuous desire, and yet was called 'amor' by the wise."[43] As they reach the heavens Juno Pronuba appears and reveals to Philology the many *daimones* of the sublunar regions. Passing upward through the spheres they arrive at the throne of the Sun, where Philology is moved to reverence by the "fountain of etherial radiance flowing forth from its secret source."[44] Finally they arrive at the level of the Empyrean, and she beholds the sphere by which the universe is moved, "not unmindful that the god and author of this vast engine and its great scheme has withdrawn himself even beyond the power of the very gods to discover." Here, at the outermost limit of the universe, she kneels,[45]

> ac tota mentis acie coartata diu silentio deprecatur ueterumque ritu uocabula quaedam uoce mentis inclamans secundum dissonas nationes numeris uaria, sono ignota, iugatis alternatisque litteris inspirata ueneraturque uerbis intellectualis mundi praesules deos eorumque ministros sensibilis sphaerae potestatibus uenerandos uniuersumque totum infinibilis patris profunditate coercitum . . . quandam etiam fontanam uirginem deprecatur . . . atque illam existentem ex non existentibus ueritatem toto pectore deprecata tum uisa se cernere apotheosin sacraque meruisse. . .

and mustering all the forces of understanding she prayed in silence, uttering in her inner mind certain words hallowed by ancient usage, words whose accent varies among the diverse nations, and whose intonation is obscure, inspired words, their letters joined or intermingled; and she uttered prayers to the

[42] *Ibid.*, 2.140, p. 61.
[44] *Ibid.*, 2.185, 192, pp. 73-74.
[43] *Ibid.*, 2.144, p. 62.
[45] *Ibid.*, 2.203-06, pp. 76-77.

gods who preside over the *mundus intellectualis* and their ministers, to whom the forces of the sensible universe do homage, and to that universality which is governed by the profound deliberation of the all-embracing Father . . . to a certain virgin fount, too, she offered prayers . . . and having invoked wholeheartedly that truth which exists by virtue of powers beyond existence she seemed to realize herself immortal and worthy of this sacrament . . .

From this climactic vision she descends to the court of Jove, where all the immortals await her, including the "souls of the blessed ancients," philosophers and poets. Even here the sages quarrel about the nature of things, and the all-consuming harmony of the Muses is necessary to drown their *rabulatu*. The decree of marriage is read, and the seven wise virgins who comprise Mercury's gift to his bride are presented. In a brief final poem the author announces the completion of the *mythos*.

From the *De nuptiis* the twelfth century derived two closely related ideas which greatly affected their own literary activity. First, like the *De consolatione* of Boethius, but far more explicitly and schematically, the *De nuptiis* dramatizes the theme of intellectual pilgrimage from the sensible world to the level of vision and theology, "per creaturas ad creatorem." As we will see this theme assumed epic dimensions in post-Chartrian literary theory and was regarded as virtually the archetypal theme of all serious poetry. Second, Martianus presents a universe in which cosmology and mythology are perfectly integrated, the *coniugia sacra* of the gods are part of the nature of things, and mythographical analysis involves no more than a simple translation from one set of terms to the other. Fulgentius, whose *Mitologiae* are largely concerned with the cosmological rationale of mythology, seems to have drawn many hints from Martianus,[46] and there is no doubt that the cosmic pantheon of the *De nuptiis* was authoritative for the middle ages.

At the same time there are ambiguities in Martianus' use of

[46] See Courcelle, *Les lettres grecques en Occident. De Macrobe à Cassiodore* (Paris, 1943), pp. 206-09.

myth. The relation of the Apuleian *Cupido*, captor of Psyche, to to "sapiential" *amor* who attends Philology on her journey to heaven was a vexed question for medieval commentators on the *De nuptiis*, and is of course part of a larger problem regarding the nature of love which is at least as old as Plato's *Symposium*. Pallas' reluctance to associate herself with the nuptial proceedings, and Venus' attempt to disrupt them,[47] together with the rather cumbersome erotic nuances with which Martianus embellishes his allegory, add further complication, and we may perhaps consider them as a pedantic equivalent to the cosmic doubts and complaints of Boethius' prisoner.

But despite these calculated inconsistencies, the *De nuptiis* was accepted by the twelfth century, and by the Chartrians above all, as an authoritative presentation of the stages of intellectual fulfillment. Martianus' suggestive metaphors—the "locus purgatioris uibratioris luminis" which is the abode of Pallas, the "globosa animataque rotunditas" in which Philology receives the draught of immortality, the "fontana uirgo," source of all existence—express the kinds of insight for which the Chartrians labored in vain to find a satisfactory rationalistic form, but which they recognized as reflections of the elusive secrets they pursued. Their sensitivity to the hints of profundity in the *De nuptiis* may be illustrated by the following passage from John of Salisbury, no curious seeker of elaborate interpretations. In the *Metalogicon* John recalls Martianus in a passage which climaxes his discussion of the Platonic notion of truth:[48]

Every man desires confirmation of his beliefs, for the love of truth is intimately related to, even innate in human reason, and with Philology, as Martianus says, "invokes wholeheartedly that truth which exists only by virtue of powers beyond existence." This truth in nowise manifests itself unless some drop of divine wisdom, in the outpouring of grace, enters and illu-

---

[47] See esp. *De nuptiis* 8.804-07, pp. 423-26, where the ceremonial gathering is invaded by Silenus and a mob of satyrs, who usher in Venus.

[48] *Metalogicon* 4.36 (Webb, p. 208).

mines the mind of one who seeks and loves it. For this is truly that "virgin fount" whence Martianus declares the aforesaid truth to flow; nothing is truly knowable unless it issues forth from this source, nor does anything false emanate therefrom; for this fountain, which [Martianus] wraps in a cloud of poetic fiction, is of a virgin purity, and innocent of all corruption and falsehood.

In such a context Martianus' metaphors become philosophical *integumenta* and assume the sort of authority accorded by Guillaume de Conches to the imagery of the *Timaeus*. But the larger form of the *De nuptiis* was of great importance as well, and the clearest indication of its significance is provided by the commentaries of Bernardus Silvestris. In the remainder of this chapter I will consider Bernardus' commentaries, together with that of Guillaume de Conches on Boethius, as evidence of new insights into literature and literary expression which constitute a critical counterpart to the new poetry of the middle and later twelfth century.

3. Psychology in Guillaume's Glosses on Boethius

I will deal with the glosses on Boethius only in a highly selective way. Their format is basically that of the *Glosae super Platonem*, and they are comparably diverse, ranging from moral platitudes and mythographical commonplaces to a bold interpretation of the *anima mundi*, evoked by the "O qui perpetua."[49] They do not pretend to a coherence of their own, though there is a consistent point of view and certain recurring themes are given special emphasis. The significant feature of the compilation for our purposes is the attention Guillaume devotes to the psychological aspect of the philosopher's experience, and the features of the *De consolatione* which are given detailed treatment as a result. For though Guillaume is chiefly concerned with the revelatory aspects of the work, and indeed seemed to some contemporaries to have made too

[49] See above, ch. 1, n. 61. The text of Guillaume's glosses on the "O qui perpetua" is printed by Parent, *La doctrine de la création*, pp. 124-36.

much of them, he is also acutely sensitive to the struggle of conflicting desires and the tension between human frailty and the discipline necessary to philosophical contemplation which runs through the dialogue, and this leads him to a number of striking insights into the literary aspects of the work.

This concern of the commentary appears in the opening gloss. Boethius, says Guillaume, shows himself to be in need of consolation by bemoaning the loss of earthly pleasures. "For he is miserable whose spirit is altered by alterations in material things, exalted when they are prosperous, downcast if they go badly,"[50] and Philosophy comes to him as his own better wisdom, speaking for the spirit against the flesh. The wilful, self-imposed element in the prisoner's grief is emphasized in Guillaume's gloss on the Muses, the "lacerae Camenae" who inspire his song:[51]

> They are called "Camenae" as "singing sweetly" ("canentes amene") knowledge of any kind. But some muses are sound, others are "wounded." The declarations of philosophy are sound because they preserve man in the soundness and constancy of reason. Those of poetry, that is, of the art which invents and depicts things in meter, are wounded, because they tear apart men's hearts, and deal faithlessly with them by recalling pleasure or sorrow to the memory, rather than guiding or consoling.

The recourse to poetry is thus opposed to the true process of consolation. Boethius recognizes Philosophy only after the clouds of

[50] London, B.M. Egerton 628, f. 165v: "Boetius tractaturus de philosophica consolatione primum ostendit se talem qui indigeat consolationem, scilicet ostendendo se miserum. Miser est cuius animus mutatur mutatione temporalium, extollendo si fiant prospera, deprimendo si fiant aduersa." All references to Guillaume's glosses, except in the case of certain published excerpts, will be to folios of this manuscript.

[51] (f. 166r) "Camene dicuntur quasi 'canentes amene' quelibet scientie. Sed sunt alie integre, alie lacere. Integre sunt philosophice sententie, quia integritate rationis conseruant hominem et constantia. Lacere dicuntur poetice sententie, id est, scientie fingendi et describendi metrice, quia lacerant corda hominum et inconstancia reddunt, reducendo ad memoriam uel uoluptatem uel dolorem, non instruendo uel consolando."

93

his self-absorption have been dispelled and the Muses of poetry banished, for "he who grieves over temporal things cannot possess understanding."[52]

Guillaume proceeds to locate the "seat of Philosophy" in the brain, the functions of which he distinguishes as *ingenium, ratio*, and *memoria*.[53] The last two present no difficulty, but *ingenium* is a complex notion, and since a knowledge of its nature is essential for our purposes, a brief digression is necessary at this point. Guillaume defines *ingenium* simply as "that mental power which perceives things immediately," but it is discussed at length by John of Salisbury who, in the *Metalogicon*, reports the teaching of Bernard of Chartres on the subject.[54] Bernard had subdivided *ingenium* itself into three forms: *aduolans*, which flits from one perception to another, "nec in aliqua sede inuenit requiem"; *infimum*, which seems to be unalterably bound to man's lower nature; and *mediocre*, the aspect in which *ingenium* is related to reason, "adapted to the work of the philosopher," and in which, says John, "it is not only competent to comprehend the Arts, but may discover a straight and unhindered path to things which are, so to speak, naturally inaccessible." The probable source of this conception is Apuleius' summary of Plato's view of *ingenium* as a faculty "neither wholly good nor wholly bad, but readily tending in either direction," and capable of refinement through education.[55]

We may, I think, regard this compound view as authoritative for the Chartrians. *Ingenium*, then, is a vital link in human consciousness, uniting the highest and the basest capacities of will and curiosity. It is closely related to imagination, the power of mind

[52] (f. 176r) "*Respicio Philosophiam*. Et notandum quod remoto dolore, diductis tenebris, defixo intuitu Boetius agnoscit quam ante non potuit agnoscere, quia non potest ille scientiam habere qui de temporalibus dolet nec qui ab ea oculos remouet uel qui perseueranter circa eam se non exercet."
[53] f. 167v. On the sources of this tripartite classification and its use in twelfth-century texts, see the references gathered by Silverstein, "Fabulous Cosmogony," p. 98, n. 34.
[54] *Metalogicon* 1.11 (Webb, pp. 28-29).
[55] *De platone et eius dogmate* 2.3 (Thomas, p. 105).

by which things absent are perceived,[56] and thus to "fantasies" of all sorts, from the wildest dream to the highest state of vision. In the *Glosae super Platonem*, Guillaume illustrates this by the myth of Vulcan's frustrated love for Pallas, and the spending of his seed upon the earth, which brought forth Erichthonius.[57] Vulcan stands for "fervor ingenii," and his love of wisdom is corrupted by corporeal frailty. The impulse of *ingenium*, partly visionary, partly carnal, produces Erichthonius, half man, half dragon.

This basic concept of Chartrian psychology seems to me to underlie a number of interpretations in the glosses on Boethius. Thus in analyzing human perception, Guillaume explains the sense in which Philosophy "exceeds" the stature of man in terms of two *excessus* which characterize human experience: for man, basically mortal and rational, can become immortal by pursuing wisdom, or irrational when drawn by vice to emulate the beasts.[58] This opposition of desires is of course a concern of Boethius himself, and a reader with Guillaume's psychology in mind could not fail to be provoked by such passages as that in Book Three where Philosophy challenges man to act on the basis of that faint intuitive tendency toward wisdom which is his birthright. "Nature leads you toward true good," she says, "but manifold error turns you away."[59] Thus, too, the figures of Ulysses and Hercules and, nega-

---

[56] The terms *imaginatio* and *ingenium* are often treated as synonymous equivalents for the Greek φαντασια; see Silverstein, "Fabulous Cosmogony," p. 98, n. 34. Guillaume (f. 167v) locates *ingenium* in the first cell of the brain, where resides the "uis intelligendi que uocatur phantastica." *Ymaginatio* is defined (f. 168r) as "uis anime qua percipit homo figuram rei absentis."

[57] *Glosae super Platonem*, pp. 93-94. In the glosses on Boethius, Guillaume gives a similar interpretation of the myth of Ixion's deception by Juno and his coupling with her image to beget the centaurs: (f. 192r) "Cadit semen in terram quia intentio actiuorum maxima ex parte in terrenis est. Inde nascuntur monstruosa animalia in parte rationabilia, in parte irrationabilia, quia facta illorum, id est cogitationes, aliquin cum ratione, aliquin sine ratione. . ."

[58] (f. 167v) "excedit hominem cum per uirtutem et sapientiam sit immortalis, et tunc rationalis et immortalis. Et hoc est quod inuenitur sapientes homines deificari, cum ad hoc quod deus est ascendunt. . . . Est alia extasis, scilicet cum per uicium fit homo irrationalis. . ."

[59] *De consolatione* 3, pr. 3, p. 41.

tively, Agamemnon illustrate the psychological challenges and conflicts which confront the seeker of truth.[60]

A central image for both author and commentator is the figure of Orpheus, and Guillaume's long exposition of this fable is also his most elaborate application of the psychology I have tried to document. Guillaume is evidently aware of breaking new ground: his gloss is introduced by a brief tirade against those "lackeys" who cannot recognize the complexities of meaning of which a great philosopher is capable,[61] and closes with the reminder that, though his account of Orpheus differs from that of Fulgentius, "one must not be troubled if interpretations differ—that is rather an occasion for joy—, but only if an interpretation contradicts itself." His reading seeks to show how the story illustrates the moral that "when one is wholly given over to temporal things one can neither know nor love the highest good." Orpheus is the wise and eloquent man who seeks, having learned the emptiness of temporal life, to fix his desire on higher things.[62] This desire or *concupiscentia* is represented by Eurydice, and Guillaume's explanation of her significance is the crux of his interpretation:

[60] Guillaume glosses the sacrifice of Iphigenia as a foolish pursuit of "inanis gloria" (f. 191v). Hercules' apotheosis represents his transition from the active to the contemplative life, and can only take place "deuictis omnibus monstris," for "nullus debet contemplationi celestium uacare nisi extincto uicio" (f. 194r).

[61] ". . . nec credendum est a tam perfecto philosopho, scilicet Boecio, aliquid superfluum uel pro nichilo posuisse in tam perfecto opere. Sed nostri gartiones garrulitati intenti et nichil philosophie cognoscentes, et ideo significationes ignorantes integumentorum, erubescentes dicere 'nescio,' querentes solacium sue imperitie, aiunt hoc exponere trutannicum esse. Tamen, ne eis consentiendo similes simus, qoud nobis uidebitur inde exponemus integumentum." This passage and the entire gloss on the story of Orpheus are quoted by Jeauneau ("L'usage de la notion d'integumentum," pp. 45-46) from Troyes 1381, f. 69rv (Egerton 628, f. 187rv). The two sentences beginning "Sed nostri gartiones" are omitted in Egerton 628.

[62] "L'usage de la notion d'integumentum," p. 46 (Egerton 628, f. 187v): "Orpheus ad inferos descendit ut uxorem extrahat cum sapiens ad cognitionem terrenorum descendit ut uiso quod nichil boni in eis est, concupiscentiam inde extrahat."

Eurydice is his wife, that is, a natural desire which is imposed upon everyone: for no one, not even a child one day old, can exist in this life without it. Hence too poets have invented the notion that there is a certain god called a "genius" who is born with each of us and dies with him. This genius is our natural desire. But this natural desire is rightly called "Euridice" or "judgment regarding good," because each of us desires what he judges to be good, whether it is truly so or not. This desire, then, straying through the fields, is amorously pursued by Aristaeus. Aristaeus stands for virtue. . . . And this virtue seeks the love of Eurydice, that is, of natural desire . . . and pursues her, because virtue always seeks to withdraw natural desire from earthly things. But Eurydice flees Aristaeus because natural desire goes against virtue in its longing for its own pleasure, which is contrary to virtue. Thus she dies and descends to the lower world, or to earthly delights. But Orpheus grieves for his dead wife; for when a wise man sees that all the things that engage and delight him are temporal, it displeases him.

It seems plain that this natural desire, this "genius" committed by nature to pursue as its proper good whatever is most pleasing, is basically identifiable with *ingenium* as described above. The union of Eurydice with Aristaeus would mean the fulfillment of that noble destiny claimed by John of Salisbury for the *ingenium mediocre* of Bernard. But Eurydice is coltish and intractable, like Bernard's *ingenium aduolans,* and if not incorrigibly carnal like the *ingenium infimum,* has nonetheless a precipitate tendency toward earthly things. And Orpheus the philosopher seems powerless to resist this tendency and extricate his *ingenium* from its involvement with the world. "It is harder to conquer one's self than to overthrow a citadel," comments Guillaume,[63] and elsewhere he alludes to those who fall short of wisdom because, sorrowing over temporal things, "they remove their eyes from her."[64] Thus Or-

[63] f. 187v.   [64] See the passage quoted above, n. 52.

pheus fails to accomplish his mission and becomes, as Guillaume rather harshly observes, "ut canis reuersus ad uomitum."[65]

Though Guillaume is explicit only about the nature and relations of desire and virtue, I think we may see his version of the fate of Orpheus as a comment not only on the hardness of the path which the Boethian wise man must travel, but on the profoundly ambivalent relation of will and imagination to the task. Orpheus is ostensibly an ideal embodiment of the union of wisdom and eloquence, and his ransoming of Eurydice is a triumph of these qualities.[66] But he is also a poet, and his finally unsuccessful descent to the underworld, in showing the earthward tendency of his will and affections,[67] also shows him to be much like the prisoner of Book One, whose heart is torn by the faithless Muses of memory and lost joys. In any case, I think we must recognize in Guillaume's analysis a sensitivity to complexities in the poetry of Boethius which defy facile moralization.

Ingenium and its mythic representation are also a major concern of Bernardus Silvestris in his commentary on Martianus, but before taking up Bernardus' work I would like to conclude this brief review of the glosses of Guillaume by suggesting their possible relevance to a remarkable and very difficult lyric which has recently received the close attention of three competent scholars, the "Parce continuis."[68] This poem is found in two versions, one no later than

[65] f.189v. Cp. *Proverbs* 26:11.

[66] "L'usage de la notion d'integumentum," p. 46 (Egerton 628, f. 187r): "Orpheus ponitur pro quolibet eloquente et sapiente, et inde Orpheus dicitur quasi 'Oreaphone,' id est 'optima vox.'"

[67] See Guillaume's analysis of the senses, moral and psychological, in which the idea of a descent to the underworld may be understood (quoted by Jeauneau, "L'usage de la notion d'integumentum," p. 42); cp. Macrobius, *In Somn. Scip.* 1.10.17 (Willis, p. 45).

[68] The poem is printed and discussed by F.J.E. Raby, "*Amor* and *Amicitia*: a Medieval Poem," *Speculum* 40 (1965), 599-610; Dronke, *Medieval Latin and the Rise of European Love-Lyric* II, 341-52; Brian Stock, "*Parce continuis*: Some Textual and Interpretative Notes," *Medieval Studies* 31 (1969), 164-73. The text that I have followed is that of Stock, though I have differed from him, as well as from the others, on numerous points of translation and interpretation.

98

the early twelfth century,[69] the other evidently from the third quarter of the century. I will concentrate on the second, much longer version, which I take to be almost certainly, as Stock suggests, an independent reworking of the first.[70] The poem may be divided in various ways, but I have found it most convenient to treat it as three sections followed by a brief coda. The first section describes the power and effect of love; the second deals with friends and lovers separated by death; the third tells the story of Orpheus and Eurydice. The poem seems to be addressed by an experienced lover-poet to a friend who is feeling the pains of love for the first time, with the purpose of convincing the friend that his situation is a universal one by describing the power and effect of love and illustrating its "authority" by a catalogue of famous lovers. I would suggest, however, that on a deeper level the poem is concerned not simply with *amor*, but with its relation to the creation and experience of poetry.

"Cease your continual lamentation," says the speaker, "for you are not in chains," and he describes the imperviousness of Love to such sorrows. He is "not of our kind," and laughs at what is painful to mortals. I, too, am bound to serve him, the singer adds, apparently contradicting the "neque uincularis" of the opening stanza, and it is a high honor, but the service is hard. Then as if recognizing that such generalities cannot be meaningful to a novice, he turns to the examples of famous lovers, prefacing the catalogue with the following lines:

> herent et uerba   non altis sermonibus,
> nobis tandem unica.   solis loquor fidibus.

And finally special words are what hold us. I do not employ lofty eloquence, but only lyric song.

[69] This version is treated separately by Dronke, "The Return of Eurydice," *Classica et Medievalia* 23 (1962), pp. 198-212.
[70] Stock shows clearly that the variants of the later text (which Dronke tends to regard as garblings of the original) make sense in their own context. We may then ask how much the second poet, like Jean de Meun, expected his audience to appreciate his adjustments, using the earlier, simpler poem as a foil.

Then follows the lyrical evocation, first, briefly, of Nisus and Eury-
alus, Theseus and Pirithous, Tydeus and Polynices; then, in more
detail, of David and Jonathan, Pyramus and Thisbe, Hero and
Leander; and finally of Orpheus and Eurydice. At the end he turns
from the sorrowing Orpheus to reflect:

Vincit amor omnia,	manus, aures, oculi
regit amor omnia.	strenua paci
fuga tantum	uix negant cupidini.
fallitur amantum.	Do quietem fidibus;
fraude subdola	finem, queso, luctibus
subnectendo modula	tu curas alentibus.

Love conquers, love rules all. Only by the flight of lovers [i.e., from
loving] is he foiled. Sly and deceitful, hands, ears and eyes, contribu-
ting their nuances, can hardly restrain desire from undergoing hard-
ships.

Now I silence my lute; do thou, too, I pray, give an end to the
sufferings that nourish care.

The poet begins and ends his history of ill-starred lovers with
references to the complicity of love's victims in their own misery.
It is we who make and enjoy love songs, songs which draw us to
love, "unica uerba"; and it is our own hands, ears, eyes, "subnec-
tendo modula," employing their own lyric language, which draw
us to the "strenua," the hard service of love. We live poems of our
own, as well as write them; there is a sense in which to give *quies*
to the lyre is to silence love itself.

Love in this sense is a self-delusion, something which has its
truest existence in the mind of the lover. The love-tragedies of the
central portion of the poem seem at first to contradict this view,
but their cumulative effect is to reinforce it. Dronke has com-
plained, with some justice, that the added stanzas disrupt the tone
of the poem, but it seems to me that the expanded version is uni-
fied by a gentle irony. All the examples show love betrayed. Nisus,
Theseus, and Tydeus lost their beloved companions in seeking to
help them; David laments the loss of Jonathan as he sits "amid
the ruins of Ziglag, victor over Amalek," the emptiness of his vic-

tory only intensifying the sense of loss.[71] The futility of the love of Pyramus and Thisbe, a theme whose poignancy had possibly been somewhat dulled by its popularity as a subject of school-poetry, is shown, as Stock remarks, by a sort of metaphysical conceit, perhaps compounded by a play on *spiritus*:

> optimus colloquiis, disparabat corpora
> sed infidus osculis, paries, spiritibus
> solis quidem peruius.

Ideal for conversation, but denying kisses, the wall separated their bodies, allowing only their spirits to pass.

The hard fact of separation and the element of human folly which leads to disaster are brought together in the *aestus*, emotional and elemental, which cause the death of Leander. His hapless situation is juxtaposed with that of his beloved in the concise final lines:

> Sestias in speculis,
> ponto perit iuuenis.

The Sestian maiden dies on her tower, as the youth perishes in the sea.

Hero is lost with Leander; loss is itself a kind of dying, and can make us wilfully seek to cross the barrier ourselves in the hope of reunion and revival. This at least is one reflection which these exempla seem calculated to provoke, and it is the one which the concluding example of Orpheus seems to develop. Uniquely endowed, and uniquely beloved, Orpheus learns the vanity of both gifts when Eurydice dies in attempting to protect herself from any other lover:

> Orpheus illam modulis
> urget insolabilis.

The very thrust of "urget" serves ironically to show the poet's help-

[71] See *I Samuel* 30, *II Samuel* 1. Cp. Abelard's *Planctus David super Saul et Jonatha*, st. 9c (ed. G. M. Dreves, *Analecta hymnica* 48, Leipzig, 1905, p. 232): "Infausta victoria/Potitus interea/Quam vana, quam brevia/Hinc percepi gaudia!"

lessness. But Orpheus, like the narrator of the poem, is bound to persist in his "unica uerba":

solam uates non adesse queritur Euridicen.

ingemit Euridicen: atque semel fidicen

retulit Euridicen.

The poet laments that his one love, Eurydice, is gone. He sighs for Eurydice; and at once the lutanist brought back Eurydice.

With these lines the shorter version of the poem ends in apparent triumph. But in the later version the lines are used very differently. The lutanist echoes the lover almost mockingly; his song recovers Eurydice only as any song of lost love revives that love, and the recovery leads to a still greater loss. At the end of a Boethian recounting of his descent into Hades, Orpheus reappears, almost lifeless, "luridus ab inferis." The thin line between loss and death has been all but eliminated. At this point the narrator intervenes with the concluding reflections quoted above.

The ending of the poem amply bears out the opening declarations about love's cruelty, but it does more; for the story which has left Orpheus wan and miserable has not, presumably, had the same effect on us. The rhythm of the succession of brief narratives, the reiterated tale of love and loss, bracketed by the narrator's unself-conscious reflections on the complicity of art and will, has the effect of drawing poet and audience into continuity with the revolving story. Then, when we shift from the sorrows of Orpheus to the larger context of the narrator's own situation, and that of his audience, we realize that loss is not the only significant fact of Orpheus' experience: love is cruel, and in the end it robs us, but poetry can restore something of what we have lost. Pyramus "lives yet," says the narrator; our will to love and suffer outlasts the experience itself and lives on to inform the experience of others. The insight of the anonymous poet is close to that examined by Gottfried von Strassburg in the prologue to his *Tristan*, where he dwells on the need of "noble hearts" to dwell on the legends of love's martyrs. The "Parce continuis" is finally a dramatization and a vindication of the lyric impulse itself.

Whatever their actual relation, I think it is possible to see in the "Parce continuis" a working out of certain ideas implicit in Guillaume's treatment of poetry and psychology in the glosses on Boethius. The poet and the lovers he describes are bound to love, and to the rehearsal of desire and loss, even to the point of death. Like Boethius' prisoner, they collaborate in rendering their misfortune vivid and overpowering, and like Orpheus they do so in response to what seems an incorrigible tendency of will. The difference of course is that the poet of the "Parce continuis" affirms what Guillaume can only view as a hindrance to the pursuit of wisdom. The universal lover who emerges from the poem has something of the dignity, the power to grow larger through the very fact of suffering, which Abelard bestows on the heroes and heroines of his *Planctus*.[72]

Guillaume does not elaborate any but the moral implications of his insights into the situation of Boethius' prisoner and his use of the figure of Orpheus. It would thus be presumptuous to deduce a precise intention, or make his reading of Orpheus and Eurydice the basis for a fuller explication of his theory of human *ingenium*. What must be emphasized, however, is that the richness of Guillaume's psychological interpretation and the freedom with which he abandons traditional authority in order to develop it are something new in the medieval treatment of classical literature, and that the direction in which his innovations tend is that of poems like the "Parce continuis," with its new and striking insights into the function of poetry. Taken in conjunction with the *ingenium*-centered psychology which I have suggested as a determining factor in his interpretations of Boethius' imagery, this originality brings the Chartrian "integumental" mode of interpretation closer to the subjective spirit of Abelard. The two meet in Bernardus Silvestris' glosses on Martianus Capella, and constitute a vital

[72] Abelard, too, it is worth noting, could present arguments strikingly like Guillaume's comment on the *Camenae* against the effects of poetry, and echoes Augustine and others in excluding poetry from the category of useful studies. See *Introductio* 2.2 (PL 178.1040-46) and *Theologia christiana* 2 (PL 178.1209-12).

precedent for the sort of poetry to be discussed in the following chapters.

4. The Commentaries of Bernardus Silvestris

On the evidence both of his writings and of what can be deduced about his career in the schools, Bernardus comes close to being the historian's delight, a perfect transitional figure. He was the friend and disciple of Thierry of Chartres, and he had already composed his greatest work by 1147, when the great masters of the School of Chartres were still active.[73] On the other hand he seems to have been associated mainly with Tours, and possibly Orleans, centers of grammatical and rhetorical study, where he lectured and wrote a treatise on the *ars dictaminis,* and where his poetry was later to be used by Matthew of Vendome to illustrate the *ornatus difficilis* to aspiring rhetoricians.[74] Even the most typically Chartrian of his writings, the commentaries on the *auctores,* seem to belong to a late stage of the School's development, when expression is becoming more important than profundity; and in fact the formulation in deceptively clear and simple terms of the thought of his predecessors was one of Bernardus' more significant achievements. There is original and adventurous thinking in his works; he was well aware of the dangers in which Chartrian thought tended to become involved, and can be seen to have taken sides in a number of important controversies. He dissented from certain tenets of Chartrian rationalism even as he exploited the freedom of Chartrian syncretism,[75] and he was by no means uncritical in his synthesis of the thought of the School. But nearly all his important insights are expressed poetically; they are inseparable from their literary context. The most interesting feature of his work, aside

[73] The *De mundi universitate* was read before Pope Eugene III ("and won his favor") in 1147; see Silverstein, "Fabulous Cosmogony," p. 115, n. 165.

[74] See Edmond Faral, *Les arts poétiques du xiie et du xiiie siècles* (Paris, 1923), pp. 1, 174-76; "Le manuscrit 511 du 'Hunterian Museum' de Glasgow," *Studi medievali* 9 (1936), pp. 69-88.

[75] Silverstein, "Fabulous Cosmogony," pp. 98-115; Jeauneau, "Notes sur l'École de Chartres," pp. 846-49.

from its literary quality and some highly original contributions to medieval mythography, remains his genius for formulating imaginatively the results of the often laborious demonstrations by which Thierry and Guillaume expressed their perception of complex relationships.

The qualities which Silverstein has noted as typifying his poetry are present as well in his commentaries:[76] he is lucid and simplistic, discreetly ambiguous about the scope of rational enquiry, and highly imaginative in many of his interpretations. But the commentaries have an importance for later literature which transcends their frequent shallowness and facility. Not only were Bernardus' exercises in mythography a rich source of material for later poets, but his readings of Vergil and Martianus in terms of the intellectual pilgrimage from earthly to divine knowledge defined a basic element of later medieval allegory, Latin and vernacular.

The commentary on the first six books of the *Aeneid* reduces Vergil's narrative to a series of *integumenta* showing the growth of understanding under the influence of Chartrian paideia. Vergil's authority is established by the citing of Macrobius' declaration, "et veritatem philosophiae docuit et figmentum poeticum non praetermisit."[77] As Bernardus' analysis develops, the *Aeneid* comes to sound strangely like the *De nuptiis*. The reasons for this are various. Bernardus has a limited precedent in Fulgentius' *Virgiliana continentia*, and his educational reading is not wholly alien to the poet's own intentions: Vergil's Aeneas, like Martianus' Mercury, undergoes a definite psychological education in the course of his

[76] For present purposes I take for granted the attribution of these two commentaries, though as Jeauneau observes, the evidence is not conclusive. The attribution of the *Aeneid* commentary is accepted by Silverstein ("Fabulous Cosmogony," p. 97 and n. 33) and by Padoan (see below, notes 78 and 97); Jeauneau has shown decisively that the commentary on Martianus is by the same author, and that this author was in close touch with the activity of the Chartrians. In any case, the most important thing is the deep affinity between the thought of the commentator and that of the author of the *De mundi universitate*.

[77] *Commentum Bernardi Silvestris super sex libros Eneidos Virgilii*, ed. W. Riedel (Greifswald, 1924), p. 1; cp. Macrobius *In Somn. Scip.* 1.9.8 (Willis, p. 41).

wanderings, and his journey through the underworld is rewarded by a magnificent cosmological explanation of the *cupido lucis* which pervades all life.[78] This passage occurs, unfortunately, just after the point at which Bernardus' commentary breaks off.) And as we will see the association of the two works corresponds to a basic tendency of Bernardus' criticism in general.

Vergil, says Bernardus, describes *sub integumento* "what the human soul, placed for a time in a human body, achieves and undergoes."[79] Aeneas, as the soul, is the son of the Father of all life, represented by Anchises, and of Venus, who stands for the *musica mundana*, and whose name also denotes the carnal appetite which is mother of *Iocus* and Cupid, unnatural and natural sexuality. Bernardus regards the death of Anchises and Aeneas' reunion with him as a major theme of the poem, and as demanding that Aeneas overcome the carnal element in his heritage.

The first five books of the poem depict the states of infancy, boyhood, adolescence, young manhood, and maturity, and illustrate the problems created by the soul's submergence in the body. Thus in Book One Aeneas "feeds" on the "inani pictura" of the Trojan War, revealing his helpless submission to his senses.[80] In Book Two he becomes articulate in answer to an inner prompting, but mixes true and false in all that he says (for Dares tells us that Aeneas, describing the fall of Troy, put his people in a favorable light).[81] Book Three surveys the means whereby the human spirit survives its voyage through the sea of worldly vices. Polydorus, Anius, and the Trojan Penates direct Aeneas' course, but by the end he has closed his mind to thoughts of God, as shown by the death and burial of Anchises.[82] Thus in Book Four his rational faculties are wholly inoperative, and he gives himself to hunting and love. But Mercury's eloquence prevails over the hero's wilful oblivion; he abandons Dido, who is consumed by fire: "for lust,

[78] See Giorgio Padoan, "Tradizione e fortuna del commento all'*Eneide* di Bernardo Silvestre," *Italia medioevale e umanistica* 3 (1960), p. 239; de Lubac, *Exégèse médiévale* II.ii, pp. 242-45.

[79] *Commentum*, p. 3. [80] *Ibid.*, p. 12.
[81] *Ibid.*, p. 15. [82] *Ibid.*, p. 23.

once abandoned, grows weak, and, consumed by the heat of man-liness, is reduced to embers, that is, to mere thoughts."[83] The games of Book Five are Aeneas' grounding in *practica*, or ethics, a necessary stage in his preparation for philosophy, and Bernardus is at pains to show how the various contests illustrate the mustering of temperance, fortitude, prudence, and justice. But the Trojan ships are burnt at the instigation of Iris, the rainbow, "many-col-ored and obstructive of the sun," who stands for the bewildering variety of sense impressions which rebel against the ordering of wisdom.[84] At this point, in a new and compelling appeal to reason, Anchises summons Aeneas to the underworld.

The descent is the key to liberation from the dominion of sense, for it represents the penetration of *mundana* by reason, and leads to knowledge of God. The death of Palinurus shows the final rejec-tion of deceitful sense, and introduces the more formal educational allegory of Book Six, where Vergil reveals his more profound philo-sophical purpose.[85] Bernardus begins his analysis by alluding, prob-ably via Guillaume's glosses on Boethius, to Macrobius' discussion of the significances of the idea of a *descensus ad inferos*.[86] Vergil, he says, uses the motif to depict the descent of wisdom to consider earthly things, so that it may see their insignificance and turn to the study of *invisibilia*. The line "Iam subeunt Triviae lucos atque aurea tecta" sets the tone of the allegorizing to follow.[87] *Trivia* refers to eloquence, subject of the *trivium*, and the proper means of access to the temple of Apollo, whose *aurea tecta* are the arts of the *quadrivium* which shelter the gold of philosophy. As Aeneas approaches the temple he is detained by the fables and histories inscribed on the doors. These are the works of the *auctores* who, now that he has passed through the grove of *Trivia*, can be appre-

[83] *Ibid.*, p. 25. [84] *Ibid.*, p. 27.

[85] *Ibid.*, p. 28: "et quia profundius philosophicam veritatem in hoc vo-lumine declarat Virgilius, ideo non tantummodo summam, verum etiam verba exponendo in eo diutius immoremur."

[86] *Ibid.*, pp. 28-30. The close parallel with Guillaume's account is demon-strated by Jeauneau, "L'usage de la notion d'integumentum," p. 42. See above, n. 67.

[87] *Commentum*, p. 30.

ciated at their full value as "introductorii ad philosophiam."[88] At this point Achates ("tristis consuetudo," the painful effort of study) appears with the Sibyl ("Sibylla," i.e., " 'scibile' divinum consilium," or "intelligentia"), who summons Aeneas into the temple.

The transition to the realm of true philosophy is shown by the violent experience of the Sibyl under the influence of the god.[89] The sudden changes in her face are a first revelation of the infinite ways in which the divine expresses itself to the intelligence. The disarray of her hair shows how all rhetorical adornment is abandoned by philosophers when they seek to express their perception of the divine. Her madness indicates her transcendence of human reason, and like Boethius' Philosophy she assumes superhuman size to deal with *coelestia* which exceed reason's power to comprehend.[90]

After the Sibyl has foretold the obstacles he must face, Aeneas pleads for divine aid, "ut per creaturarum agnitionem creatorem agnoscat."[91] In a long digression based on the brief allusion in his prayer he is compared with Orpheus in terms borrowed from Guillaume.[92] The plucking of the golden bough is his maiden essay in the discernment of philosophical truth through the *umbrae* of the world.

Though the analysis of the underworld journey itself is incomplete, and the mass of legendary data to be explained causes the allegory to disappear at times, certain landmarks may be observed. One is the comparison of Aeneas' quest with those of his precursors—Hercules, Perseus, Theseus, and Pirithous—all of whom are shown to have prevailed by force of intellect. Perseus slew Medusa with the aid of Mercury and Pallas, for "mala operatio" can only be overcome by the civilizing power of education. Hercules' capture of Cerberus shows the imposition of order and pur-

[88] *Ibid.*, p. 36.   [89] *Ibid.*, p. 40.
[90] Cp. Guillaume's gloss on the stature of Philosophy, quoted above, n. 58.
[91] *Commentum*, p. 51.
[92] *Ibid.*, pp. 53-55. See Jeauneau, "L'usage de la notion d'integumentum," pp. 45-49.

pose on undisciplined eloquence. The demigod Theseus represents the cooperation of divine *theorica* and human *practica* to form philosophy, while the mortal Pirithous, *eloquentia*, stands for the perishable medium of speech. They descend to Hades together, for both delight "circa mundana philosophari," but only Theseus returns; "sapientia sua sapientem educit; solum eloquentem garrulitas sua magis vincit."[93]

Within the underworld itself judgment is imposed upon the abusers of intellect. Minos, *sapientia*, distinguishes the wise from those who scorn wisdom. The weeping multitude of "infant souls" awaiting his judgment consists of those who set out to become philosophers but were seduced by the "atra dies" of worldliness. The citadel of Tartarus shows the abuse of wisdom by ignorance and falsehood.[94] The iron tower stands for the "mens elata," and Tisiphone, guarding the entrance, is "sermo malus in ore pravo." But within the citadel is a greater horror, the Hydra ("ignorantia") with its fifty gaping mouths ("infinitis quaestionibus"), a conception borrowed, perhaps with a certain grim humor, from Boethius.[95] The point is reinforced by the image of Titius, stretched over nine acres of ground which stand for the three tripartite disciplines of *theorica*, *practica*, and *rhetorica*. He is a figure of the dedicated scholar, whose anxiety to seek out the "arcanam rerum naturam," represented by the vulture which eats out the liver of Titius, is so engrossing as to "consume" his immortal mind.[96]

The commentary breaks off just as Aeneas and the Sibyl are preparing to enter the gates of Elysium—when, that is, "visibilibus

[93] *Commentum*, p. 88. Cp. the treatment of these two figures in the commentary on Martianus (Cambridge, University Library Mm. 1.18, f. 1va): "Sed alter semideus, alter uero ex toto mortalis inuenitur quia sapientia in theorica interminabilis, in practica uero transitoria, eloquentia uero tota cum animalis interitu dissoluitur."

[94] *Commentum*, p. 107.

[95] *Ibid.*, p. 108 (cp. Boethius' use of the Hydra figure, quoted above, n. 17).

[96] *Ibid.*, p. 110. Bernardus' interpretation seems to be a refinement of Guillaume's treatment of Titius in his gloss on *De cons.* 3, metr. 12 (Egerton 628, f. 189v): "Vultur dicitur iecur illius comedere quia cura semper comedit cor intenti diuinationi."

peragratis, restat invisibilia perquirere."[97] The Cyclops' wall becomes a figure of the firmament, and a detailed review of the roles of invention, reason, and memory prepares Aeneas for the new effort of mind which will be required in the consideration of heavenly things. The placing of the golden bough on the threshold (the consignment of philosophy to the chamber of memory) completes Aeneas' preparation for the study of *invisibilia*.

Riedel and Skimina have shown how much of the *Aeneid* commentary is mere compilation, from Servius, Macrobius, Fulgentius, and the later mythographers.[98] When the further borrowings from Guillaume de Conches are taken into account, Bernardus' own contribution is reduced to the harmonizing and elaborating of these various sources. Perhaps the most significant feature of the work is the very ingenuity of Bernardus' adaptations; we are left with the sense that almost any meaningful narrative could be reduced and "translated" in a similar way. Bernardus even provides an emblem of the adaptive process in his comment on the priest-king Anius, who reveals the inner "claritas" concealed by the words of the Delian oracle. He stands, says Bernardus, for *ethimologia*, and is both ruler and priest because "ethimologia divina aperit et practica humana regit."[99] This is hardly an exalted view of the

[97] *Commentum*, p. 114. In the Cracow manuscript of the commentary the analysis *ad verbum* is carried on through the rest of Book Six, though a definite break occurs at line 636, and the sustained allegorical interpretation breaks off at this point. See Stanislaus Skimina, "De Bernardo Silvestre Vergilii interprete," in *Commentationes Vergilianae* (Cracow, 1930), p. 209. Padoan, who has examined this portion of the Cracow manuscript, asserts that "il metodo, le convinzioni, la cultura, lo stile sono proprio quelli del Silvestre" ("Tradizione e fortuna," p. 233). The third known manuscript breaks off at the same point as Riedel's; see M. de Marco, "Un nuovo codice del commento di Bernardo Silvestre all'Eneide," *Aevum* 28 (1954), p. 178; Padoan, "Tradizione e fortuna," p. 229.

[98] See Riedel's "Index auctorum," *Commentum*, pp. 131-35, and Skimina, "De Bernardo Silvestre," pp. 210-37.

[99] *Commentum*, p. 19. Cp. Bernardus' gloss on the ascent of Apollo and Mercury in the *De nuptiis*, with its similar emphasis on the "introductory" role of poetic language (Cambridge U.L. Mm. 1.18, f. 24va): "In hoc ascensu cum Mercurio et virtute Apollo incedit, quia in itinere ad creatorem quid bonum est sapientia concipit, eloquentia aperit."

evocative power of poetic language, and at worst it is a pedantic debasement of it.

But as I have suggested, the psychological emphasis of the analysis of the first five books of the *Aeneid* is true to one aspect of Aeneas' experience, though the moralizations, owed largely to Fulgentius, are cumbersome; and there is a genuine insight as well as an indulgence in conventional Neoplatonism in the emphasis on initiation in Bernardus' treatment of the Sibyl and her surroundings. In the commentary on Martianus Capella these positive qualities are more prominent, partly because the theme and structure of the *De nuptiis* are better adapted to the methods of the commentator, and perhaps also because this commentary was written later, when Bernardus' own thought had matured. In any case it shows Bernardus handling allegory and myth in a way that is both more original and more serious than in the *Aeneid* commentary.

Pending the discovery of still another commentary, on the *Timaeus*, to which it frequently alludes,[100] the commentary on Martianus must also be viewed as Bernardus' philosophical *summa*, his most scientific essay in Chartrian philosophizing *super auctores*. This purpose is particularly apparent in the excerpts published by Jeauneau, who is concerned to establish Bernardus' intellectual position vis-à-vis Guillaume de Conches, rather than his contribution to literary studies. He gives us Bernardus' discussions of such topics as the nature of the elements, the *anima mundi*, and the origin of the human soul. These were living questions for Bernardus, and Jeauneau has shown how he opposed Guillaume de Conches over the particular question of the existence of waters above the firmament (seemingly implied by *Genesis* 1:6), the literal truth of which Guillaume had rejected.[101] Bernardus supports his defense of the letter with references to Scripture and the Fathers, and would thus seem to be distrustful of Guillaume's willingness to substitute his own readings *secundum physicam* for the letter of Scripture.

[100] Jeauneau, "Notes sur l'École de Chartres," p. 846.
[101] *Ibid.*, pp. 847-51; *De philosophia mundi* 2.3 (PL 172.58B); *Glosae super Platonem*, p. 139.

But in other areas Bernardus exercises his own kinds of freedom and tends toward a syncretism which, while it produces identifications of pagan and Christian doctrines which recall and even exceed those of Guillaume in their explicitness, relies much more on intuition than on philosophical demonstration. A number of formulations recall the quasi-theological paradigms of Alain and Garnier, while others suggest Abelard's interpretation of the World Soul. It is this syncretism that I wish to consider in detail, and it may be divided into three kinds, epistemological, mythographical, and thematic.

The first is most apparent in the prologue to the commentary, where, like Garnier, Bernardus adopts Hugh of St. Victor's classification of the stages of *theorica philosophia*, and discusses the mind's ascent through these in terms which also recall, somewhat impressionistically, the Neoplatonism of the opening of Boethius' *De arithmetica*.[102] Noting with Boethius the role of the *quadrivium* in guiding the mind from sense perception to "a surer understanding of things," he explains that by this Boethius means theological understanding, and that the Arts have a special function in "illumining once again the darkened eye of the mind." This conception recalls the *Didascalicon* as well as Garnier's pseudo-hierarchy,[103] but its attribution of a certain autonomy to the pursuit of wisdom through the Arts implies a literal acceptance of the Neoplatonist ideas and imagery of both Boethius and Martianus which is closer

[102] Cambridge, U.L. Mm. 1.18, f. 1ra (ed. Jeauneau, "Notes," p. 856). The text of all passages from the commentary discussed in this chapter, with the exception of short excerpts included in the notes, is given in the Appendix (pp. 267-72 below), where the passage cited here appears as No. 1. On the division of *theorica* cp. Hugh, *In Hier. Coel.* 1.1 (PL 175.927-28); *Epitome Dindimi in philosophiam* 2.20 (ed. Baron, *Hugonis de Sancto Victore opera propaedeutica*, Notre Dame, Indiana, 1965, pp. 195-96); also Bernardus, *Commentum*, p. 41.

[103] Hugh does not allude directly to the *De arithmetica*, but very similar ideas are expressed in the opening books of the *Didascalicon*. See, e.g., *Didascalicon* 2.1 (Buttimer, p. 23): "Hoc ergo omnes artes agunt, hoc intendunt, ut diuina similitudo in nobis reparetur, quae nobis forma est, Deo natura, cui quanto magis conformamur tanto magis sapimus. tunc enim in nobis incipit relucere, quod in eius ratione semper fuit, quod in nobis transit, apud illum incommutabile consistit."

in spirit to Garnier. This suggestion is strengthened by Bernardus' explanation of the form of the *De nuptiis*, which is that of a sustained *integumentum*. This occasions a somewhat simplistically lucid definition of the relationship between *integumentum* and *allegoria* which goes beyond the implications of Chartrian practice in stressing the mutual exclusiveness of the two modes, and at the same time their closely related functions. *Allegoria*, says Bernardus, exists only in writings which express historical truth (that is, the truth of sacred history as revealed in Scripture), while *integumenta* are proper to the deliberate fictions of poets and philosophers.[104] Both fable and history, *integumentum* and *allegoria* have a special function—as Bernardus says, their "ministerium occultum"—but they lead to truth by separate paths.

Bernardus' distinction is probably only a version of the Augustinian distinction elaborated by Hugh, between verbal and real signification. But Bernardus does not imply any limitation in the scope of *integumentum* as compared with *allegoria*, only that its subject matter is of a different kind.[105] Thus, despite the reservations noted by Jeauneau about the freedom of Guillaume vis-à-vis the authority of Scripture, it is hard to detect any clear exclusiveness in Bernardus' formula. His own discussion of the World Soul seems to admit its equation with the Holy Spirit, and he echoes Abelard in combining philosophical and prophetic testimonies in support of his identification.[106] In discussing the origin of the human soul he draws on Guillaume to show the compatibility of the Platonic view with the "sententia catholicorum." Thus, when

[104] See Appendix, No. 2.

[105] The passage just cited is followed by the Macrobian distinction between *fabulae* (i.e., *integumenta*) and the *similitudines et exempla* to which philosophers resort when they presume to speak of the very highest truth; see Macrobius, *In Somn. Scip.* 1.2.14 (Willis, p. 6). Abelard makes this distinction (*Introductio* 1.20, PL 178.1022D; *Theologia* 1, PL 178.1153-54), but neither he nor Bernardus attempts to apply it. Bernardus alludes later in his commentary to the philosophers' custom of speaking "modo aperto modo mistico sermone" (see Appendix, No. 14), but "misticus sermo" seems to mean no more than the use of poetic equivalents for philosophical and theological terms.

[106] See the passage from f. 22r printed by Jeauneau ("Notes," pp. 862-64).

set in relation to his practice, the decisive tone of his definition of the *integumentum* does not appear to be accompanied by any real gain in clarity or precision of application.

But Bernardus' formula assumes a significance of its own in the light of his treatment of mythography, which involves both distortions of, and departures from mythographic tradition. His interpretations are sometimes mere lists of conventional identifications, more crudely schematic than anything in previous mythographical writing.[107] Sometimes he introduces complex analyses of traditional myths to explain portions of Martianus' text where no allusion to these myths can be discerned.[108] Most striking of all are his Christianizations, which put the entire commentary and its subject in a new perspective. For if Bernardus is firm in defense of the letter of Scripture, he is remarkably free in using Scripture, Christian doctrine and homiletics to explain the *arcana* of the pagan allegory which is his text. Considered in the light of his interpretations of Castor and Pollux, Vulcan and Venus, Jove, Pallas and Juno, the modes of expression which he calls *divina* and *philosophica pagina* come to appear, more than for Abelard or any of the earlier Chartrians, as two approaches to the same essential truth.

This mythographical syncretism appears in a gloss on the opening hymn to Hymenaeus, in which the "complexus sacer" and the "dissona nexa" of cosmic marriage are associated, by way of a radical digression, with what seems an unmistakable reference to the sacrifice of Christ:[109]

> *Joined by a sacred bond*: that is, united by proportion; for divine is united with mortal in temporal life just as mortal is united with divine in eternity. This is aptly illustrated by the story of Pollux and Castor. For Pollux means "perdition" and

[107] See, e.g., Appendix, No. 6.

[108] See, e.g., the discussions of Theseus and Pirithous (f. 1va; quoted above, n. 93) and Castor and Pollux (Appendix, No. 4).

[109] See Appendix, No. 4. Cp. the much briefer version of this interpretation in the *Commentum*, p. 55. See also Appendix, No. 5, where the brothers are compared to the contemplative and the active life, and made to illustrate the elevation of the human spirit from action to contemplation.

Castor "utmost evil." The human spirit is called "perdition" because, just as seeds consigned to the earth first die that they may later come to life, so does the soul when united with the body. And the body is called "utmost evil" because, as I explained in glossing Vergil, those who have classified all existence have encountered nothing lower than the body. . . . And Pollux is called a god because spirit is a rational and immortal substance, while Castor is mortal because bodily substance is sluggish and subject to decay. The god underwent mortal death that he might confer his godhead upon mortality; for spirit dies temporally that flesh may live eternally.

This striking suggestion of an analogy between the "eternizing" effect of continuity in nature and the eternal state accessible through grace is a theme which we will see explored in various ways in the poetry of Bernardus and Alain. It is one of several mythographical conceptions which converge in their treatment of the "genius" figure, and it is central to their allegorical view of the broader relationship between the natural and divine orders.

More complex, and more suggestive of a systematic syncretism, is Bernardus' handling of Venus and Vulcan, whose relations suggest a sort of psychomachy, closely bound up with the effects of the fall.[110] The basis of his interpretation is Martianus' description of the gifts bestowed upon Psyche, the human soul, by the two divinities:[111] Vulcan provides "unquenchably enduring fires, lest she be overwhelmed by shadow and dark night," while Aphrodite "introduces the pleasurably nagging itch of lust." The association of Vulcan with the effort of the spirit to preserve its awareness in the prison of the flesh is the aspect of the text which Bernardus elaborates in his gloss. Vulcan stands, he says, for the *animus* or rational soul, wounded but not wholly excluded from the pursuit of wisdom:[112]

---

[110] A curious gloss in the *accessus* to the commentary (f. 1ra) explains that the author is called "Martianus": "tamquam erudiens nos in marte spirituali, id est uirtutum uitiorumque conflictu perpetuali."

[111] *De nuptiis* 1.7, p. 8.

[112] Appendix, No. 8. The tradition of the "inner feet," in which the left

Lame in his right foot he is supported by the left because, hindered in his attempt to consider the eternal, he is wholly devoted to the consideration of temporal things. He was granted by Jove the freedom to claim Pallas, because he possesses from the creator a natural capacity whereby wisdom may be united with him. For he possesses innate ingenuity ("ingenium"), the natural ability to understand all things; reason, the natural ability to distinguish all things; and memory, the natural ability to retain all things. And if he does not pursue perfect knowledge by these means, he is at least capable of doing so . . . though he see nothing, he does not lack the capacity for vision.

Bernardus then treats Vulcan specifically as a figure of human *ingenium*, endlessly engaged in "the conception of things," and concludes with a vivid Pauline view of this faculty in its present state, like a brute animal which unearths precious stones only to reject them and tunnel instead into the dung-hill:[113]

So too if our *ingenium*, straying amid random thoughts, encounter some worthy object, it is hardly able to linger over it. When, for example, praying in church, I strive to fix my thoughts upon heavenly matters, I suddenly discover them to have descended in an instant to fasten upon some unclean thing. . .

This view of *ingenium* conforms to the psychology discussed above in connection with the glosses of Guillaume, but Bernardus' first person intrusion has the effect of bringing it to life in a special way. We recognize the general situation as close to that of Guillaume's Orpheus, but there is also a subjective insistence which, if

---

represents natural stasis and the right is the aspect of the will which seeks to transcend nature and the "crippling" influence of the body, is explored at length by John Freccero, "Dante's Firm Foot and the Journey without a Guide," *Harvard Theological Review* 52 (1959), 246-81.

[113] Appendix, No. 8b.

less eloquent than that of Augustine in the *Confessions*, has something of the same quality. Similarly Heloise writes to Abelard:[114]

> So sweet for me were those lovers' pleasures which we enjoyed together that they cannot now displease me nor be erased from my memory. Wherever I turn they present their blandishments to my sight, and they do not cease to delude me when I am asleep. Amid the very solemnities of the Mass, when one's prayers should be purest, the obscene imagining of those pleasures so captures my most miserable soul that I devote myself more to such foulness than to prayer; and when I ought to grieve at what I have committed, I rather sorrow for what I have lost.

The emotional force of Bernardus' characterization of Vulcan, the sense it gives of a will seeking endlessly to rise above the limitations of its condition, will reappear in the *De mundi universitate*, in Bernardus' characterization of Nature herself.

In relation to this debilitation of mind and will the *illecebrae* of Venus stand for the effects of original sin. Bernardus develops this theme, distinguishing the natural gifts bestowed upon Psyche, the soul, by Jove, Juno, Pallas, and Vulcan from the alien traits introduced by Venus,[115] and then illustrates the effect of these traits on the senses by several biblical examples of the perversion of the sense of taste.[116] Mars is then introduced as a good man corrupted by Venus, and the capture of the pair by Vulcan is made to show "how the fire of concupiscence fetters virtue with the unbreakable bond of habit."[117]

The general tendency of Bernardus' interpretation of Venus and Vulcan is anticipated in a gloss of John Scotus Eriugena on the

[114] Second letter to Abelard, ed. J. Monfrin, *Abélard: Historia calamitatum* (Paris, 1959), p. 122.

[115] See Appendix, No. 9.

[116] See Appendix, No. 9a. None of the other senses is treated in detail.

[117] See Appendix, No. 9b. Cp. Mythogr. ii, 30 (ed. Bode, p. 85). For further references and discussion of this motif, see Thomas D. Hill, "La Vieille's Digression on Free Love," *Romance Notes* 8 (1966), 113-15.

same passage of the *De nuptiis*; here Vulcan, as *ingenium*, is said to be imparted to all mortals "that they be not altogether deprived of knowledge of their creator, and of their own natural dignity, but rather, illumined by a perpetual inner light, seek out themselves and God in a relentless quest for truth."[118] Remigius of Auxerre had made explicit the connection between Venus' gifts and original sin.[119] What Bernardus adds to these insights, aside from a more detailed analysis of the implications of man's corruption, is continuity; for his interpretation points up the full complexity of the relationship of Vulcan and Venus, both to the cosmic idealism which provides the setting of the *De nuptiis*, and to the allegory of intellectual pilgrimage which is its theme. The focal point of this complexity is Vulcan, but before giving further consideration to this figure it is necessary to look briefly at the larger context in which Bernardus' interpretation serves to place him.

Bernardus takes pains to make us see in Vulcan's debilitation and the corrupting role of Venus not simply a moral exemplum, but a pivotal event, a disruption of the "system" of classical mythology comparable to the disruption of the angelic hierarchy by the fall of man. For the cosmic order depends on the "sacra coniugia" of the gods, and its integrity is violated by Venus' adulteries just as Psyche's by the effect of her involvement with Cupid.[120] In emphasizing this point, Bernardus is pointing up a lacuna in mythographic tradition, the absence of a consensus as to the role and significance of such myths as that of Vulcan, Venus, and Mars, which, if taken seriously, can only reflect a disruption of the order of things. Macrobius had declared that philosophers "prefer to

[118] *Annotationes in Marcianum*, ed. Cora E. Lutz (Cambridge, Mass., 1939), p. 13: "naturale ingenium . . . omnibus viritim in hoc mundo nascentibus distribuitur mortalibus, ne et conditoris sui et naturalis dignitatis cognitione omnino priventur, sed semper interiore lumine illustrati et seipsos et deum assidua veritatis indagine inquirant."

[119] *Commentum in Martianum Capellam, Libri I-II*, ed. Lutz (Leiden, 1962), p. 79: "Per illecebrosa Veneris donaria significantur omnia vitia quae merito originalis peccati rationali animae ingeruntur."

[120] Of the "sacra coniugia" of the gods (*De nuptiis* 1.3, p. 5) Bernardus observes (f. 7ra): "ponit 'coniugium' large pro 'coniunctione,' sed ad excludenda deorum adulteria."

overlook" fables which show the gods behaving indecently;[121] Calcidius, followed by Guillaume de Conches and the mythographer Albericus, offers the view that such stories represent a perversion by poets of the ancient philosophers' custom of teaching the unlettered law and reverence by inventing supernatural beings to represent cosmic phenomena.[122] Another common view preserves the integrity of the cosmic pantheon by means of the Platonic notion of "two Venuses," celestial and earthly.[123] But these same commentators were of course aware that myths of divine adultery and violence could not be ignored. Thus Macrobius, having, in his commentary on the *Somnium Scipionis*, rejected the myth of Saturn's castration of his father Caelus as unworthy of serious analysis, nonetheless provides a definitive interpretation of this myth in his *Saturnalia*, giving a cosmological rationale for its association with the birth of Venus and the beginning of time:[124]

> It is said that Saturn, having cut off the privy parts of his father, Heaven, threw them into the sea, and that from them Venus was born and received the name Aphrodite from the foam (αφρος) out of which she was formed—a myth from which we are meant to understand that while chaos lasted, times and seasons did not exist, since time has fixed measurements and those are determined by the revolution of the heavens. Cronus then is held to be the son of Heaven, and he, as we said a moment ago, is Time. And since the seeds of all things which were to be created after the heavens flowed from the heavens, and since all the elements which could comprise the complete universe drew their origin from those seeds, it followed that, when the universe had been provided with all

[121] *In Somn. Scip.* 1.2.11 (Willis, p. 6).

[122] Calcidius, *Commentarius* 128 (Waszink, p. 171); Guillaume de Conches, *Glosae super Platonem*, pp. 201-02; Mythogr. III, 5.2 (Bode, pp. 171-72).

[123] On the "two Venuses" see Bernardus, *Commentum*, pp. 9-10; Eriugena, *Annotationes*, p. 67; Remigius, *Commentum*, p. 69; Dronke, "L'amor che move il sole e l'altre stelle," pp. 398-408.

[124] *Saturnalia* 1.8.6-8 (ed. Willis, pp. 35-36; tr. P. V. Davies, New York, 1969, pp. 64-65).

its parts and members, then, at a fixed point in time, the process whereby seeds from the heavens caused the elements of the universe to be conceived came to an end, inasmuch as the creation of those elements had now been completed. However, the power of creating an everlasting succession of living creatures passed from the heavenly fluid to Venus, so that thereafter all things were created by the intercourse of male and female.

Macrobius' gloss emphasizes the harmony of cosmic and human creation, the link between the heavenly origin and the sexual office of Aphrodite, and this emphasis is present in many Neoplatonic accounts of Venus and generation.[125] But as a Christian mythographic tradition took shape it was the disruption of cosmic harmony and the imposition on man of the burden of physical necessity that became the dominant associations of the myth. Saturn's mutilation of Caelus was conflated with the Vergilian theme of Jove's overthrow of Saturn, and so with the idea of the loss of a primaeval *aurea aetas*.[126] The association of Venus and procreation with lust and mortality is stressed by Fulgentius, whose terse observation "saturitatis abundantia libidinem creat" sums up the paradox of man's relation to the sources of cosmic vitality and renewal.[127] For the act which Macrobius seems to see as affirming man's role in the cosmic harmony also involves his subjection to a disorienting and destructive passion.

It is this insight which Bernardus, taking his cue from Martianus and Eriugena, develops in his interpretation of the figure of Vulcan—an interpretation which, like that of Castor and Pollux, is both

[125] See Dronke, "L'amor che move," pp. 397-405.

[126] The substitution of Saturn for Caelus and of Jove for Saturn occurs at least as early as Fulgentius (*Mitologiae* 2.2, Helm, p. 39). Both versions were transmitted by the mythographers; see Mythogr. I, 105; II, 30; III, 1.7 (Bode, pp. 34, 85, 155). Mythogr. III, noting the existence of the two versions, sensibly observes, "De hac tamen diversitate nonnisi idem sentimus." On the relation of the myth to the Vergilian account of the Italian Golden Age see Mythogr. I, 105; III, 1.2, 7 (Bode, pp. 34, 153, 155).

[127] *Mitologiae* 2.2 (Helm, p. 40).

a tentative Christianization and a response to an essential quality
of the myth itself. Vulcan is *concupiscentia* in a complex sense,
at once *ingenium* and *vis ignita*, a link between the physical and
mental levels of *conceptus rerum*, and also, as Eriugena suggests,
a link between man's original immortal condition and his present
immersion in mortality, devoid of the capacity for true vision.[128]
The paradox of his situation is dramatized in the myth of his frus-
trated love for Pallas, and the emission of his seed onto the earth
to produce Erichthonius. Bernardus' gloss on this myth is no doubt
largely inspired by Guillaume, but he goes further in bringing out
the irony of Vulcan's situation:[129]

> Being lame, he is rejected by Pallas, for while he possesses the
> debility mentioned above he does not attain wisdom. When in
> their struggle he urges himself upon her, she flees, since when-
> ever he seeks her out in his studies she withdraws herself. For
> the more we come to understand, the more things we realize
> remain beyond us. Thus the Psalm says "Man will come to the
> depth of his own heart, and God will be exalted." [*Ps.* 63:7]
> Seed is poured forth intemperately when teaching is uttered

[128] Vulcan's relation with the *ignis terrenus* is discussed by Eriugena, *An-
notationes*, p. 13; Remigius, *Commentum*, p. 79; Mythogr. III, 10.4 (Bode,
pp. 223-24). Eriugena compares the pervasive influence of the element of
fire with that of human *ingenium*, "a higher kind of speculation," as he
remarks, than that which associates Vulcan simply with the *calor voluptatis*.
But this last is inseparable from any total understanding of the figure of
Vulcan. One may speak of "two Vulcans" as of "two Venuses," but only
with the recognition that the two meet in Vulcan's role as *ingenium*, and
that their division reflects man's loss of the state of perfect psycho-physical
integration which he enjoyed before the fall. The same relation to a primor-
dial condition can of course be established for the two Venuses also; this is
the effect of the treatment of mythology in Alain's *De planctu naturae*.

[129] Appendix, No. 8a. Cp. Guillaume's gloss on the stature of the figure of
Philosophy (Egerton 628, f. 168v): "*Respicientium hominum* [*frustrabatur
intuitum*], quia, ut ante diximus, deficit circa ipsum [deum] humanus intel-
lectus. Unde psalmista: 'accedet homo ad cor altum et exaltabitur deus,' quia
quanto aliquis cogitat altiori corde de creatore, tanto magis cognoscit eum
incomprehensibilem, et ita exaltatur deus." See also Guillaume's accounts of
Erichthonius and Ixion (cited above, n. 57).

presumptuously, for man observes that his knowledge is of no value if he, so profound a being, has not the knowledge to know himself.

The implicit equation between man's inability to grasp the full significance of the pursuit of wisdom and his inability to fathom his own desires and motives recalls Hugh's homilies on *Ecclesiastes*, with their deep pessimism about the efficacy of human knowledge. The workings of the *cor altum* are very largely subconscious, and its manifestations in action are profoundly ambiguous.

The implications of the figure of Vulcan are developed in various ways in twelfth-century poetry, but the central paradox of his situation remains as presented in Bernardus' commentary. His Vulcan, like Guillaume's Orpheus, is at once the embodiment of a subjective view of human experience and an objective exemplum of that experience. Like Orpheus, and like the *Cupido* of Alain de Lille, he testifies to both the futility and the inevitability of certain patterns in human behavior—he demands and at the same time suspends moral judgment. As in the *De consolatione* and Guillaume's reading of it, one is left feeling that the tension between the philosophical context and the poetic interplay within it has not been fully resolved. The complexities of Vulcan are not fully assimilated to Bernardus' analysis of the quest for wisdom. For this very reason the dilemma as he states it seems to constitute a starting point for poetic treatments of Vulcan and the psychology for which he stands. The complex of ideas which Bernardus associates with him seems also to surround the enigmatic genius figures of his own poetic allegory and the *De planctu naturae*, and Vulcan himself is prominent in other Latin and vernacular poems.

No hint of irresolution is apparent in the later stages of Bernardus' commentary, which clearly define the stages of Mercury's ascent to truth.[130] The philosophical culmination of the *De nuptiis* is the vision of the *mundus intellectualis*, and it is at this point that Bernardus' commentary breaks off (even as the *Aeneid* commen-

---

[130] See Appendix, Nos. 11-14a.

tary leaves its hero on the threshold of Elysium),[131] after a discussion of the presiding deities of this transcendent realm, Jove, Pallas, and Juno. This discussion is the most striking instance of Bernardus' concern to reconcile pagan *figurae* with Christian doctrine, in this case the doctrine of the Trinity. He begins by describing how reason led the philosophers to recognize the existence of three divine powers, *artifex*, *uoluntas*, and *scientia*, and to consider the possible unity among them. He then proceeds to enumerate the ways in which these are named by the *auctores* in *philosophica pagina*:[132]

> Philosophical writing employs both direct and mystical terminology. Thus in direct terms it refers to God as "the Father," as Scripture does. Where Scripture calls God's wisdom "the Son," philosophy speaks of "Noys" or "Mind". . . . And where Scripture refers to "the Spirit" philosophy refers to the "World Soul." (For earthly things owe their life to the spirit of God, as was explained elsewhere.). . . . Philosophy, then, refers to the Trinity directly by these names: Father, Mind, World Soul. But in mystical terms Jove is the name of the divine potency, Pallas of the divine wisdom, Juno of the divine will. . . . Thus Jupiter seeks the assent of Juno and the advice of Pallas regarding the act he is about to perform; for God's will urges and his wisdom orders what his potency brings to accomplishment.

The directness and facility of these equations recall that of the

[131] Bernardus' summary of the *ordo operis* at the beginning of his commentary (f. 1rb) covers the whole of Martianus' first two books, but his reference to the episode in which Mercury and Virtue encounter Apollo as the "ultima distinctio," that by which the attainment of real knowledge is confirmed, suggests the possibility that his commentary is consciously ordered around this subordinate theme, and that its breaking off so soon after the vision of the philosophical "trinity" is not wholly an accident of transmission. The general shape and sudden termination of the *Aeneid* commentary invite similar speculation, though in both cases the absence of a clearer manuscript tradition robs such internal evidence of real conviction.

[132] Appendix, No. 10. Cp. the discussion of *theorica* in the *Commentum*, p. 41, and Macrobius, *In Somm. Scip.* 1.14.6-7 (Willis, p. 56).

discussion of *integumentum* and *allegoria* in Bernardus' prologue. But it brings his reading of the *De nuptiis* to an appropriate conclusion, and it provides a nice instance of the ease with which his kind of criticism leaps over problems which would have seriously engaged Thierry or Guillaume. Elsewhere in the commentary he elaborates his philosophical trinitarianism with arguments which have a deceptively scholastic ring, but these, like the biblical references which illustrate the *illecebrae* of Venus, are introduced more or less gratuitously.[133] It is two sets of labels that are assimilated here, not the doctrines which they imply. The linkage serves only to emphasize certain metaphorical implications of the *De nuptiis*, and to suggest in a schematic way analogies which assume more importance when brought to life by the poetry of the *De mundi universitate*.

One final instance of syncretism, equally characteristic and much more important for literary purposes, is worth mentioning: the relationship which Bernardus intuits between the *De nuptiis* and the soul-journeys of Vergil and Boethius. In his prologue, commenting on Martianus' purpose in the *De nuptiis*, he asserts:[134]

> The author's purpose is imitation, for he takes Vergil as his model. For just as in that poet's work Aeneas is led through the underworld attended by the Sibyl to meet Anchises, so Mercury here traverses the universe attended by Virtue, to reach the court of Jove. So also in the book *De consolatione* Boethius ascends through false gods to the *summum bonum* guided by Philosophy. Thus these three *figurae* express virtually the same thing. Martianus, then, imitates Vergil, and Boethius Martianus.

In this comparison historical, intellectual, and moral themes are reduced to images for the same spiritual experience. The three works do, to an extent, illuminate one another: Vergil's purpose

---

[133] See his equation of *Endelichia* with the divine wisdom, Appendix, No. 7.

[134] Appendix, No. 3 (also ed. Jeauneau, "Notes sur l'École de Chartres," p. 857).

is in some respects clarified by the translation of his poem into the terms of late-classical Neoplatonism, and the implications of Martianus' mythology are sharpened and become more profound when applied to the moral and philosophical concerns of the *De consolatione*. But in Bernardus' hands they become, as it were, the "types" of a kind of allegory which, though many of its characteristics are perceptible in Martianus and Boethius, is fully realized only in the twelfth century. In his *De mundi universitate* Bernardus takes these authors—lovers, and, as it seemed to him, imitators of Plato —as his models. His poem is a genuine response to the challenges presented by theirs, and so extends a chain of influence and reaction which links together the work of these *auctores* and, in a real sense, brings the twelfth-century Chartrians into a living relationship with the *Timaeus*. This was the classical tradition for Bernardus and his contemporaries; so Alain de Lille will imitate Boethius, Vergil, and Martianus in his *De planctu naturae* and *Anticlaudianus*, and will declare that the philosophical allegory of the latter work, dealing with the regeneration of man, is more truly an epic subject than the conventional themes, Troy and Alexander, treated by his contemporaries. We will see twelfth-century authors of vernacular romance coming to terms in various ways with Bernardus' definition of the heroic theme, and in succeeding centuries the *Roman de la Rose*, the *Vita nuova*, and the *Comedia* will reveal in countless points of theme and structure the enduring vitality of this tradition for the later middle ages.

CHAPTER THREE

THE POETRY OF THE
TWELFTH-CENTURY SCHOOLS

1. Humanism and Subjectivity

The most striking features of Bernardus' commentaries, his exploitation and systematization of mythography, and the strong sense of a Platonist allegorical tradition which coordinates his insights, have their counterparts in the "learned" poetry of the later twelfth century. In satires, didactic and comic "visions," and a host of occasional lyrics, the subtleties of Martianus, the intensity of Boethius, and the insights of their commentators are assimilated to the uses of original creation, sometimes reduced to the level of witty conceits, sometimes made to symbolize deeply felt tensions and contradictions.

Social as well as intellectual and literary influences were, of course, very important in this new literary movement. Much of the finest poetry of the period anticipates Villon in its awareness of paradox and incongruity, and the sense of alienation from the established order of things which it projects, and thus reveals an inevitable consequence of the immense cultural advances of the century. The development of stable social institutions, with the attendant benefits of increased education and an increased leisure for the patronage of art and scholarship, made the schools a very attractive alternative to the monastery and the world, and so the supply of budding scholars came to exceed the demand for them. There emerged what Bolgar has called the "intellectual proletariat," learned and basically serious-minded, but frustrated by their lack of a functional role in society, angered by the corruption of civil and ecclesiastical structures in which they were denied preferment, and for many reasons perpetually tempted by cynicism and dissipation.[1] From this group was recruited the "ordo vagorum,"

---

[1] *The Classical Heritage*, pp. 178-88. See also Jacques Le Goff, *Les Intellectuels au moyen âge* (Paris, 1957), pp. 35-40.

the wandering scholars made famous in modern times by Helen Waddell, and they were, no doubt, largely responsible for the proliferation of unorthodox views of love, nature, and society. Their perspective and experience, which received epic treatment in the *Architrenius* of Jean de Hanville, expressed itself in a variety of attitudes, as diverse as the lyrics of two poets whose names symbolize the special situation of the intellectual and man of letters in the twelfth century, Abelard and the Arch-Poet. Abelard's *Planctus* seem at times almost to dissent from divine justice, while the Arch-Poet's famous "Confession" is outrageous comedy. But both dramatize the difficulty of containing and legislating the activity of the will. Abelard's Dinah pleads in defense of her ravisher, Sichem,[2]

> Coactus me rapere
> mea raptus specie,
> Quovis expers veniae
> non fuisses judice.

Forced to ravish me, ravished yourself by my beauty, you could not have been refused the mercy of any judge.

The Arch-Poet exploits biblical authority in his own way to explain how, "avid for pleasure more than for salvation," he commits adultery in his heart, and becomes in the process a living anti-type of the Christian life.

Of course the "ordo vagorum" is at least in part a literary invention. Architrenius himself was the creation of an apparently well-established schoolmaster, and as Dronke points out,[3] the spirit of the order is as well expressed by the occasional lyrics of the professor Walter of Chatillon as by Hugh Primas and the Arch-Poet. But the concern of solid citizens with the same social injustices and inner tensions which were the preoccupation of the *vagantes* indicates that these were general problems, and gives authority to the new concern with the experience of the individual.

The humanist spirit basic to this literary milieu, and the problems it confronted, are perfectly illustrated by the anonymous

---

[2] *Planctus Dinae, filiae Jacob,* st. 3ab (ed. Dreves, *Analecta* 48, p. 223).
[3] *The Medieval Lyric,* pp. 21-22.

Metamorphosis Goliae episcopi,[4] written around the year 1142.[5] The author was clearly steeped in the educational ideals of Chartres and in the sort of literary study represented by Bernardus' commentaries. His poem seems at first sight loose and imbalanced, a sort of abortive *Streitgedicht* so awkwardly concluded that its debate theme is scarcely allowed to develop. But this is a conscious effect, a way of dramatizing the poet's theme, the embattled state of humanism.

The poem opens on a spring morning with the poet asleep under a tree. In a dream he enters a grove where beauty and vitality are unaffected by time or chill, and where he hears a harmony which represents the order of the planets. At the center of the grove is a palace, the work of Vulcan, lavishly adorned with precious metals and jewels, and with pictures conceived, says the poet, wholly as *involucra* and *figurae*.[6] It is Ovid's *regia solis*, set in Martianus' grove of Apollo; various levels of meaning have been telescoped so that myth and cosmology are thoroughly intermingled. Vulcan's artistry is described:[7]

> Hic sorores pinxerat novem Elyconis,
> et coelestis circulos omnes regionis;
> et cum his et aliis eventum Adonis,
> et Gradivi vincula et suae Dionis.

Here he depicted the nine sisters of Helicon, and all the spheres of

[4] The title bears no clear relation to the poem, and was no doubt added later because of the poem's similarity to other "Goliard" verse.

[5] On the poem's date and background, see R. L. Poole, "The Masters of the Schools at Paris and Chartres in John of Salisbury's Time," *English Historical Review* 35 (1920), 336-42.

[6] *Metamorphosis Goliae Episcopi*, line 44 (ed. Thomas Wright, *Latin Poems attributed to Walter Mapes*, London, 1841, pp. 21-30). All references will be by line to Wright's text. The poem has been reedited on the basis of a newly discovered manuscript by R.B.C. Huygens, "Mitteilungen aus Handschriften," *Studi medievali* 3 (1962), pp. 764-72, and I have silently incorporated several of his readings.

The association of *involucrum* and *figura* is one of several details in the poem which recall Bernardus' commentary on Martianus, though of course the chronology of the two works would be hard to establish; see Appendix, No. 2, and below, notes 9 and 15.

[7] *Metamorphosis*, lines 45-48.

the celestial region, and, amid these and other details, Adonis' fate, and the fettering of Mars and his Dione.

These apparently discordant details are passed over for the moment, though they will prove to be significant, and the positive significance of the palace is made explicit:[8]

> Ista domus locus est universitatis,
> res et rerum continens formam cum formatis,
> quas creator optimus, qui praeest creatis,
> fecit et disposuit, nutu bonitatis.

This mansion is the seat of the universe, containing things and the forms of things with what is formed from them, which that best creator who exists beyond creation made and disposed as an expression of his goodness.

From the palace comes the joyful sound of the "concordia rerum." Within, Jove and Juno are seen presiding over creation:[9]

> Per hunc rebus insitus calor figuratur,
> quamvis hic et aliud eo designatur;
> per hanc tota machina mundi temperatur,
> arbor fructus parturit, terra fecundatur.

By Jove is figured the vital warmth infused into creation (albeit here he also stands for something more); through Juno all the universe is temporally ordered, trees bear fruit, the earth waxes fertile.

Pallas, "mens altissimi," hovers nearby, her countenance veiled to all but Jove, through whom her divine wisdom "ordains the laws and destinies of nature." Mercury and Philology are present,

---

[8] *Ibid.*, lines 49-52. The association of Vulcan with *forma* and *formata* suggests that his role is comparable to that of the cosmic Genius of Bernardus' *De mundi universitate.* See below, pp. 174-75, 183-84.

[9] *Ibid.*, lines 65-68. With line 66 cp. Bernardus' commentary on Martianus, f. 27ra: "Aliter tamen intentio figurarum quas in his nominibus supra exposuimus; quamuis enim totum hoc integumentum trinitatis (f. 27rb) consensum exprimat, tamen alioquin Iunonem aerem uel uitam practicam, Palladem theoricam poteris accipere. . ." Bernardus seems to be referring to the list of interpretations given on f. 7va (see Appendix, No. 6).

Here and in lines 103-04 the *Metamorphosis* poet seems to hesitate in attributing spiritual meanings to his imagery, suggesting a fresh awareness of the sort of censure encountered by Guillaume de Conches, Abelard, and Gilbert de la Porrée.

dressed in their marriage robes, and the importance of their marriage is briefly explained. Then Philology's crown, the gift of *Phronesis* and a symbol of wisdom, is described in detail, and compared rather boldly to the sun:[10]

> Sol sublimis capite suum gerit sertum,
> hinc et hinc innumeris radiis refertum;
> nichil huic absconditum, nichil inexpertum,
> sed quid hoc significet, satis est apertum.

> The sun on high wears a garland of his own, manifested on every side by countless beams of light; nothing is hidden from him, nothing exceeds his knowledge—but I have said enough about the significance of this.

The sun is the sensible manifestation of the power exercised by the divine wisdom through Jove and Juno, and at the same time symbolizes the power of the human mind. So, too, the concord of the Muses stands both for the music of the spheres and the harmonious faculties of the soul.[11] The survey of cosmic and mental order is completed by the introduction of the Graces, who embody both the consummation of that harmony represented by the Muses and at the same time a *largitas* of spirit which expresses itself in charity.[12]

The poem thus far has presented an ideal view of the elements of philosophical study, and of the relations of the philosophizing mind with the divine order. Everything responds to the *sacra coniugia* of the gods. But as if to offer a reminder of the practical unattainability of such intellectual perfection, the iconographic clarity of the scene is disrupted by Silenus and a mob of satyrs, ushering in Venus and Cupid, whose appearance raises the question of the place of love in a universe ruled intellectually by Pallas. Venus presses her claims, with the result that "Pallas novercatur," she assumes the role of a "noverca," a nagging, inhibiting presence.[13] As the goddesses confront each other, a dispute breaks out among their supporters. As if by way of presenting evidence in the matter, the poet enumerates in one stanza four instances of love

[10] *Ibid.*, lines 101-04.
[11] *Ibid.*, lines 125-28.
[12] *Ibid.*, lines 133-36.
[13] *Ibid.*, lines 153-54.

among the gods, and follows in the next with a brief mythographical comment on each of them:[14]

> Nexibus Cupidinis Psyche detinetur;
> Mars Nerinae coniugis ignibus torretur,
> Ianus ab Argyone disiungi veretur,
> Sol a prole Pronoes diligi meretur.
>
> Psyche per illecebras carnis captivatur;
> sors in Marte fluctuat, Nereus vagatur;
> opifex in opere suo gloriatur;
> quid fiat in posterum Deo scire datur.

Psyche is held by the snares of Cupid; Mars takes heat from his bride Nerina; Janus fears to be divided by Argyone; Apollo earns the love of the daughter of Providence.

Psyche is captured by fleshly temptation; the fortunes of war shift, [just as] Nereus ebbs and flows; the maker rejoices in what he has made; what may one day come to pass is known only to God.

Psyche's mishap represents simply the power of temptation. Mars' union with a sea-nymph illustrates the shifting tides of war. Janus, as "deus principii," and so a type of the creator, is drawn to Argyone, in whom is imaged the beauty of his handiwork, suggesting the deep attractiveness of earthly beauty.[15] Finally, the love of *Mantice* for Apollo teaches us that knowledge of the future rests with God.

These "sacra coniugia" do not fit easily into the cosmic system, and their purpose seems to be to suggest the ambiguity with which any attempt to evolve a consistent system from the myths of the *auctores* must deal. As Pound and Propertius observe, the gods have brought shame on their relatives: there is no way of linking all their actions to the expression of a single ideal of world har-

---

[14] *Ibid.*, lines 161-68. Both Wright and Huygens read *sola prole* in line 164, but the true reading is clear from Martianus, *De nuptiis* 1.6, p. 7. On this and other borrowings from Martianus, see Karl Strecker, "Kritisches zu mittellateinischen Texten," *Zeitschrift für deutsches Altertum* 63 (1926), pp. 111-15.

[15] In Bernardus' commentary on Martianus (f. 10va), Janus is glossed as "Dei sapientia eterna," and Argyone as "mundana machina," and Bernardus explains: "*Janus*, ille archetypus mundus, *miratur Argionem*, miratur sensilem speram." Cp. *De nuptiis* 1.7, pp. 5-6.

mony. The root of the problem is in the version of the corruption of love inscribed by Vulcan on the walls of the palace of Jove. At the risk of over-interpretation I think we may see in the juxtaposition of the death of Adonis with the adultery of Venus and Mars a delineation of two phases of human experience. The first, represented by the thwarted idyll of the love of Venus and Adonis seems to stand for a lost ideal, a primordially pure union sundered by violence and death. The second is love in a fallen world, and is crystallized as an archetype of human folly, first by the *vincula* of Vulcan, and now by his art.[16]

Having illustrated the case to be tried, the poet introduces a host of witnesses: first the great philosophers,[17] each with the emblem of his contribution to the study of nature; then the ancient poets, each with his love, vying with one another in the grace and complexity of their songs; finally the famous scholars of modern times. The poet's bias emerges in his praise of liberals like Thierry of Chartres, Gilbert de la Porrée, and Peter Lombard,

> quorum opobalsamum spirat os et nardum,
> et professi plurimi sunt Abaielardum,

as well as the fact that the sole figure singled out for censure is the quarrelsome monk Reginaldus, whom some commentators have identified with the arch-foe of humanism, Cornificius, against whom John of Salisbury directed his *Metalogicon*.[18] Then the poet introduces one who is both philosopher and lover, Abelard:[19]

[16] This reading of the Adonis story is perhaps reinforced by the naturalistic associations of the myth, in which the death of Adonis represents the annual declination of the sun *ad australes circulos*, while Venus, as "Terrae superficies" or "pulchritudo" mourns the loss of his vital warmth. See John Scotus Eriugena, *Annotationes*, pp. 13-14; Remigius, *Commentum*, p. 94. The relationships of Venus with Mars and with Adonis seem also to be contrasted in the *Roman de la Rose*.

[17] *Metamorphosis*, lines 169-72. This passage, garbled in Wright's manuscript, was reconstructed by Strecker ("Kritisches," p. 112) on the basis of *De nuptiis* 2.213, p. 78. Strecker's readings are confirmed by Huygens.

[18] On the identities of the teachers mentioned see Poole, "The Masters of the Schools," pp. 336-42; Huygens, "Guillaume de Tyr étudiant," *Latomus* 21 (1962), pp. 814-15, 822-29. On Reginaldus in particular see Poole, "The Masters of the Schools," p. 339, and Webb, ed. *Metalogicon*, p. 8.

[19] *Metamorphosis*, lines 213-16.

> Nupta querit ubi sit suus Palatinus,
> cuius totus extitit spiritus divinus;
> querit cur se subtrahat, quasi peregrinus,
> quem ad sua ubera foverat et sinus.

The bride [i.e., Philology] asks where her man of Pallet may be, in whom resided a spirit wholly divine; she asks why he has withdrawn himself, like one in an alien land, he whom she nursed at her breasts and clasped to her bosom.

The forsaken bride of the passage is of course Philology herself, but one thinks inevitably also of Heloise, and the poet's deep sympathy with her complaint is clear. The recollection of Abelard's fate introduces a comdemnation of St. Bernard and his followers, whose suppression of one seems to threaten all; for the tradition of intellectual freedom is the tradition of Abelard. Accordingly it is his scholars who make the accusation, taxing "that hooded tribe who wrap themselves like onions in three cloaks" with superstition and hypocrisy. This condemnation is climaxed by a *tour de force*, as the gods themselves, the powers of cosmic love and order, unite to give the final condemnation:[20]

> Dii decernunt super hoc, et placet decretum,
> ut a suo subtrahant hunc a coetu coetum,
> et ne philosophicum audiat secretum,
> studii mechanici teneat oletum.

The gods decree in this case (and the decree is applauded) that they must exclude the monkish throng from their gathering, and that lest these should hear the mysteries of philosophy discussed, they must be confined to the dungheap of the mechanical arts.

The poem ends with the poet's prayer that the monks may be banished from the schools.

Certain of the poem's transitions are hard to follow, but the poet's control over the final stages seems to me complete and highly suggestive. The debate is effectively suspended by the discovery that Abelard is not present, and this discovery precipitates the shower of denunciation which concludes the poem. The fate of Abelard, whose "martyrdom" was due both to love and to his insistence on intellectual freedom, is a particularly appropriate il-

[20] *Ibid.*, lines 229-32.

lustration of the problem posed by the debate, and his significance is enhanced by the way in which he is introduced. "Nupta querit": for a moment Abelard becomes the object of the bride's appeal, a striking and daring piece of allusion, for it makes us think not only of Abelard as a worthy substitute for Mercury, but also of the yearning of the scriptural Bride. The lament of Philology, moreover, and her inevitable association with the tragic figure of Heloise,[21] recall Abelard's own *Planctus*, whose Old Testament subjects express a suffering which is very close to Abelard's own and that of Heloise in the course of their "history of calamity."[22] Like the *Planctus*, and like those passages of the *Historia* in which Abelard presents himself as a Susannah, a Jeremiah, even a Christ, his pivotal role in the *Metamorphosis* seems to argue on behalf of human feeling, to suggest that the causes which have withdrawn him from the fellowship involve more than depravity. Venus and Pallas have been set at odds in Abelard's own life, but the allegory of the poem's earlier portions has offered a rich natural and humanistic context for the debate between them, and the sudden shift to denunciation of the monks which follows the lament of Philology suggests that a misapplication of certain monastic standards has led to the betrayal of all the values at stake in the poem. The final effect of the *Metamorphosis* is to suggest a need for tolerance, and a recognition of the complexities of nature in dealing with human problems. It is a tentative and in some respects a deliberately evasive definition of the problem, but one which is reinforced by such poems as the *Architrenius*.

Reserving for a later chapter the famous *Altercatio Phyllidis et Florae*, based on the *Metamorphosis* and relevant to its themes and concerns, I would like to look next at a lyric that might be said to carry out the debate of Venus and Pallas which the abrupt conclusion of the *Metamorphosis Goliae* had left in suspense. The

[21] The association would of course be strengthened by Heloise's own great reputation for learning.

[22] The autobiographical element in the *Planctus* is discussed, and perhaps exaggerated, by Giuseppe Vecchi, ed. I *"Planctus" di Pietro Abelardo* (Modena, 1951), pp. 8-16. See also von den Steinen, "Les sujets d'inspiration," pp. 363-73, and Dronke, *The Medieval Lyric*, pp. 53-55.

poem opens with a description which stresses the harmonious joy of spring, though the reference to the satyrs suggests an uneasy peace and anticipates the disruption of this harmony:[23]

1a.	Dant ad veris honorem
	    arida florem;
	flos in amorem
	    spirat odorem.
	En valor et calor
	    est modo rebus,
	zodiaci petit
	    ardua Phebus,
	omnia dant sua gaudia.
	    . . .
		1b.	Color est Iridi
			    ilaris serene,
			quia nunc viridi
			    omne madet pene;
			saltant satiri
			    voce Philomene
			quos dire diu
			    vinciunt habene.
			Nunc contendunt
			    Venus et Minerva.
			Pugnat Pallas egide
			    proterva;
			clamat: Iovis me paterne
			    serva!

2a.	Tonat, prestat illi Parcas
	et decanas et tetrarchas,
	Musas ducit Stilbon Arcas,
	    anxiat Apollo.
		2b.	Iuvant partes Citharee
			Ceres, Bachus, natus Ree,
			omnes simul fere dee
			    adiuvant in bello.

3a.	Bello fera dat innumera Venus vulnera; tenet ethera, perimit Tartara.	3b.	Terga dat plane pompa Diane, capto Titane, teque, bifrons Iane.
4a.	Fles tu, o dia Filologia, flesque, Talia,	4b.	casus Limitane. Catenato Pane rides, Volicane.

In spring's honor the barren places flower, the flower breathes its perfume into love. See the power of life, the warmth that is now in the world; Phoebus seeks out the high regions of the Zodiac, all things give forth their joys.

Serene Iris has a joyous color, for now on the green nearly everything is moist. Satyrs leap at the sound of Philomena, satyrs whom cords have long and grievously held bound. Now Venus and Mi-

[23] Ed. and tr. Dronke, *Medieval Latin and the Rise of European Love-Lyric* II, pp. 367-68.

nerva conflict. Pallas fights with her fearful Gorgon-shield. She cries out "Aid me, Father Jupiter!"

He thunders, he offers her the Fates, and the decans and the tetrarchs; Arcadian Stilbon (i.e., Mercury) leads forth the Muses, Apollo is ill at ease.

Ceres, Bacchus, and the son of Rhea help Cytherea's side; almost all the goddesses at once join in battle.

Venus, fierce in war, inflicts countless wounds. She holds sway in heaven and ravages hell.

Diana's host turns tail entirely once the Titan is captured, and you, two-faced Janus.

You weep, Goddess Philology, and you, Thalia, weep at the calamities of Diana of the Crossways. And you laugh, Vulcan, because Pan is chained.

Cosmic order, represented by Pallas and Jove, the governing principles of the elements, Mercury and the Muses, is overthrown. Venus, says the poet, "tenet ethera,"[24] and a helpless Philology is reduced to tears. The one surviving vestige of order is the apparent ability of Vulcan to contain the lust of Pan and the satyrs.[25] Perhaps the poet intends us to see in the chaining of Pan the channeling of lust into procreation, and the suggestion that lust, though ineradicable, can be curbed, and chaos avoided. This would be to give Vulcan as *concupiscentia* a role like that of the *genii* of sex-

[24] I cannot agree with Dronke's suggestion (p. 369) that Venus' triumph means that she is "the goddess of 'ethereal' love, *Venus caelestis*." She is a cosmic power, but it seems clear enough that in relation to Pallas, the Satyrs, and Vulcan, taken as elements of human nature, she stands for the power of physical desire. That she "holds sway in heaven" only indicates the extent of her disruptive effect.

[25] "Did the poem originally finish here?" Dronke asks. I suspect that it did, and that the ambiguity of Vulcan's eleventh-hour intervention is the poet's carefully calculated last word. The ambiguity is compounded if we see Pan, whom Vulcan fetters, not simply as lust (Dronke's sensible suggestion) but as the whole of nature. This is one of his common roles: see Servius, *Commentarii in Aeneidem*, ed. Georg Thilo and Hermann Hagen (Leipzig, 1884) II, 99; Guillaume, *Glosae super Platonem*, p. 107; Mythogr. III, 8.2 (Bode, p. 200). This would suggest more fully the effect of Venus' onslaught —and make Vulcan's smile a very private thing indeed.

uality in the *De mundi universitate,*[26] and complementary to the preservative function of Vulcan as *ingenium* in the commentary of Eriugena. But in any case the role of Vulcan is ambiguous. Vulcan the controller of lust is very close to Vulcan the artist, and we may see the chains he forges as corresponding to such rich, profound images as the "locus universitatis" of the *Metamorphosis Goliae,* or the shield of Vergil's Aeneas, images through which he defines and in a sense controls the forces and capacities which give order and purpose to human life. But he is also Vulcan the husband of Venus, the cuckolded first person of what has been called the "bourgeois trinity," and in this light the fettering of Venus and Mars, or of Pan, may seem to do no more than give an ironically authoritative definition to the forces which betray his sense of the possibilities of human life. In any case, as artist, as sexual desire, or as *ingenium,* his inspiration and the truth he seeks to realize are outside the perimeter of normal human consciousness, deeper than sensuality in the "cor altum," or beyond the limits of the patterns of order which reveal themselves to rational understanding.

A more simply ironic view of the adulteries of the gods, and one which provides a convenient summary of the problems they raise, appears in a mock-sermon addressed by an anonymous chaplain to the nuns in his cure.[27] His concern is to explain Ovid's *Metamorphoses* in such a way as to make them suitable for ladies whose only schools are the "castra pudoris," and he begins his rather complicated prologue with a subtly distorted version of the grammarian's maxim that it is a good thing not to explain everything:[28]

> Rectius ignoras   aliquid quam scire laboras.
> —"Plus id ego credam?   quod non ignoscere quedam
> Aut ignorare   melius possim reputare."—
> Sepe recensentes   dicenda viri sapientes
> Hoc decrevere   melius quam multa: tacere.

Better not to know something than be over anxious about it.— "Shall I really believe this? For I could not imagine that over-

---

[26] See below, ch. 4, pp. 182-84.
[27] "Profuit ignaris," ed. and tr. Dronke, *Medieval Latin* II, 452-61.
[28] On the grammatical precept alluded to, see above, ch. 1, n. 37.

looking certain things or not knowing them is better (than knowing)."—Often wise men, considering what should be said, have found silence even better.

At the very least, the author declares, he will help his audience to deal directly with his words by remaining anonymous, like the Apostle. This will also help him escape shame if the verse is judged bad, and guilt if it is considered lewd. The effect of all this is to establish a rationale for the ensuing commentary which is a perfect parody of the assumptions on which the "reverent exposition" of the authors was founded. Far from a repository of ethical wisdom, it is suggested, the writings of the poets are a Pandora's box. We are left to wonder what motive can have suggested such a pursuit to the present author.

In any case, the author meets his subject head-on. What are we to make, he asks, of incest, bloodshed, adultery on the part of the Olympians? And what do human marriage vows mean if the very gods betray them? This brings up the subject of divine incursions into human life. The rape of Semele and the cuckolding of Amphitryon are described in terms which recall Prudentius' burlesque of the "divus amator" in his *Contra Symmachum*. But the author lingers over the latter episode, and gradually a new note is heard; the ponderous assault becomes something more positive, even magnificent:[29]

> Passa deum meta   maiore fit Hercule feta,
> Et triduum totum   consumpsit amabile votum.
> Continuata mora   tridui, prolixior hora
> Debuit impendi,   quo gloria concipiendi
> Maior haberetur,   semen celeste daretur
> Ad tante molis,   tante primordia prolis.

Suffering the god's embraces for a longer course (than normal), [Alcmene] becomes pregnant with Hercules. The answer to the lover's prayer took three whole days. When his visit had lasted three days, a longer time had to be imposed that the greater glory of conceiving might be realized, that a heavenly seed might be implanted in the first born of such might, of so great a race.

[29] "Profuit ignaris," lines 49-54.

138

The new emphasis introduces a new train of thought: if this kind of love has thus affected the gods, it cannot be bad. Rather it must have a message for man. Why do we censure in ourselves what is freely practiced by higher beings? Indeed, can we not make an analogy between gods and goddesses on the one hand and monks and nuns on the other? Like the gods (in their cosmological aspect) we are bound to an ordered, canonical life, but when we stray into adultery we have also their precedent. Even if we descend to fornication with the laity, are we not imbuing secular life with our own *virtus* and *maiestas*, even as Jove scattered his *celeste semen*?

Such comminglings are ordained, we are told, by that power "qui mundum vicit," and the author proceeds to establish a cosmological framework for his theme. Ovid, he tells us, began the *Metamorphoses* with a cosmogony to show how all the forces of life were originally harmonized. But then came the flood, the presumption of Phaethon, the tears of the Heliades, the unholy lusts of the gods. The purpose was to show us how Nature has been defiled and corrupted, and thereby to define the alternatives open to man. Through philosophy we may seek again the original order of things as expressed in the courses of the planets, and we may conceive the celestial origin and destiny of the soul:[30]

> Hec de virtute, de vera verba salute
> Quando tractamus, ad sidera mente volamus:
> Sic celum petimus, non ut ferat Ossan Olympus.

When we expound such things about virtue and true salvation, in spirit we are flying to the stars. Thus do we (truly) seek heaven— this is not to pile Ossa on Olympus.

But then we revert to the state of our mortality again, the god in us overcome by earthly desire:[31]

> Hunc habitum mentis tunc rursus ad impia sentis
> Prave mutari, scortari, luxuriari.
> Mortales actus Iovis implet ad infima tractus,
> Mens vitio victa peccat virtute relicta.

Then again you feel this state of mind changing, turning to im-

---

[30] *Ibid.*, lines 155-57.   [31] *Ibid.*, lines 158-61.

piety, wantonness, and luxury. Jove, drawn deep down, fills human action, the mind sins, overcome by vice, casting virtue aside.

And yet, the poet concludes, there *is* a meaning in this vacillation, a correspondence between the activities of our own inner "Jove" and the processes which coordinate the different levels of cosmic life. For what are these but the couplings of divine powers?[32]

> Vis elementorum,   concors operatio quorum
> Rerum naturas   dat, rebus habere figuras,
> Et quid agat spera   celestis, et illa serena
> Sidera que rapidi   cursum moderantur Olympi,
>
> . . .
>
> Quidquit in hoc mundo   crudeli sive secundo
> Sidere versantur,   et quidquid in hec operantur,
> Ex quibus omne genus   rerum constare videmus,
> Quod sapis et sentis,   quod ab his fit et est elementis—
> Hoc opus istorum   coitum dixere deorum.

The power of the elements, whose concordant working determines the nature of the world and allows things to have their own forms; the activity of the heavenly sphere and of those bright stars that regulate the course of swift Olympus, . . . whatever comes to pass in this world under a cruel or kindly star, whatever has influence on these, from which we see every created form established, whatever you know and feel, whatever is begotten and exists by virtue of these elements—all this men saw in the sexual unions of these gods.

In a sort of coda, the author offers his ideas as occupation for the leisure of ladies, apologizes for any faux pas he may have committed, and reflects smugly that at least he is safe in his anonymity.

Though mainly a comic exercise, the poem is not without intellectual substance. As Dronke observes, it raises serious questions about the value of human love and its compatibility with commitment to higher things.[33] In a world ruled by the *amor* here described, "incarnation" means the immersion of mind in sensuality,

---

[32] *Ibid.*, lines 164-67, 173-77.

[33] *Medieval Latin* I, 232. However, Dronke's interpretation seems to me to exaggerate the philosophical seriousness of the poem at the expense of its broad comedy.

and the relation of human activity to cosmic order, seemingly implied by the metaphorical significance of the gods, has become dubious. The "authority" of the traditional myths has undergone a metamorphosis, so that the literal fact of adultery is made to seem more profoundly significant than the metaphorical implication of divine harmony. Thus the "Profuit ignaris" is finally a celebration of that very instability of mind and will which is at the heart of the drama of the *De consolatione philosophiae* and Bernardus Silvestris' characterization of Vulcan.

Like the self-caricature of the Arch-Poet, the mock-pedantry and outrageous comedy of this poem are potentially misleading, and it is important to see how it reflects human concerns like those of the great lyric poets of the period. A lyric found only in the fourteenth-century Arundel collection,[34] but which clearly reflects the concerns of the twelfth century, may serve to suggest the relation between such scholastic performances as the *Metamorphosis Goliae* and the "Profuit ignaris" and poetry of a more personal kind. A "learned" poem, and useful as an example partly because of the rather schematic nature of its presentation, it opens with an erotic panorama couched in the imagery of Martianus and the *Streit-gedichte*, but proceeds to translate the general statement into auto-biographical, or at least subjective, terms, concluding with ironic reflections on the philosophical implications of the experience described. In the opening stanza, the heavens smile, and "the happy influence of Dione's star visits her own." In the second, the order of things is disrupted: Jove rejects Juno and seeks new loves, Janus yearns to descend to Argyone, Ceres laments Pluto's theft of Proserpine. In the third, the painful effects of Cupid are described, and the solaces of Venus, with which the poet's own Florula had once consoled him. The fourth stanza tells of the winter of separation and confusion which has wholly displaced their spring. It is the poet's reflection in the fifth and final stanza that gives the poem its complexity:

[34] "Dum rutilans Pegasei," ed. Wilhelm Meyer, "Die Arundel Sammlung mittellateinischer Lieder," *Abhandlungen der kgl. Gesellschaft der Wissenschaften zu Göttingen* 11 (1909), p. 22.

Vivat amor in ydea,   Dabit adhuc Cytherea
   ne divulgetur opere.   videre, loqui, ludere:
vivam tuus, vive mea,   nos pari iungat federe
   nec properemus temere!   relacio Dionea.

Let the idea of love live on, but let it not be divulged in action. I will live for thee, live thou for me, but let us not proceed rashly. Cytherea will allow us this much: to see, to converse, to play. May Venus' communion preserve us in mutual trust.

So long as love is confined to the level of the ideal, it is suggested, its equilibrium can be preserved, and the *par foedus* of Venus be realized. Once descended to the physical plane, however, it is subject to human frailty, mistrust, and accident.[35] The ironic implication of this, the apparent impossibility of permanence in human love except through sublimation, or the crystallization of poetry, is explored further in the brooding and difficult lyrics of Walter of Chatillon, and defines a basic theme of medieval and renaissance love poetry.

But if the thematic continuity of the Arundel poem with those we have been considering is clear, it is also clear that the concern to establish the place of love in the universe runs deeper than the faintly cynical conclusion of this poem would suggest. Whether considered "clinically," in terms of the strangely lyrical movement of its physical and psychological ebb and flow, as in the "Dum Dianae vitrea," or deified as a power capable of drawing the very gods from their thrones, love and its disruptive effects are increasingly taken for granted as a fact for which any optimistic humanism must allow.

The "marriage of humanism and subjectivity" cannot be described with too great precision, or related too simply to the Chartrian milieu. That stress on personal experience which Abelard's

[35] There is a certain ambiguity in the lines "Dabit adhuc Cytherea/videre, loqui, ludere," which may mean that sexual fulfillment is possible *if* the lovers proceed cautiously, or that Venus is all too favorable and that *therefore* the lovers must proceed cautiously (assuming in both cases that "ludere" refers to something more than "petting"). But in the context of the poem as a whole I think that however we read these lines the implication is that to become too deeply involved is to court disaster.

Planctus and the lyric just quoted exemplify is already present in the eleventh-century Cambridge songs, and appears in many kinds of twelfth-century verse, religious and secular.[36] Much of the concern with the relation of mental and physical, human and cosmic life and experience which the fully developed lyric reflects, and which seems to reflect the influence of Chartrian thought, is also present in a more precise form in the medical writings current in the period. Nonetheless the broad correspondence between the spread of Chartrian humanism and the growing importance of subjective points of view in poetry is plain. Guillaume de Conches and Bernardus Silvestris accord a special status to literary expression in their interpretation of Plato, Boethius, Martianus, and Vergil. They define a metaphorical *tertium quid* between literal discourse and genuine *allegoria,* and extend the authority of the *integumentum* to such complex figures as Orpheus and Vulcan. Like the incorporation of poetry into philosophy, the use of the flexibility of poetry to bring the subjective and the philosophical together led to new insights and new ways of formulating them.[37] When human feeling is given an intrinsic significance, as in the "emotional sainthood" delineated by Abelard, and when metaphor is granted a status approximating that of *allegoria,* new kinds of literary expression become possible. Love poets adapt their analyses and exaltations of erotic experience to an authoritative world view grounded in the cosmology of the *Timaeus,* while a philosophical poet, Bernardus Silvestris, begins his allegory of the creation with a passionate appeal by the goddess *Natura* in which the learned rhetoric of Boethius and Ovid's *Heroides* is animated and transformed by a desire,

[36] See Dronke, *Medieval Latin* 1, 264-85; Franco Munari, "Tradition und Originalität in der lateinischen Dichtung des XII. Jahrhunderts," *Romanische Forschungen* 69 (1957), pp. 319-23.

[37] The special role of poetry in this period is explored in two excellent studies: Richard McKeon, "Poetry and Philosophy in the Twelfth Century: the Renaissance of Rhetoric," *Modern Philology* 43 (1945–46), 217-34; Eugenio Garin, "Poesia e filosofia nel Medioevo latino," in his *Medioevo e Rinascimento* (Bari, 1954), pp. 48-65. Garin's emphasis on the "sottile sottinteso sacro" of even the most pagan and Platonizing of serious medieval poetry is elaborated by Vincenzo Cilento, *Medioevo monastico e scolastico* (Milan, 1961), pp. 171-82.

partly erotic and partly spiritual, which is of the essence of twelfth-century lyric.

2. Poetry and Pedagogy

As the poets of the schools began to exploit the resources of the *De nuptiis* and the Roman poets with a new confidence, another group of twelfth-century *litterati* were attempting to systematize the resources themselves, pedagogical, mythological, and linguistic, which the *auctores* provided. The recently edited *Ordo artium* is one of a number of allegories which took the Liberal Arts themselves as a theme.[38] This long exercise in goliardic stanzas begins with a lucid and attractive discussion of the *Timaeus*, proceeds to analyze the "arbor artium" along whose branches all knowledge is disposed, and concludes with a discussion of the functions of the individual Arts and their hierarchical cohesion. The author shows a close knowledge of Bernardus' commentary on the *Aeneid*, and perhaps the *Metamorphosis Goliae* as well as the *Fons philosophiae* of Godfrey of St. Victor, and seems to have derived certain of his organizing motifs from Bernardus' allegorization,[39] but he has excised virtually all mythological allusions and reduced the allegory to its barest pedagogical outlines.

A development which complements the production of such pedagogical epics is the attempt to systematize the *integumenta* of classical myth. Foreshadowed in Bernardus' commentary on Martianus, this purpose is made explicit in the prologue of Albericus,

[38] "Der Leipziger *Ordo artium*," ed. Ludwig Gompf, *Mittellateinische Jahrbuch* 3 (1966), pp. 94-128. Other examples of this genre include Godfrey's *Fons philosophiae*, in which the Arts are subordinated to theology; the anonymous "Somnium cuiusdam clerici," ed. Wilhelm Wattenbach, "Beschreibung einer Handschrift der Stadtbibliothek zu Reims," *Neues Archiv* 18 (1893), pp. 496-504, in which Philosophy, having introduced the hero to the Arts, gives way to Hope, who alone is able to guide him to the marriage bed of Fronesis; and the "In commune theatrum" of Étienne de Tournai, ed. Lucien Auvray in *Mélanges Paul Fabre* (Paris, 1902), pp. 284-90, in which the Arts, together with the gods, present gifts to a child born to Jove and Juno.

[39] See Gompf, "Der Leipziger *Ordo artium*," pp. 99-106.

the third of the "Vatican Mythographers," to his elaborate com-
pendium, where he declares that the work is intended to provide
an introduction to poetry (though its materials will also prove to
be "of no small value in philosophical study") through a fuller
compilation of "authenticae traditiones" concerning the gods than
has yet been undertaken.[40] The work is especially concerned with
the cosmological order to which the legends of the gods correspond,
a concern present also in the Ovidian commentaries of Arnulf of
Orleans. Arnulf classifies his interpretations of Ovidian fable as
moral, historical, and "allegorical," a category which corresponds
to the scope of the Chartrian *integumentum*, and reflects Arnulf's
close familiarity with the writings of Guillaume de Conches.[41]

The purpose of such writings as the *Ordo artium* and the treatise
of Albericus is to bring the stability of something like scientific
method to the study of poetry. For another kind of pedagogue who
begins to appear in the middle and later twelfth century, the very
elusiveness of the imagery and diction of Martianus and the *auc-
tores* was of consuming interest in itself. Among practitioners of
the *ars dictaminis* and those who labored to produce imitations of
classical verse, the sensuous *blanditiae* of Martianus, Claudian, and
other late-classical authors were cultivated with scant regard for any
higher meaning they might be made to yield. At the same time a
certain acknowledgment was made of this higher notion of poetry:

[40] "De his ergo tractatum non praesumtionis meae ostentaria commentitia
vel adinventione, sed authenticarum commodiore traditionum aggregatione
publicae utilitatis studio suscepi . . . . In hoc ergo opusculo licet ad poemata
introductorie non nihil tamen et philosophicis subservientes tractatibus
utrasque fabularum species, quas posuimus postremas, quantum se ad prae-
sens facultas dederit, iuxta veterum maxime vestigia persequemur." Pro-
logue to "Alberici Poetria" (i.e., the compendium of Mythogr. III), ed. F.
Jacobs and F. Ukert, *Beiträge zur ältern Literatur der Herzogl. öffentlichen
Bibliothek zu Gotha* (Gotha, 1835) I.ii, pp. 202-04. On the identity of the
author see Eleanor Rathbone, "Master Alberic of London, 'Mythographus
Tertius Vaticanus,' " *Medieval and Renaissance Studies* 1 (1941–43), pp.
35-38.
[41] See the *Allegoriae super Ovidii Metamorphosin*, ed. Ghisalberti, "Ar-
nolfo d'Orléans" (cited above, ch. 1, n. 2), p. 201. On Arnulf's knowledge
of the writings of Guillaume de Conches, see Berthe M. Marti, ed. *Arnulfi
Aurelianensis Glosule super Lucanum* (Rome, 1958), pp. xlv-xlix.

Martianus had declared in the portion of the *De nuptiis* devoted to rhetoric that allegory ("translata uerba") had the dual function of augmenting the expressive power of words and providing ornamentation ("cum res aut sua non inuenit uerba aut cum uolumus splendidius aliquid explicari").[42] It is often difficult to tell which purpose Martianus' own representations are intended to serve, but it was an article of twelfth-century critical belief that the two were intimately related. Though the decorative function tended increasingly to dominate, and "allegory" was often used in wholly profane contexts where it could hardly pretend to serve any remotely philosophical purpose, it depended on the traditional aura of the philosophical conception of poetic language for a certain amount of its appeal.

This pseudo-philosophical purpose is well illustrated by the *Ars versificatoria* of Matthew of Vendome, and is effectively symbolized by the little vision which introduces the portion of the *Ars* devoted to poetic diction ("ornatus verborum"). Matthew imagines himself dwelling in "the abode of fine writing" ("locus venustatis") created by Flora to show her special partiality to scholars. The description of the place, which is intended to enhance its significance as the setting for the delivery of Matthew's rhetorical doctrine, is strongly reminiscent of Martianus:[43]

> I seemed to perceive, when the barrier of wintry inactivity had been broken, that Flora, portress of spring, as she purpled the lap of earth with its varied mantle of flowers, poured forth the sweet signs of her favor in the haunts of learning more than in other places, that the subtle sweetness of their scent might bring to the seekers of wisdom a relief from their labors and a renewal of their zeal, or, more exactly, that when the surface of earth had been thus adorned, and its sweet scent, spreading abroad, been borne by the carriage of smell to the chamber of

[42] *De nuptiis* 5.512, p. 251.
[43] *Ars versificatoria* 2.2, ed. Faral, *Les arts poétiques*, pp. 151-52. Matthew's view of creativity involves the same tripartite conception of mental activity employed by Guillaume and Bernardus. The source of the "favilla oblivionis" is ultimately the spark of *ingenium*.

reason, the attendant tongue might more readily bring forth, with the assistance of the faithful memory, whatever should slumber there, lulled asleep by the dying embers of oblivion.

Here Philosophy refreshes herself in company with the Arts. She is described in the elaborate manner of Martianus' descriptions of the complexions of the planets, the individual Arts, and the gods, with emphasis on the power of her gaze, the flush of intense activity in her complexion and the firm set of her lips. But when it comes to her perfectly woven robe, says Matthew, "humanum languescit ingenium," for the gown has evidently been mended since Boethius' day, and the secret of its integrity is divine. For all her devotion to the dissemination of knowledge, Philosophy likes to intermingle with her handmaids, the Liberal Arts, a leavening of the "facundi pectoris delicias." Thus the literary genres are present as well, and come forward in procession. Tragedy declaims, satire sneers in unblushing nakedness, comedy offers the delights of the everyday, and then elegy, who comes last "not from any inferiority but because of the inequality of her feet," proceeds to explain to the poet the secrets of "polished words" and the colors of rhetoric.

The passage is of course evidence of the decadence of the Chartrian tradition in the schools; Matthew's debt to Martianus is a matter of their common facetiousness. Moreover, he evidently saw himself as a modern Ovid rather than a Martianus, and it is perhaps merely ironic that he should have found the latter so readily adaptable to his purpose. But the passage is significant, and I have presented it in such detail, because it represents the first attempt by a medieval critic to convey, albeit in this highly impressionistic way, a sense of the quality of the poetic language of the *auctores*. No philosopher himself, Matthew seems nonetheless to have been fascinated by the allusiveness of the style of the *De nuptiis*, and by its effect on the humanist thought and poetry of his own day. Indeed, much of the *Ars* seems to me to be best understood as an attempt to assimilate to the purposes of the classroom something of the new richness with which poets like Bernardus and Alain de

Lille had imbued their allegories.[44] Recognizing in it something more than rules could explain, he was led to create a little allegory of his own to bring his perception to bear on the otherwise pedestrian purposes of the *Ars versificatoria*. The recollections of Martianus, the introduction of allegorical personifications to suggest the cosmic and quasi-spiritual significance of the doctrine to be set forth, the allusions to visions beyond the power of imagination to conceive, and the attribution to the literary genres of a certain connection with the Liberal Arts, all of these suggest Matthew's concern to emphasize the continuity of his *summa* with the traditions of twelfth-century humanism.

The same general purpose appears in the technical portions of the treatise, particularly where description and disposition are in question. Chenu has pointed to Matthew's concern with metaphor as a minor but authentic manifestation of the twelfth-century "mentalité symbolique,"[45] and it is possible to discern in his summarial remarks on the intended effect of *descriptio* a desire for something like the multi-leveled, organic effect of the *integumentum*:[46]

[44] Matthew was plainly influenced by Bernardus, whom he mentions with pride as his teacher (see Faral, *Arts poétiques*, p. 1), and cites several times in the *Ars*. Raynaud de Lage, noting the many stylistic correspondences between the *Ars* and the *De planctu naturae*, concluded that Alain had been influenced by Matthew (*Alain de Lille: poète du xii⁰ siècle*, Paris and Montreal, 1951, pp. 137-63). But Mlle. d'Alverny has shown that the *De planctu* must be dated before 1170 (the *Ars* was written before 1175) and feels that Matthew was the borrower (*Alain de Lille: Textes inédits*, pp. 33-34). This view seems to me to be further strengthened by the wholly conventional nature of Matthew's references to *Natura* and *Genius*, which suggest timid allusions to Alain's profound conceptions (see below, n. 48).

[45] *La théologie*, pp. 171-72 (Taylor-Little, pp. 118-19).

[46] *Ars versificatoria* 1.74-75, p. 135. The passage bears a curious resemblance to a gloss of Matthew's arch enemy Arnulf of Orleans on *Metamorphoses* 1.8 (printed by Ghisalberti, "Arnolfo d'Orléans," p. 182): "*unus vultus nature*, rerum naturalium, i. elementorum. *Vultus*, noticia, quia in vultu habetur sola noticia de homine, modo multe sunt noticie nature quia iam res multa creavit natura per quas possumus habere noticiam de ea." On the relations of Matthew and Arnulf (insulting references to whom clutter

Note that the description of any person may be of two kinds: one superficial, the other inward; superficial when the shapeliness of the limbs, or the outer person, is described; inward, when such characteristics of the inner man as reason, faith, patience, probity, harshness, pride, wantonness, and the other conventional labels for the inner man (which is to say the soul) are exposed for praise or blame.

It should also be noted that in the description of a person on the basis of his occupation, or sex, or character, or rank, or state of life, or age, the face should be used most of all to illustrate these things.

Again:[47]

And if it be permitted to compare material things to words, just as we may consider three aspects of man, namely his inner vitality, the attractiveness of his bodily fabric, and the style in which he conducts his life, and as none of these is exclusive of any other, but rather all appear to better advantage, and have a more pleasing effect, when considered together; similarly in poetry the attractiveness of the inner content, and the outward arrangement of the words, and the style of expression enjoy cordial relations one with another, and rarely if at all does one of them come to assume an isolated position without the company of another.

The same concerns are apparent in Matthew's own exercises in *descriptio*, even though they tend to be conceived as bait for the pedantic "lector deliciosus" who knows his Ovid. The informing presence of *Natura* is a recurring theme, and gives a certain sense of underlying unity to the clusters of mock-classical marmorealities, but the appearances of traditional motifs and concepts obviously reflect deference to convention, and rarely have a serious function.

---

the pages of the *Ars* and other of Matthew's works) see Marti, ed. *Glosule super Lucanum*, pp. xviii-xxii.

[47] *Ars versificatoria*, 3.50, p. 179.

Thus in a set piece describing a beautiful grove the four elements are enumerated ("quia tellus concipit, aer/Blanditur, fervor suscitat, humor alit"), and the final couplet seems intended to suggest a certain ideal significance, but is almost perversely obscure:[48]

> Praedicti sibi fontis aquam, sibi floris amicat
> Blanditias, genii, virgo, studentis opus.

In Matthew's writing the influence of Martianus and Chartrian thought has merged with that of the ornamental rhetoric of such *novercae* as Claudian and Sidonius Apollinaris; we are never far from poetry on subjects like the Hermaphrodite, or the "Debate of Rhetoric and Poetry."[49]

But such excesses must not blind us to the positive side of the *Ars versificatoria* or lead us to dismiss Matthew as an amusing grotesque. His concern with language is real, and in certain ways reflects the concerns of the Chartrians. Bishop Adelbert of Mainz, a student of Thierry of Chartres, is said by his biographer to have been versed in "verba poetica, sive platonica."[50] The formula suggests the ideal conception of poetic language toward which Matthew is groping in the *Ars versificatoria*, and which, as we will see, amounts to a unifying theme of Alain's *De planctu naturae*. These twelfth-century *litterati*, like their legitimate heirs, the Platonists of the Italian Renaissance, conceived of the true poet in such terms as Macrobius had used to characterize Vergil:[51] he is an authority

---

[48] *Ibid.*, 1.111, p. 149. The lines may tentatively be translated, "The virgin (i.e., Nature, the virgin goddess) makes the water of the fountain and the alluring beauty of the flowers, the work of a zealous genius, favor her." Genius reappears as a studious artisan in a brief *descriptio naturae* interpolated into the vision discussed above (*Ars* 2.3, p. 152).

[49] See Faral, *Les arts poétiques*, pp. 8-9.

[50] Anselm of Havelberg, *Vita Adelberti II Moguntini*, in *Bibliotheca Rerum Germanicarum* III, ed. P. Jaffe (Berlin, 1866), p. 572; cited by Paul Salmon, "Über den Beiträg des grammatischen Unterrichts zur Poetik des Mittelalters," *Archiv für das Studium der neueren Sprachen* 199 (1963), p. 75.

[51] Macrobius, *Saturnalia* 5.1.18-19 (Willis, p. 243). See also E. R. Curtius' valuable excursus on late antique literary studies, *European Literature and the Latin Middle Ages*, pp. 443-45. The image of a religious mystery, used by Macrobius to characterize the *involucrum* (see above, pp. 37-38), appears again in the *Saturnalia*, where Symmachus is made to declare: "Sed

in every branch of learning, and his knowledge imbues even single words with deep meaning; he is almost divine, a type of the creator, and his work shows a deep affinity with the "divinum opus mundi." It is with something like Macrobius' beautiful intuition in mind that Geoffroi de Vinsauf characterizes the poet's work of creation, his disciplining of recalcitrant words as the divine wisdom once tamed and disposed the elements.[52]

Such ideal poetry is no more attainable than the sort of philosophy dreamed of by Martianus, describing Philology's ascent to the Empyrean. The systematizing of Albericus, the celebration of epistemology in the *Ordo artium*, Matthew's attempts to capture in precept and example the elusive secrets of poetic language, all are partial contributions to an impossible synthesis. But at the same time the very existence of such a synthesizing tendency as these works suggest is itself indicative of an important achievement: for these authors reveal a common sense of a vision accessible through the medium of poetry which, if not divine, has nonetheless a wholeness, self-consistency, and universality of its own. It is, in short, a fully realized poetic "world," the "locus universitatis" implicit in the poems discussed earlier in this chapter, and it becomes itself a major theme in the *De mundi universitate* of Bernardus Silvestris.

---

nos, quos crassa Minerva dedecet, non patiamur abstrusa esse adyta sacri poematis, sed arcanorum sensuum investigato aditu doctorum cultu celebranda praebeamus reclusa penetralia." (*Sat.* 1.24.13; Willis, p. 130.)

[52] See Geoffroi's *Poetria nova*, lines 44-49, 60-61, 136-41, 214-18, ed. Faral, *Les arts poétiques*, pp. 200, 201, 203. He alludes to the first two sections of the *De mundi universitate*, and more specifically to Alain, *Anticlaudianus* 1.15-17, 2.375-79, 3.350-58 (ed. Robert Bossuat, Paris, 1955, pp. 57, 83-84, 99), where Bernardus' cosmic drama has been reduced to a figure of the relations of form and matter.

CHAPTER FOUR

FORM AND INSPIRATION IN THE POETRY OF BERNARDUS SILVESTRIS

In the course of the preceding three chapters we have seen how the cosmology of Plato's *Timaeus* established itself as the framework of Chartrian thought, at once a manifestation of the divine wisdom and a measure of the scope and dignity of the mind of man. We have seen the emergence of a rich new sense of the capacities of human reason and imagination on the one hand, and on the other, the more or less simultaneous recognition of the complex, and at times the almost hapless psychological situation in which man's immortal yearnings seem to place him when confronted with an unfathomable providence, a harsh necessity, an ineradicable sensuality. Finally we have seen the study of the *auctores* and the poeticizing of philosophy combining to give rise to a conception of poetry and poetic form as embracing a "world" of meaning with a certain integrity of its own—the "integumental" world of the *Timaeus*, the *Aeneid*, the *De nuptiis*, with the pantheon of mythology and the complexities of human motivation at large within it.

All of these large themes have their place in the world of Bernardus' poetry. His great theme is the place of man in nature, and involves both a comprehensive synthesis of Chartrian Platonism, and a searching critique of certain of its assumptions. He goes further than any of his twelfth-century predecessors in illustrating both the elevating and the inhibiting effects of man's cosmic environment on his realization of his condition. Bernardus is preeminently the poet of natural aspiration, the will of created existence to realize a higher destiny, and his allegory is capable of expressing simultaneously the profoundly natural source of the yearnings and passions of man, the *malignitas* in earthly life which thwarts and inhibits his attempts to achieve vision and freedom, and the divine purpose which comprehends and gives continuity to his imperfect achievements.

Bernardus' conception of the relations of man and nature always involves a certain tension between human will and the containing universe, and this tension is effectively expressed in the forms of his two major poems. In the *Mathematicus*, blocks of conventional declamation are disposed with marked, if cumbersome, efficiency to delineate the tragedy of Patricida; an idealizing rhetoric is set in tension with a poetic form which points up its excesses and reveals inexorably its inability to express the full situation of man. Similarly in the *De mundi universitate*, the very detail with which the birth of the universe is described is made to imply the forces within it which will conspire to alienate man from the perfect integrity of its order, and the rhetoric of humanism is set against the limits of a form which is that of Nature herself.

1. The *Mathematicus*

The *Mathematicus* or *De Parricida* is so little known that it seems best before discussing the text to summarize the plot.[1] A Roman knight and his wife, happy in all other respects, have no son. The wife consults an astrologer who foretells the birth of a son who will be perfect in every way, but who will slay his father. The knight commands his wife to slay the child at birth, but in the event, overcome by the boy's beauty, she entrusts him secretly to foster parents. The boy, who bears the cryptic name Patricida, grows up, perfect in learning, character, and chivalry, becomes a soldier, saves Rome from Carthage, and becomes king of Rome, by popular acclaim and the voluntary abdication of the former king. His mother learns of his elevation and, torn between mater-

[1] The *Mathematicus* appears in PL 172.1365-80, where it is attributed to Hildebert of Lavardin, and in a superior edition by Barthélemy Hauréau (with the *Passio Sanctae Agnetis* of Peter Riga, Paris, 1895). All quotations are from Hauréau's edition. The poem's astrological aspect is discussed by Lynn Thorndike, *A History of Magic and Experimental Science* II, 106-08. Its relation to the themes and concerns of later twelfth-century poetry is suggested by von den Steinen, "Les sujets d'inspiration," pp. 373-83.

nal pride and conjugal concern, finally reveals the truth to her husband. He stoically accepts the fate foretold, and asks only that he may once meet and embrace his son. His wife gains an audience and an emotional meeting takes place, after which the father utters a long encomium on his son, declaring his readiness to die and forgive. But the son refuses to accept a tyrannous determinism which thus denies human dignity. He convokes the Senate and elicits their promise to grant any favor he may name. He then reveals that what he seeks is the privilege of taking his own life, and justifies his wish in lofty terms. But the Senate dissolves in a babel of protestation, incurring the scornful rebuke of Patricida, who then briefly announces his abdication, thereby asserting his freedom to choose his own destiny. At this point the poem ends abruptly.

From the beginning, Patricida represents human perfection. At the moment of his birth he appears "so much the image of a god that he may scarcely be believed a man of flesh and blood," and as the lineaments of mature perfection appear in the first stirrings of infancy,[2]

> Exit et interior vi rationis homo.

To the king whom he saves from the Carthaginians he is a perfect synthesis of worth and beauty, such that fortune, in favoring him, proves herself no longer blind. The very order of the universe labors to bear him on to the *culmina rerum*, and both his parents hail him as a predestined savior.[3]

All of this, of course, only makes it harder to understand the strange curse which shadows him: his mother, preparing to inform her husband that his son is still alive, first inveighs against the treachery and incorrigible wickedness of womankind. But her husband sees in the chain of events the workings of a providential destiny, and accepts that he must be sacrificed to it. The two concur in accepting the situation as unalterable, and the husband is consoled by the thought that he will live on in his son:[4]

[2] *Mathematicus*, line 112 (Hauréau, p. 18; PL 172.1368).
[3] *Ibid.*, lines 147-52, 501-12, 543-50 (Hauréau, pp. 19, 28, 29; PL 172.-1368, 1374-75, 1375).
[4] *Ibid.*, lines 437-42 (Hauréau, p. 26; PL 172.1373).

Sed moriens ego non moriar, totusque superstes
   Totus et in tali prole renatus ero.
Quod de fatali descendit origine rerum
   Non dicas fieri fraude vel arte tua;
Fatum me perimit, fatum servavit eumdem
   Quem servasse putas; omnia lege meant.

But in dying I shall not die; I will survive wholly and be wholly re-
born in such an offspring. Do not suppose that what descends to
us from the source of destiny comes about by any deceit or con-
trivance of yours. It is fate that has determined my death, fate that
has preserved him whom you suppose yourself to have saved. All
comes about by law.

"Omnia lege meant": these words define the astrological point of
view toward the situation of the poem. But they are flatly contra-
dicted by Patricida himself, who refuses to let fate determine his
actions. He resolves to deny the meaning of his name and rise
against the tyranny of the stars:[5]

Nostra quid aethereis mens est cognatior astris,
   Si durae Lachesis triste necesse ferat?
Frustra particulam divinae mentis habemus,
   Si nequeat ratio nostra cavere sibi.

Why is our mind so closely aligned with heavenly powers, if it must
suffer the grim necessity of harsh Lachesis? It is in vain that we
possess a portion of divine understanding, if our reason is unable
to provide for itself.

His father has a wholly fictive conception of immortality, and his
thoughts about death center on "chaos and the dim realm of Sty-
gian Jove."[6] But Patricida asserts man's affinity with celestial pow-
ers. Death, he argues, will be a release from prison, a reward, a
return to his true home:[7]

Corporis invisi caecis excedere claustris
   Non trepidat meritis mens mea tuta suis.
Carnis ab excesu superos migrabit ad axes,
   Sideris in numerum restituenda sibi.
Jucundum felixque mori. . .

[5] *Ibid.*, lines 639-42 (Haureau, p. 31; PL 172.1377).
[6] *Ibid.*, lines 449-50 (Haureau, p. 26; PL 172.1374).
[7] *Ibid.*, lines 799-803 (Haureau, pp. 35-36; PL 172.1379-80).

155

My mind, secure in the sense of its own merits, does not fear to depart from the dark prison of the hateful body. From the aberration of carnal existence it will journey back to the summit of heaven, to reassume its rightful place in the number of the stars. It is pleasurable and blessed to die. . .

The contrast between Patricida's vision and his father's serves to focus the larger implications of the poem, and of its use of rhetorical commonplace. For it is rhetoric that defines the impossible situation of the poem. Patricida is perfect in natural endowments, learning, political and military skill. His father is a perfectly blameless man, his mother both a perfect mother and a perfect wife, incapable of choosing between two such claims on her affection. But the parents' rhetorical view is earthbound. They cannot see the larger implications of the "forma deitatis" which shines forth in their son, or see his evolution to maturity and greatness as capable of extending beyond the attainment of the "culmina rerum," the lordship of Rome. Patricida, however, is able to see further, and to intuit the source of the topoi which define his perfection in a primordial state in which man had his place among the governing principles of the universe, realized his own divine origin, and the affinity of his mind with the divine wisdom, and so saw beyond the cosmic forces of fate and necessity which impinge upon human life. Thus, when the Senate objects to his intended suicide, he accuses them of seeking to seduce him with the corrupted arts of logic and rhetoric with which they themselves had been seduced by the Greeks. He has sought, he declares, to show them the way back to the simple integrity of the Romans of old, who had used open and unadorned speech, but they insist upon living within the web of their own sophistry. The vision of a lost simplicity and purity are not just commonplaces of political oratory for him, and so he is wholly immune to the elaborate protestations of the senators. Their formulae and syllogisms are hidebound, and in seeking to make their king less than a king, by denying him sovereignty over himself, they are seeking to alienate him from his true nature as a man. All that this implies about the corruption of human society is symbolized by Patricida's gesture as he removes his robes of state and goes forth to his death, sustained only by the dignity of his own manhood. By this gesture he transcends the power of any determinism and the finite limits imposed upon his evolution by the form and rhetoric of the poem. The final line, "Liber et explicitus ad mea vota meus," with its plays on "liber" and "explicit," emphasizes the sense in which the poem's formal resolution is at once a conclusion and a release.[8]

The opposition between Patricida's vision and his father's is paralleled by the relation of Bernardus' poem to its source, the fourth Declamation of the pseudo-Quintilian. There the point of the dilemma is in its insolubility: the hero (who, unlike Bernardus' Patricida, has known all along of the astrologer's prophecy) resolves on suicide only after having taken every possible risk in an attempt to die honorably in battle, and has no higher reason for taking his own life than that it will spare his father's. Even then he fears that his suicide may cause his father to die of grief.[9] In relation to this negative purpose, the vision of Bernardus' hero comes as virtually a new dispensation from God, and the suggestion of such an analogy is surely one purpose of the poem. Patricida's act and his sense of its implications are a refutation of the order of things as paradoxical as the passion of Christ, and leave his people with a humanist counterpart to the challenge of faith. Suicide is the only way of removing the curse of determinism, and reaffirming the virtues of primitive *Romanitas*: in a similar humanist spirit Dante makes Cato of Utica the warden of his Purgatory, and it has affinities as well with Bernardus' treatment of Castor and Pollux in the commentary on Martianus.

More generally, we may see in Patricida's intuition of the spiritual implications of rhetoric the reflection of a widespread concern of later twelfth-century poets. The heroic poem of his life testifies, as I have suggested, to an impulse toward the recovery of lost perfec-

[8] It will be obvious that I accept without question that the hero goes on to take his own life. Hauréau argues compellingly for this view (ed. *Mathematicus*, pp. 7-8). See also von den Steinen, "Les sujets d'inspiration," pp. 378-79.

[9] Pseudo-Quintilian, *Declamatio* 4.4, 23 (*Quintiliani quae feruntur Declamationes XIX Maiores*, ed. G. Lehnert, Leipzig, 1905, pp. 71, 88).

tion, an imitation by the human spirit of its original wholeness. But it is only an imitation, and the syntheses it creates all too often fall short of integration with the reality they seek to express, just as the earthly eminence achieved by Patricida is finally a denial of what it seeks to dignify, a betrayal of the true meaning of the aspiration which had achieved it. And of course we cannot simply accept Patricida's confident assertion of his own destiny; for it is a translation into directly spiritual terms of an intuition and an impulse which in the earthly state of man are fated to remain unconscious. But we can see in his action the image of a self-assertion which claims an intrinsic value for itself in just the subjective way of the heroes of Abelard's *Planctus,* and expresses the aspiration of a profound humanism. To recognize the depth and meaning of this aspiration is perhaps to see new implications in the many twelfth-century lyrics which dramatize the flights and vacillations of erotic feeling, endlessly seeking to align itself with the ongoing order of nature. This attempt is closely akin to that of the chivalric hero, striving toward the clarity of purpose necessary to achieve social order, to refine away the shadows and neutralize the tensions of the *silva* of earthly life. Whether the inspiration be love, chivalry, a humanistic or religious ideal, there is a sense in which the conscious object, and the degree to which it is realized, are less important than the origin of the impulse itself in the vestigial survival of man's original perfection.

2. The *De mundi universitate*

In Bernardus' major allegory the impulse to perfection is traced to its source in the original emergence of ordered life from chaos— one cannot simply say the imposition of order on chaos, for Bernardus is at pains to emphasize the collaboration of the principles involved. The human condition is the central concern of the *De mundi universitate,* but it appears only in the context of an account of the creation which begins, in the fullest sense, at the beginning. The fact of the nonexistence of time in the eternal prelude is exploited boldly and ingeniously: matter exists already *in forma con-*

fusionis, and Nature, present as a kind of primordial aspiration toward formal existence, pleads on behalf of the *primordia rerum* that something more beautiful be made of the primal chaos, the *silva.* The boldness of her appeal, her sense of a dignity and destiny which demand form and order for their fulfillment, are, as it were, presentiments of the humanist vision to which Patricida gives expression in the *Mathematicus,* and when Noys, the figure of divine wisdom to whom she appeals, speaks of Nature as "uteri mei beata fecunditas,"[10] echoing the salutation to Mary, their common task acquires quasi-sacramental implications, and Nature assumes a role in some sense analogous to that of the *figlia del suo figlio.*

The introductory dialogue between Nature and Noys gives a good illustration of the breadth and complexity of Bernardus' allegory. Nature is to become the principle of harmony between soul and body, and the overseer of the processes of generation and renewal in the universe. But for the moment, with her domain sprawled about her, she represents an unformed desire, the "spirit," as it were, of a physical universe which is itself unformed. She feels and expresses the plight of the *silva,* "nurse" and receptacle of the existence to come:[11]

> Debetur nonnullus honos et gratia silvae
> Quae genitiva tenet gremio diffusa capaci.

[10] *De mundi universitate* 1.2, line 3 (ed. C. S. Barach and J. Wrobel, Innsbruck, 1876, p. 9). All reference will be to line and page in this edition. For purposes of reference I refer to the work by the title given it in the Barach-Wrobel edition, but the evidence of the manuscripts suggests that the proper title was *Cosmographia,* and the two books of the work were very often cited by their own titles, *Megacosmus* and *Microcosmus.* At several points I have emended the Barach-Wrobel text on the basis of a text of the *Megacosmus* prepared by Peter Dronke, based on Oxford, Bodleian Laud. Misc. 515, and my own examination of this manuscript. I have also consulted the critical edition of the *De mundi* (*Cosmographia*) by André Vernet (dissertation, Paris, École des Chartes, 1937). I would like here to acknowledge the kindness of Mr. Dronke in providing me with a copy of his text of the *Megacosmus,* and of Professor Brian Stock of the Pontifical Institute of Medieval Studies, Toronto, in allowing me to consult his copy of Vernet's edition.

[11] *De mundi universitate* 1.1, lines 37-40, p. 8.

Has infra veluti cunas infantia mundi
Vagit, et ad speciem vestiri cultius orat.

No small honor and grace are due to Silva, who contains the original natures of things diffused through her vast womb. Within this cradle the infant universe squalls, and cries aloud to be clothed with a finer appearance.

The dramatic impact of Nature's subjective and somewhat irrational appeal is made to convey a number of suggestions. A restrained but audible irony, an accusatory tone and a sense of offended dignity give her the presence of a tragic heroine:

Quid prodest quod cuncta suo praecesserit ortu
Silva parens, si lucis eget, si noctis abundat
Perfecto decisa suo, si denique possit
Auctorem terrere suo male condita vultu?

What does it avail Silva, mother of all, that her birth preceded all creation, if she is deprived of light, abounds in darkness, cut off from fulfillment? If, finally, in this wretched condition, her countenance is such as to frighten her very creator?

Such a passage both enhances the dignity of Nature and her appeal and suggests a certain feminine frailty. The complex tone is appropriate to a highly complex pattern of allusion. The very humanness of Nature's appeal, the theological absurdity of the final reproach and the desire "to be more pleasing in thy sight," the hint of self-righteousness and the sense of wrong, recall both the *Heroides* and the Psalms, with their impassioned appeal for a new sign of God's favor. ("How long wilt thou forget me, O Lord, for ever? How long wilt thou hide thy face?") We may think of Vergil's Venus, pleading with Jupiter that her son may find peace after the toil and violence of his long odyssey. There are echoes of the great prayer of Boethius' Philosophy for stability and illumination, and Martianus' invocation of the unifying power of Hymen. And, of course, there is the hint of a typological significance in the anticipated impression of *silva* with the impress of the divine wisdom:

. . . ascribe figuram,
Adde iubar: fateatur opus quis fecerit auctor.

The religious undertones hint at the dignification of a specifically human nature, and yet the implications of human frailty are fully as evident: for the Ovidian elements in Nature's appeal extend not only to the *Heroides* and the opening cosmogony of the *Metamorphoses*, but to the second book of the *Ars amatoria*, where the soothing and disarming of a reluctant mistress is compared to the imposition of heavenly order on the *confusa moles* of the primordial chaos.[12]

The *De mundi* will incorporate the implications of all these themes and sources. Like the *De nuptiis* and on a deeper level Bernardus' allegory describes a philosophical marriage, a union of divine and earthly which will culminate in the uniting of the soul and body of men. Nature must be educated to the point at which she will be capable of cooperation with a celestial *ratio*, a process which involves both a Chartrian schooling in the meaning of the creation and an emotional experience of the struggle of cosmic life against the threat of dissolution comparable to that dramatized in the *De consolatione* of Boethius.

The cosmogony of the *De mundi* proceeds rhythmically, reiterating at every stage the archetypal pattern of creation. We pass from chaos to order, are given dark hints of the danger of dissolution, and see the tension between order and *malignitas* neutralized by the pervasive influence of providence and continuity. This rhythmical movement has an important thematic function: on the one

---

[12] See *Ars amatoria* 2.467-70, and Silverstein, "Fabulous Cosmogony," p. 99, n. 39. The sexual element in Bernardus' account recalls not only the *Asclepius* but Calcidius' paraphrase of Aristotle, *Physics* 1.9 (*Commentarius* 287, Waszink, pp. 291-92): "Superest ergo, ut silua cultum ornatumque desideret, quae deformis est non ex se, sed ob indigentiam. Est enim turpitudo siluam cultu formaque indigere; sic quippe erit uidua carens specie, perinde ut carens uiro femina. Proptereaque et, inquit, appetit speciem, ut sexus femineus uirilem, quoque sit in aliqua posita deformitate, formam atque cultum, simul cupiens perire atque exolescere quod est in semet ex indigentiae uitio, contraria siquidem haec duo sibi et repugnantia, species et item carentia, quorum quod obtinuerit alterum perimit. Cupiditatem uero negat esse talem, qualis est animalium, sed ut, cum quid coeptum atque inchoatum, dicitur perfectionem desiderare, sic, opinor, etiam silua speciem cupit; potest enim florere eius consortio."

hand it dramatizes the ceaseless vitality and self-renewing power of Nature, the continual victory of life over death; on the other hand it conveys in a rich and often ironic way the paradoxical nature of man's relations with this ongoing order. For Nature, continuity is a virtual immortality, but for man it implies both death and life. Moreover, the integration of Nature, equipoised between Providence and *malignitas*, never giving way to formlessness and never transcending herself, points up the inevitable and potentially tragic disintegration in the life of man, the barrier between human consciousness in its "natural" state and the ultimate sources of purpose and meaning in human life.

These themes begin to appear in the long prose section which describes the response of Noys to the demands of Nature. Noys is a highly complex figure, referred to as both the "ratio" and the "providentia" of God, sprung "utique de se alteram se," an intelligence "idem natura cum Deo nec substantia disparatum."[13] But as Silverstein has shown she cannot be simply identified with the Verbum Dei, which is plainly referred to separately.[14] She has traces of Martianus' Pallas about her, as well as the "Natura creatrix" of the *Asclepius* and the ordering Wisdom of the *Book of Wisdom* and *Ecclesiasticus*. We can probably do no better than to settle for Silverstein's summarial characterization of her as the "figurative representative" of the second person of the Trinity.

With a fine sense of decorum Bernardus first shows us Noys as she slowly emerges from deep thought to respond, "vultu blandiore," to the appeal of Nature.[15] In words as ponderous and arcane

[13] *De mundi* 1.2, pp. 9, 13.

[14] "Fabulous Cosmogony," p. 110. Silverstein's careful distinction between the "fabulous" Noys and the actual *Verbum Dei* is a refinement on the position of Étienne Gilson, "La cosmogonie de Bernardus Silvestris," *Archives d'histoire* 3 (1928), pp. 12ff., who had simply identified the two. This position is defended against Silverstein's by Mlle. d'Alverny, "Alain de Lille et la *Theologia*," in *L'Homme devant Dieu* (cited above, ch. 1, n. 156), II, 121. But her arguments ignore the fact that Silverstein is concerned as much with a figural technique as with a theological position.

[15] *De mundi* 1.2, lines 1-3, p. 9. The phrase "vultu blandiore" suggests that Noys had been sad up to this moment. In any case the vision of the creative principle brooding over the barren emptiness of the pre-creation is an appro-

as Nature's had been swift and vivid, she commends the "filia providentiae" and praises her devotion to the cause of material life. After reminding Nature of the "rigid and invincible necessity" which makes the task difficult she agrees to undertake the formation of the universe. Even she, however, cannot wholly perfect the ambiguous condition of material existence, suspended "between good and evil"; for there is an ancient and ineradicable *malignitas* in matter which can be dissipated or restrained but never eliminated,[16] and which will always resist the bonds of peace and love with which Noys curbs the elements.

Having thus presented us with a cosmic analogue to original sin, Noys proceeds to her initial task, the separation of the elements, each of which assumes its natural character. Fire leaps upward first from the confusion of chaos, and "instantly dissipates the primeval darkness with darting flames." Then earth, "refixior et corpulentiae grossioris," eases itself into position at the center of things. Air and water are made to express the condition of created life, suspended between these two extremes:[17]

> Prodit liquentis aquae clara substantia, cuius plana et lubrica superficies figuras reddit aemulas umbrarum incursibus lacessita. Tractus aereus subinfertur levis quidem et convertibilis: nunc consentire tenebris, nunc suscepto lumine resplendere, calore et frigore nunc rigescere nunc dissolvi.

> Forth came the gleaming substance of clear water, whose level and shimmering surface gave back rival images when sullied by the intrusion of shadows. Then the vast region of the air was interposed, volatile and subject to change; now giving itself to shadow, now gleaming at the infusion of light, now growing crisp with frost, now languid with heat.

---

priate prelude to Bernardus' dignification of material existence. One thinks of the description of Saturn which opens Keats' *Hyperion*.

[16] *De mundi*, 1.2, pp. 9-11. Cp. Calcidius, *Commentarius* 287-98, Waszink, pp. 291-300; J.C.M. Van Winden, *Calcidius on Matter, His Doctrine and Sources* (Leiden, 1959), pp. 117-28.

[17] *De mundi* 1.2, lines 105-10, p. 12.

The words convey a sense of more than merely physical mutability. The emphasis on the tenuous nature of the phenomena described recalls the evanescent *fortunae* in Martianus' grove of Apollo, and suggests the unstable nature of our perception of reality in a way which we will see again in Bernardus' treatment of the World Soul.

The coherence of the universe and its continual peace depend on a perfect *tenor* and *firmitas* among the elements. This is contrasted in Boethian terms with the plight of "the hapless race of men," whose elemental balance is imperfect and who, as a result, live in constant fear of external accident. "For whenever heat from without aggravates the heat of man's nature, his inner peace is disrupted, and what had existed in a state of calm becomes aroused to destructive activity."[18] This disturbing reflection concludes Bernardus' account of the *ornatus elementorum*, and Noys proceeds to the creation of the World Soul, *Endelechia*.[19]

Bernardus' treatment of this crucial concept gives an excellent illustration of his poetic perspective on Chartrian philosophy. The World Soul was the central concern of the Chartrians, and in particular the justification for their preoccupation with cosmology, for it was seen as the link between God and creation, and hence between the divine wisdom and the human mind. Bernardus' treatment is at once reverent and highly oblique; he begins by dwelling at length on the source of the World Soul in Noys' deliberations on universal life. The solemn tone suggests the difficulty of comprehending a system so vast, and the divinity of a wisdom which can contain it whole:[20]

Illic in genere, in specie, in individuali singularitate conscripta, quicquid hyle, quicquid mundus, quicquid parturiunt elementa. Illic exarata supremi digito dispunctoris textus temporis, fatalis series, dispositio saeculorum. Illic lacrimae pauperum fortunaeque regum. Illic potentia militaris, illic felicior philosophorum disciplina. Illic quicquid angelus, quicquid ratio

[18] *Ibid.*, 1.2, lines 141-43, p. 13.
[19] On this figure see Silverstein, "Fabulous Cosmogony," pp. 115-16.
[20] *De mundi* 1.2, lines 157-67, p. 13.

comprehendit humana. Illic quicquid caelum sua complecti-
tur curvatura. Quod igitur tale est, illud aeternitati contiguum,
idem natura cum Deo nec substantia disparatum.

There were enrolled, in kind, in species, in individual unique-
ness, all that Hyle, that the cosmic order, that the elements
labor to bring forth. There, inscribed by the finger of the su-
preme arbitrator, were the fabric of time, the chain of destiny,
the disposition of the ages. There were the tears of the poor
and the fortunes of kings, the soldier's strength and the happy
discipline of the philosophers, all that the reason of angels or
men may comprehend, all that is gathered together beneath
the dome of heaven. What exists in this way verges on the
state of eternity, is one in nature with God and not disparate
in substance.

In the wake of this sonorous declaration the creation of the World
Soul occurs almost imperceptibly, in a single sentence:

Huiusce igitur sive vitae sive lucis origine vita, iubar et rerum
endelechia quadam velut emanatione defluxit.

From the very source, then, of this our life and light, there is-
sued forth by a sort of emanation the life, illumination and
soul of creation, Endelechia.

And Bernardus dwells on its unfathomable mystery in an elabor-
ately indirect manner which recalls both the baroque abstractions
of Martianus and Hugh of St. Victor's response to the words of
the Preacher on the vanity of philosophy:

Conparuit igitur exporrectae magnitudinis globus, terminatae
quidem continentiae, sed quam non oculis, verum solo pervi-
deas intellectu. Eius admodum clara substantia liquentis flui-
dique fontis imaginem praeferebat, inspectorem suum quali-
tatis ambiguo praeconfundens, cum plerumque aeri plerumque
caelo cognatior videretur. Quis enim tuto diffinivit essentiam
quae consonantiis, quae se numeris emoveret? Cum igitur
quodam quasi praestigio veram imaginem fraudaret, non erat

in manibus inspectantis unde fomes ille vivificus sic maneat ut perire non possit, cum separatim singulis totus et integer refundatur.

She was like a sphere of vast size, yet of fixed dimensions, and such as one might not perceive visually, but only by intellect. Her shining substance appeared just like a steadily flowing fountain, defying scrutiny by its uncertain condition, since it seemed closely akin to the atmosphere, and at the same time to the heaven itself. For who has defined with certainty that mode of being which emerges from harmony, from number? And so when one was deluded as if by magic as to its true aspect, it was beyond the reach of scrutiny to divine how this vitalizing spark should so endure that it might not be extinguished, but was rendered back whole and undiminished by each individual creature.

The passage combines the sort of scientific formulation by which Guillaume had explained the World Soul "integumentally" with the Neoplatonist imagery of the prayers of Philology to the sun and the *virgo fontana*; but it uses both only to suggest their inability to capture the essence of what they seek to define. More tenuous and subtle than the images formed in air or water, the mode of existence of Endelechia seems to demand an anagogical transformation of our perception. Thus Bernardus both vindicates the deepest insights of the Chartrians and tactfully evades any charge of presumption.

The long catalogue poem which follows deals with the adornment of the visible heavens and the creation of earthly life. Its primary emphasis is on the fact of natural plenitude itself, but it derives a certain unity also from its allusion to the countless traces of man, his nature and history, present everywhere in the universe, which suggest both the joys and possibilities and the hardships of human life. There is much charm and occasional humor, but also irony, and a sense of how man's involvement in the *silva* of experience robs him of perspective and orientation. At such moments

Bernardus' poetry may remind us of similar motifs in Vergil: of Iopas' song of "the wandering moon and the sun's labors," with its cosmic foreshadowing of the fates of Dido and Aeneas; of the long and painful history inscribed on Aeneas' shield; and of the song of Silenus in the sixth Eclogue, where an account of the cosmogony introduces a sequence of tragic legends.

The best known portion of the catalogue poem is the astrological section, in which the vicissitudes of history are said to have been foretold in the stars. There were set forth from the beginning of time the achievements of human civilization and the violence and excess which brings civilization low, the prototypes of wisdom, beauty, and strength, and of vice, vanity, and treachery. The justice and piety of Phoroneus are balanced by the discord of the sons of Oedipus and the presumption of Phaethon; Paris is paired with Hippolytus, Priam with Turnus. An attractive balance between chivalry and "clergie" is suggested by the coupling of the boxer Pollux with Cicero, a combatant at law, and of Tiphys the navigator with the geometrician Thales: we recall the juxtaposition of "potentia militaris" with the "felicior philosophorum disciplina" in the ponderings of Noys. But the corruption of this graceful ideal is suggested in a couplet contrasting the art of Vergil and Milo with the pomp and vanity of Nero.

There has been much speculation over the years about the seriousness of Bernardus' astrology in this passage, with its preordained series of events.[21] But those who have dwelt on the possible implications of determinism have paid curiously little attention to the couplet on the Incarnation with which the passage concludes:[22]

[21] See Theodore Wedel, *The Medieval Attitude toward Astrology*, pp. 34-35; Thorndike, *A History of Magic and Experimental Science* II, 105-06; von den Steinen, "Les sujets d'inspiration," pp. 373-77.

[22] *De mundi* 1.3, lines 53-54, p. 16. The couplet on Pope Eugene III which follows was perhaps interpolated at the time when the poem was read before him (see above, ch. 2, n. 73), but its outrageous flattery is ingeniously worked into the context of the catalogue, for it echoes an account of the virtues of Patricida in the *Mathematicus* (lines 505-06; Hauréau, p. 28; PL 172.1375) and thus hints that Eugene is the "perfectus homo" made possible again by the effect of the Incarnation.

> Exemplar specimenque Dei virguncula Christum
> Parturit et verum saecula numen habent.

A tender maid gives birth to Christ, at once the type and the embodiment of God, and earthly life realizes true divinity.

While the classical heroes and sages are isolated and partial embodiments of the idea of man, and their excellences are marred and obscured by their involvement in the corrupting process of history, Christ's nature joins the ideal and the actual in a more definitive way: he is at once the supreme *exemplar*, the Word, and, through the Incarnation, the supreme *specimen* as well, the perfect embodiment of ideal reality in earthly *involucrum*, and so points up by contrast the inevitable disintegration of meaning in the merely human arts of rhetoric and astrology.

In the light of this contrast between different levels of meaning we may perhaps see a certain irony in the lines which conclude the next section of the catalogue, a long survey of the constellations:[23]

> Sidera quae praesens sic vel sic nominat aetas,
> Temporis exortu caelitus ignis erant.
> Communi ne voce rei generalis oberret,
> Quae modo sunt stellis nomina fecit homo.

The stars, to which the present age gives this name or that, existed at the birth of time as heavenly fire. Lest he lose touch with their universal meaning by expressing it in common speech, man created those names which even now denote the stars.

The idea of an archetypal language transmitted from age to age for the discussion of the heavens is a noble one, but the very proliferation and variety of imagery in the heavens suggests, like the contrasts of the historical survey, the limited power of any man-made system to comprehend the meaning of so vast a design.

The catalogues of earthly nature convey a wide variety of meanings. The procession of animals is marked by a certain emphasis on the servitude and abuse to which certain species are subjected, and ends with a couplet which, in context, is horrifying in its effect:[24]

[23] *De mundi* 1.3, lines 133-36, p. 19.

[24] This couplet is not given in Barach-Wrobel. It belongs between lines 232 and 233 on p. 22.

> Carior et redolens et burse predo sabellus,
> Guttura conplectens deliciosa ducum.

Costlier still (i.e., than the beaver, prized for its fur), that ill-smell-ing plunderer of purses, the sable, wraps himself about the pleasure-glutted throats of the great.

In the catalogue of famous rivers the poet is free to adorn his verse with exempla as he chooses. As in the historical passage, good and bad are balanced: the violence and excesses of Roman imperial-ism are balanced by prophecies, in the couplets on Siloa and Jor-dan, of the sacraments and reforms of Christ, and the Rhone is associated with the heroic refusal of St. Maurice and his Theban Legion. In the concluding couplets secular pomp and power are balanced by an idealizing view of "Martinopolis," Bernardus' na-tive city of Tours, suggesting the restorative mission of heroic sainthood:[25]

> Sequana prosiluit, ubi grandia germina regum
> Pipinos, Carolos bellica terra tulit.
> Emicuit Ligeris, ubi Martinopolis inter
> Sidereos fluvios pictaque rura iacet.

The Seine flows where a warlike land has brought forth great dynas-ties of rulers, the lines of Pippin and Charles. The Loire shimmers, where the city of St. Martin lies between starlit waters and painted fields.

As other examples will show, Bernardus' attitude toward the land-scape of France and northern Europe generally is complex. He seems always to hint at a savage quality not easily tamed by the graces of Latinity and its ordering conventions. Thus, in the lines just quoted the French soil spawns warriors, as it were, by nature, and is pastoralized only by the influence of powerful sanctity.

The catalogue of famous mountains concludes on a similar but darker note. This catalogue is unified by the theme of intellectual aspiration: Olympus' summit is shielded by cloud from mortal view; Parnassus strives to behold the gods "disposing the affairs of men and the seven planets"; Ossa and Pelion recall the presump-

---

[25] *De mundi* 1.3, lines 259-62, p. 22.

tion of the Titans; Prometheus' grim vigil in the Caucasus is contrasted with Orpheus' attachment to Rhodope; the dense cedar forests of Mount Lebanon are contrasted with the open slopes of Sinai, which Moses ascended to confront God. The passage touches last on the forbidding nature of the Alps, whose lonely fastnesses freeze at sunset, and concludes with two couplets strangely suggestive of the opening lines of the *Inferno*:[26]

> Quod spatii montana tenent deperdit aratrum
>   Articuloque iacet sub breviore solum.
> Cepit enim fruticosa lupos, deserta leones,
>   Arida serpentes, pars nemoralis apros.

Such open ground as the mountains enclose is lost to the plow, and the land about their foothills lies idle. For their thickets harbor wolves, their desert places lions, the dry wastes serpents and the woodland boars.

These lines seem deliberately to recall by contrast the passage in praise of the beauties of Italy with which Pliny concludes his *Natural History*,[27] and to oppose to his idealization a nature savage and intractable, menacing human order with the *silva* of the unknown.

A more positive view of the relation of human order to the external landscape is the passage on the foresting of the earth, which begins with a rich array of fruit trees, trees sacred to gods, and trees bearing scents and spices, and overflows easily into a description of Eden, where the elements had not the power to harm, and where man dwelt "too briefly" as a guest. Here, says Bernardus, Nature's disposition of forest and verdure was carefully planned; elsewhere the *silvae* grew up at random. The distinction recalls the contrast of Sinai and Lebanon, and suggests the alien quality of the world after the Fall. Nonetheless Bernardus turns immedi-

[26] *Ibid.*, 1.3, lines 199-202, p. 21.
[27] In Pliny's conclusion Italy is said to be favored by her "positione procurrentis in partem utilissimam et inter ortus occasusque mediam, aquarum copia, nemorum salubritate, montium articulis, ferorum animalium innocentia, soli fertilitate, pabuli ubertate." (*Naturalis historia* 37.13.77.201; ed. Karl Mayhoff, Leipzig, 1870–97, v, 476.)

ately to a catalogue of famous groves, the Aonian, Pierian, and the "locus academicus" frequented by Plato. Here the harmonizing power of the mind is offered as a possible answer to the challenge of an alien nature. In the mountain catalogue the mind's transcendent aspirations are opposed to an unyielding wilderness, but here the emphasis is on the achievement of a harmony *within* nature, the use of its very diversity to recreate a higher harmony on earth. (Solomon, we may recall, used the cedars of Lebanon to raise the house of the Lord.)

Bernardus passes suggestively from this ideal view of mind and nature to the wilder groves of India, and the *Celtica terra*, whose tall trees menace the heavens, and then to the forests of France, the strange ring of whose names has appealed to all readers of the poem:[28]

> Briscelim sinus Armoricus, Turonia Vastem,
> Ardaniam silvam Gallicus orbis habet.

Brittany has Broceliande, Touraine her Gâtine, and Gaul has the forest of Ardennes.

Like the contrast of the mountain wilderness with Pliny's Italy, but far more gently, the unwieldy names seem to suggest a new challenge to the ordering and refining mind. Is it possible that Bernardus is contrasting these woods with the groves of classical poetry as a way of hinting at the special difficulties of his own poetic undertaking?

At this point the poem shifts to the more mundane relations of man and nature, cataloguing the legumes and herbs which provide his nourishment and cure him of the effects of his vices. The emphasis on excess grows increasingly vivid and the passage concludes with the quasi-human mandrake which "fetu terra novo prodigiosa tulit," before the poem abandons solid ground to conclude with catalogues of fish and birds.

Diffuse and prodigal by its very theme and structure, the catalogue states the theme of the *De mundi universitate* in a unique way by setting the refinement of chaos and the channeling of its

[28] *De mundi* 1.3, lines 351-52, p. 25.

energies in relation to the seeming chaos of human experience. It suggests that the seeds of overreaching, carnality and violence are sown in the very development of civilization, but it also offers beautiful intimations of the coming to terms with the challenge of nature through the ordering power of the mind, symbolized by the *nemora* of poetry and philosophy, and demonstrated in the controlling function exercised by the framework of the catalogue poem itself. The cumulative effect of its obliquities is to point up the need of accepting earthly life as the context within which man's higher attainments must originate, rather than seeking to divorce the quest for mental harmony from the reconciliation of mind with matter, with the body, and the *silva* of experience.

The first book of the *De mundi* concludes with a prose section which, as if to reawaken our sense of the integrity of the cosmic order, summarizes the work of creation in terms of its organizing and animating principles. The rich prose passes rhythmically over a sequence of hierarchical emanations, restating in abstract terms the plenitude described *ad litteram* in the catalogue poem, and withdrawing the narrative once again to a level on which earthly ambiguities have no place:[29]

> Ex mentis igitur vita, silvae spiritu, anima mundi, mundalium vegetatione rerum aeternitas coalescit. In Deo in Noy scientia est, in caelo ratio, in sideribus intellectus. In magno vero animali cognitio viget, viget et sensus causarum praecedentium fomitibus enutritus. Ex mente enim caelum, de caelo sidera, de sideribus mundus, unde viveret, unde discerneret, linea continuationis excepit.

> Thus from the life of the divine mind, from the spirit of Silva, from the World Soul, from the growth-principle of created life, the eternity of the universe has its rise. Knowledge reposes in God, in Noys; a rational plan eixsts in the firmament and intelligence in the stars. And so in this great animal understanding and awareness thrive, and draw nourishment from their antecedent principles. The firmament learns from the

[29] *Ibid.*, 1.4, lines 71-78, p. 31.

divine mind, the stars from the firmament, and the universe from the stars, whence their life derives and how they may discern the course of existence.

All is pervaded by intelligence and vitality; *malignitas*, and the ambiguous allusiveness of previous sections, have become indiscernible. Thought and language alike reveal the purest idealism:

> Ex mundo intelligibili mundus sensilis perfectus natus est ex perfecto. Plenus erat qui genuit plenumque constituit plenitudo. Sicut enim integrascit ex integro, pulcrescit ex pulcro, sic exemplari suo aeternatur aeterno . . .

> From the intellectual universe the sensible universe was born, perfect from perfect. The creative model exists in fulness, and this fulness imparted itself to creation. For just as [the sensible universe] participates in the flawlessness of its flawless model, and waxes beautiful by its beauty, so by its eternal exemplar it is made to endure eternally.

This rich Neoplatonic view of the rapport between creator and creation seems, like Bernardus' account of the World Soul, to show the integration of cosmic life on a level inaccessible to philosophy. It is a visionary conception of the relation of the cosmos to God, and provides a sharp contrast with the experience of Nature in the second book of the *De mundi*. After Noys has reviewed her handiwork approvingly, she sends Nature to seek out Urania, the divine *ratio* who is to collaborate with her in the creation of man.[30]

[30] Though her role in the *De mundi* is limited, Urania stands for relationships which become crucially important in later allegories. She is in intimate contact with the divine wisdom, and it is through her that man "follows Nature" in the most profound sense (hence her famous "I, Natura, sequar," 2.4, lines 53-54, p. 40). Like Nature's, her divinity is limited: the two goddesses ("Urania pariter et Natura") invoke the Trinity together (see below, n. 34), and Urania's influence, like that of Nature, is liable to the interference of human sensuality and sinfulness. Her function is absorbed by that of Nature herself, together with Genius, in the *De planctu naturae* of Alain, by Nature alone in the *Architrenius* of Jean de Hanville and by *Prudentia* in Alain's *Anticlaudianus*, but she is essentially reborn in the *Raison*

Through her association with Urania, Nature, too, will attain a certain visionary awareness of human destiny, but the search, conceived in imitation of Mercury's search for Apollo in the *De nuptiis*, dramatizes the limited vision of universal reality accessible to the human mind. Nature is invigorated by the warm light of the ethereal region, and moves upward through the spheres by sure degrees, but her search is long and exhausting, and she is made to seem a somewhat alien being, from whom the secrets of the heavens are sealed. The contrast between her world and that toward which she seeks to rise is powerfully drawn in the vision she is given of the multitude of unborn souls clustered about the house of Cancer, for whom the prospect of earthly birth seems like a descent into Hades:[31]

> Quippe de splendore ad tenebras, de caelo Ditis ad imperium, de aeternitate ad corpora per Cancri domicilium quae fuerant descensurae sicut purae, sicut simplices, obtusum caecumque corporis quod apparari perspiciunt habitaculum exhorrebant. Ad huius rei spectaculum mora consumpta est aliquanta, et quae quaeritur non inventa.

> They who were destined to descend from splendor into shadow, from heaven to the kingdom of Pluto, pure as they were and simple, from eternal life to that of the body, grew terrified at the clumsy and blind fleshly habitation which they saw prepared for them. Some little time she (i.e., Nature) spent pondering this spectacle, and what she sought was not to be found.

The sad wisdom of the Preacher seems to inform the final words of this comment on the burden and disappointment of human life.

Nature comes finally to the outer limit of the universe, where she meets the *Oyarses* or Genius who has charge of the forms of all creatures, and assigns each its special properties as the heavens devise. He himself is inscribed with the marks of great age, and his

---

of Jean de Meun's portion of the *Roman de la Rose*, who, however, corresponds chiefly to her human aspect.

[31] *De mundi* 2.3, lines 63-70, p. 37.

words to Nature express both the labor and the dignity of their common task:[32]

> Heus, inquit, o Natura, et ad axes astriferos devenisti, digna quidem tu caelo recipi, cuius qualitatibus et cuius essentiis indefessae studio sedulitatis inservis.

> "Hail, O Nature," he said, "you have come to the summit of the star-bearing sphere; and indeed you are worthy to be received in heaven, for you give your service to heavenly qualities and essences with all the zeal of unflagging devotion."

The Genius and his office, the union of form with matter, define the limits of Nature's ascent toward the origins of being. It is he who points out Urania, where she sits, gazing in wonder at the newly created firmament, and so performs the archetypal act of bringing together the celestial *ratio* and the impulse toward form represented by Nature. The importance of this union is made plain in Urania's speech of greeting, which stresses the special balance which is to be realized in the nature of man:[33]

> Velle Dei, mixtura modum, modulatio nexum,
> Nexus amicitiam pariat sacer,
> Ne pigeat mentem caecas habitare tenebras
> Hospitiumque pati grave corporis,
> Ne propria de carne queat fecisse querelam
> Spiritus imperiis subiectior,
> Ut concors sibi disparitas coniuret amice,
> Huius ad artis opus comes evocor.

It is God's will that the mixture be balanced, that balance effect a bond, that this divine bond bestow harmonious relation, lest it disgust the mind to dwell in shadowy blindness and suffer the forced hospitality of the body, lest the spirit have cause to complain of the flesh that it is too much subject to its dictates; that this concord of unlike powers may come about peaceably, I am summoned to lend my help to the project.

The relation of celestial *ratio* to natural existence is the theme, explicit and implicit, of the long journey of the two goddesses from

[32] *Ibid.*, 2.3, lines 100-03, p. 38.   [33] *Ibid.*, 2.4, lines 7-14, p. 39.

the *Aplanon* down through the universe to the earthly Paradise, *Granusion*, home of *Physis*, who will fashion the human body to which Nature will then join the soul provided by Urania. As the focus of the poem narrows to center on this crucial action, the relations of heaven and earth are reviewed through a panorama of the influences of the planets, the hierarchy of cosmic "intelligences" and daimones, and, in a highly concentrated and difficult poem, the relationship of form and matter. As in Book One extreme contrasts are drawn. Before descending, the goddesses pass briefly "outside" the universe to invoke "a certain triune majesty," a radiance so dazzling as to shield itself from their sight,[34] in an atmosphere rich with the sort of Neoplatonist imagery (here obviously recalling the pseudo-Dionysius) already exhibited in the final section of Book One. As they descend, they are increasingly reminded of the turbulent world below, and the contrast is made explicit as they pause at the circle of the moon, the point at which the influences of the planets are adapted to the exigencies of a grosser state of being, and first express themselves as fate, necessity, *vis genitiva,* and perturbation:[35]

> Supra quies intermina, serenum perpetuum, tranquillitas aetheris inconcussa. . . . Ea quidem in parte caeli, quia natura est invariabilis, mulcebris et quieta, sollers Graecia campos consentit Elysios, et felices animas, alma sacrata et numquam desitura lucis amoenitate vestiri. Infra aeris qualitas turbidior infunditur, cuius mutabilis convertitur species, quotiens expositas passionibus materias contrarietas accidentium interpellat. Unde homines, quia locum incolunt inquietum, tumultus instar veteris, motus perturbationum necesse est experiri.

> Above was endless calm, perpetual quiet, the unbroken peace of the aethereal regions. . . . The penetrating mind of Greece

---

[34] *Ibid.*, 2.5, lines 26-33, p. 41. Cp. the description of the Word in *Celestial Hierarchy* 12 (tr. Eriugena, PL 122.246C): ". . . qui in secretissimis sui Patris sinibus omnes sanctos perficit intellectus in primordialibus suis causis ac veluti ex luce divinitatis inaccessibili instar clarissimi radii procedit."

[35] *De mundi* 2.5, lines 193-205, pp. 45-46.

concluded that in this region of the firmament, since its nature is unchanging, soothing, and quiet, were placed the Elysian Fields, where blessed souls were enshrined in a gracious and hallowed state, never to be deprived of light. In the regions below were disposed the more turbid properties of the atmosphere, whose volatile appearance is altered whenever some chance occurrence offers to its passions the material they demand. So mankind, inhabiting this unquiet region, the very image of ancient chaos, must needs be subject to the force of its upheavals.

It is here, as the goddesses prepare for the final stage of their descent, that Urania addresses to Nature the poem which contains Bernardus' most profound intuitions into the relations of human life with the divine plan. In the scheme of the *De mundi* it corresponds to Anchises' discourse in the Elysium of the *Aeneid* on the all-pervading "spirit" of cosmic life and its influence on the destiny of the human soul. The Vergilian comparison is not so gratuitous as it may appear, for the whole of Nature's experience in Book Two of the *De mundi* constitutes a kind of "Aeneid," in the broad terms of Bernardus' comparison between Vergil's poem and those of Boethius and Martianus discussed above. Like Aeneas' odyssey and his descent to the underworld, Nature's long journey through the spheres, laborious and marked by ominous portents of the destiny of man, has been a preparation for the great task now to be performed. All the forces and influences of the greater universe are to come to bear on the making of a single being whose complexity will mirror them all, and whose life will somehow play a part in the ultimately positive design of creation. So Aeneas brings the forces of fate and destiny and the whole of world history to bear on the great task of the conquest of Italy and the establishment of Rome, the earthly city. In both cases the new creation gives rise to new problems which extend beyond the limits of the poetic context. The clarity and purpose so vividly expressed in the celestial regions become obscured and seemingly contradictory on the earthly level, and all the uncertainties of Nature's journey reap-

pear, like the memories of love and loss which goad and frustrate
Aeneas, in the account of the "battle against formlessness," the
ongoing process of generation which concludes the *De mundi* and,
by implication, begins human history.

The poem which introduces this final stage of the action of the
De mundi presents problems. It contains certain obscure phrases
and difficult transitions, and the evidence of the manuscripts, some
of which present a badly corrupted text and others of which simply
omit the poem altogether,[36] suggests that it was not easily under-
stood in its own day. Urania reviews the chain of divine influence
which descends from Noys' initial ordering function, and dwells
with Lucretian vividness on the love and harmony which unite the
diverse forms of created life. By an almost imperceptible transition
she then isolates the special condition of man, in whom the ex-
tremes of gross matter and *ignea mens* are brought together, "ut
res dissimiles uniat unus amor,"[37] and dwells on the tension be-
tween flesh and spirit, stressing the divine destiny of the soul "if
it exercise wisdom." Then, seeming to recall her sojourn with the
Genius of the *Aplanon*, she considers the problem in more philo-
sophical terms:

> Quid morti licitum, quae mortis causa, quis auctor,
>   Altius evolvens philosophando vide;
> Quo trahit imperio sorbetque voragine quicquid
>   Aura levat, tellus sustinet, aequor alit.
> Si tamen inspirat verum mens conscia veri
>   Rem privat forma, non rapit esse rei.
> Res eadem subiecta manet, sed forma vagatur,
>   Atque rei nomen dat nova forma novum.
> Forma fluit, manet esse rei, mortisque potestas
>   Nil perimit, sed res dissociat socias.

Pursuing philosophical enquiry further, behold what is permitted
to death, what is death's cause and who its author, by what author-
ity it draws down, in what maelstrom engulfs everything that air,
earth, or water sustains. And yet, if the mind which consorts with

[36] The poem is omitted in, e.g., Oxford, Bodl. Digby 157; Cambridge,
Trinity 1368; and Berne 710, all of the twelfth century.
[37] *De mundi* 2.8, line 28, p. 51.

178

truth inspires true understanding, [death] deprives a thing of its form, but does not steal away the essence of the thing. For the subject matter remains the same, though its form pass away, and a new form only gives this matter a new name. Form flows away, the essence of the thing remains; the power of death destroys nothing, but only disunites united parts.

The tone and movement of the lines recall both the gentle moralizing of Horace's *Ars poetica* on the fortunes of language and the loose hexameters in which Bernard of Chartres had set out his theory of being.[38] The deceptive simplicity is unique in the *De mundi*, and no passage in the work is more demanding philosophically. But the passage seems to me to be central to the meaning of the poem, for it states abstractly what is dramatized in Nature's initial appeal to Noys, that the seeds of perfection are present in material existence itself, that the imposition of form is a response to the impulse of this lower nature. One love unites *ratio* and *subiecta*: "matter alone desires adornment, just as female desires male, and what is shapeless longs for beauty."[39]

Difficult as it is philosophically, and although Bernardus' presentation is almost impenetrably concise, the thesis of these lines clearly serves to focus our attention on the critical importance of the union of opposites which defines human life, and so helps to set the stage for the elaborate account of the actual creation of man which follows. Preparations are completed when, after the goddesses have arrived on earth and been received by Physis, Noys appears to prophesy the glorious destiny of man:[40]

> Omnia subiciat, terras regat, inperet orbi:
>   Primatem rebus pontificemque dedi.
> Sed cum nutarit numeris in fine solutis
>   Machina corporeae collabefacta domus,
> Aethera scandet homo, iam non incognitus hospes,
>   Praeveniens stellae signa locumque suae.

[38] See John of Salisbury, *Metalogicon* 4.35 (Webb, pp. 205-06).

[39] Calcidius, *Commentarius* 286 (Waszink, p. 290), translating Aristotle, *Physics* 1.9. Cp. n. 12 above.

[40] *De mundi* 2.10, lines 49-54, p. 56. With lines 53-54 cp. Ovid, *Metam.* 15.839, on the apotheosis of Augustus.

That he may subordinate all to himself, rule on earth and be lord
of the universe I have established him as ruler and high priest
of creation. But when at last the tottering structure of his bodily
dwelling fails, its binding harmony dissolved, man will ascend the
heavens, no longer an unacknowledged guest, to assume the place
assigned him among the stars.

This prophecy of man's imperial destiny corresponds to that pro-
nounced by Anchises concerning the empire Aeneas is to establish
in Italy. The association is strengthened by Noys' gifts to the three
goddesses of the knowledge necessary to their roles in the creation
of man. Urania receives the "speculum Providentiae," in which cre-
ation is described in terms of its expression of ideal *exemplaria*.
Nature receives the "Tabula Fati," in which created life is shown
extended in time under the influence of the heavens, and the life
of man is shown panoramically, as in the catalogue of Book One:
poverty balances luxury, some are destined for warfare, some for
study, and the course of history may be seen "degenerating little by
little, to end at last in an age of iron."[41] The "Liber Recordationis,"
presented to Physis, shows the natures of the elements, their con-
flict and the laws which govern it, and the causes of the diversities
of created life, but it cannot ascend the scale of creation by intu-
iting higher principles. Its scope is that of natural philosophy in
a strict empirical sense: "nothing else but the intellect applying
itself to the study of creation, and committing to memory its rea-
sonings, based often on fact, but more often upon probable conjec-
ture."[42] The three authorities correspond to three themes of the
De mundi. The "Speculum" shows the universe in its quintessen-
tial purity, ideally expressive of the harmony of Noys and the
World Soul; Nature's "Tabula" shows human history as it appears
in the stars, in all its ambiguity and seeming contradiction of man's
nobler destiny; and the Book of Memory reflects the experience of
the unenlightened mind, seeking in nature for a meaning which
lies beyond.[43]

[41] *De mundi* 2.11, lines 79-81, p. 58.
[42] *Ibid.*, 2.11, lines 86-89, pp. 58-59.
[43] For the glossator of Laud Misc. 515 the three types of speculation rep-
resented are theology, astronomy, and physics (f. 211v). Of the *Speculum*

The effect of the three visions of human life is hard to reconcile with that noble view of man's destiny expressed by Noys, as the violence and hardship of Roman history, and the fact that it demands the destruction of the innocence of Saturnian Italy, are hard to reconcile with the eloquent enthusiasm of Anchises. Urania is forced to search long and anxiously before she finds the image of man in her mirror, and even in the Book of Memory he appears only "sublustrem et tenuem" on the final page. Thus the combined effect of Noys' prophecy and her gifts is to give an almost authoritative status to the Boethian doubts and ambiguities which have appeared in the course of the *De mundi,* and to consolidate what has amounted to a running critique of the Chartrian faith in the stabilizing affinities of mind and cosmos. This uncertainty inevitably lingers in our minds as we read what is in itself a painstakingly scientific analysis of the composition of the human body and its animation in the sections which follow. Again we are made to concentrate on the special balance which defines human life, and again, as Physis labors by trial and error to achieve the necessary proportions among the elements, we are reminded of the tenuous nature of this balance.

This concern to trace the implications of the union of spirit and matter to the core of human life is carried through to the very end of the *De mundi.* The poem which concludes the work is an account of the organization of the body, and deals in succession with the brain, its "ministers," the senses, then the heart, the liver, and the loins. It is the account of the organs of generation which provides the real conclusion of the work on all levels. Bernardus begins by extolling their proper exercise as a source of joy, and describes their work in powerful terms:[44]

> Saecula ni pereant decisaque cesset origo,
>   Et repetat primum massa soluta chaos,
> Ad genios fetura duos concessit et olim
>   Commissum geminis fratribus illud opus.

Providentiae the glossator of Bodl. Digby 157 observes (f. 12r) "describit per inuolucrum diuinam predestinationem."

[44] *De mundi* 2.14, lines 157-64, p. 70.

Cum morte invicti pugnant genialibus armis,
　Naturam reperant, perpetuantque genus.
Non mortale mori, non quod cadit esse caducum,
　Non a stirpe hominem deperiisse sinunt.
Militat adversus Lachesin sollersque renodat
　Mentula Parcarum fila resecta manu.

Lest earthly life pass away and the process of generation be cut off, and material existence, dissolved, return to primordial chaos, propagation was made the charge of two *genii*, and the act itself assigned to twin brothers. They fight unconquered against death with their life-giving weapons, renew our nature and perpetuate our kind. They will not allow what is perishable to perish, nor what dies to be wholly owed to death, nor mankind to wither utterly at the root. The Phallis wars against Lachesis and carefully rejoins the vital threads severed by the hands of the Fates.

The *genii* of generation, applying to the seeds of future life the images transmitted to them from the brain, "ut simili genesis ore reducat avos," recall the divine *Oyarses* of the celestial sphere, uniting matter with form to perpetuate universal life. But the labor of the *genii* of man is exhausting even as it perpetuates the race, for man has not, like nature, the power of perpetual self-renewal. A further contrast between man and universe, concluding on the note of *vanitas vanitatum* which has recurred throughout the work, brings this out:

Influit ipsa sibi mundi natura superstes,
　Permanet et fluxu pascitur usque suo.
Scilicet ad summam rerum iactura recurrit
　Nec semel ut possit saepe perire perit.
Longe disparibus causis mutandus in horas
　Effluit occiduo corpore totus homo.
Sic sibi deficiens peregrinis indiget escis,
　Sudat in hoc vitam denihilatque dies.

Nature, outliving herself, pours herself into the universe, and endures and thrives in her very ebbing away. For whatever is lost only merges again with the sum of things, and that it may die perpetually never dies wholly. But man, ever liable to affliction by forces far less harmonious, passes wholly out of existence with the failure of his body. Unable to sustain himself and wanting nourishment from without, he exhausts his life, and a day reduces him to nothing.

The implications of this final poem are extremely complex, for it is an attempt to show how the drama of human life is reflected in the human constitution. The human mind, like Noys herself, is capable of encompassing a *mundus intellectualis* evolved, so to speak, on the basis of evidence provided by the senses. The hierarchy of ordering powers which descends from the mind to become involved with the turbulent forces of man's bodily nature can be understood through an understanding of the roles of Physis, Natura, and Urania in creating him. The resistance of the body to the ordering power of mind, the fallibility of the senses as they descend into fleshly darkness and multiplicity, the passions which assail the heart, are like the *grossities* of external nature which reduce the legend of Physis' Book of Memory to probabilities and riddles. The continual struggle to maintain continuity in the face of necessity and man's own tendency to excess corresponds to the halting and retrograde movement of man's temporal existence as expressed in the *Tabula Fati*.

It may well be asked what role the *Speculum Providentiae* can possibly play in such a state of affairs; but here, it seems to me, a profound and profoundly ironical point of comparison exists in Bernardus' treatment of generation. If the two *genii* who preside over the conception of human life are recognized as analogous to the divine *Oyarses* who greets Nature at the limit of the universe, then they, too, have a certain divinity. They are more than any other aspect of human nature a part of the unalterable and incorruptible order of things, and express more truly than any rational construct or moral insight the relation of man to Nature. There is something mysterious about the presence of these *genii* at the wellhead of man's sensual nature, and about the process by which they join form and matter and transmit them insensibly from generation to generation. If their generative function is taken together with the role of the classical Genius figure as "deus humanae naturae," a tutelary presence in the soul, they may be compared with the *Speculum*, the secret perception of divine order and purpose

183

hidden deep in the soul, by which man's deepest spiritual insights are rewarded.[45] Just as the teachings of the *Speculum* remain for the most part buried by the mass of inferior mental perceptions and the bewildering evidence of the senses, so the means whereby man, laboring to overcome necessity and perpetuate himself *in genere*, obeys the dictates of the *genii*, the act in which his psychic and physical natures cooperate most strikingly to reveal the analogy between his constitution and the orderly processes of the universe, also entails his deepest involvement with the mindless forces of earthly nature. In both cases an extraordinary degree of mental control and poetic insight is required to penetrate the mystery, and its full significance is accessible only to the spiritually enlightened understanding. This is not, of course, to suggest that Bernardus is apotheosizing sexuality; the divine image transmitted through generation is a lesser thing than the soul, and the role of the *genii* is limited by the limits of the natural order. But the hint of heroic self-sacrifice in Bernardus' account of their work reminds us that the form they impose upon each human embryo is in some degree the image of the Logos, and that their office has real affinities with the divine act of creation. We recall the hints of a Christ-like sacrifice in Bernardus' interpretation of Pollux's sharing of his immortality with Castor; it is possible that he has the Gemini in mind again when he refers to the testicles as "twin brothers." Again the vivid depiction of the sexual urge as a creative impulse, endlessly at war with necessity yet never able to transcend it and achieve full expression in a life superior to death, recalls the complex figure of Vulcan, yearning to give spiritual expression to a deeply flawed *ingenium* but continually forced to compromise with lusts it cannot deny.

In terms of the theme of the *De mundi* the contrast between the brief animal act and the implications of divinity expressed by it suggest a deeper contrast between the fact of mortality and the

[45] In the course of their journey through the sublunar region Urania points out to Nature a kind of *genius* "qui de nascendi principiis homini copulatus vitanda illi discrimina vel mentis praesagio vel soporis imagine vel prodigioso rerum spectaculo configurat" (2.7, lines 82-85, p. 49). Cp. Calcidius, *Commentarius* 132 (Waszink, pp. 173-74).

tenuous thread of dim awareness which preserves man in some relation to his original nature and destiny. It expresses the uncertain and potentially tragic course of human life and at the same time recalls the transcendent significance of the yearning for form in Nature's opening appeal to Noys. Thus generation is an appropriate symbol for the uncertainty of life. It is a godlike and humanitarian function—as Jean de Meun and Geoffrey Chaucer were to testify in their very different ways. It is also liable to degradation through the rejection of man's higher nature in favor of immediate and self-destructive pleasure. Thus it expresses the condition of the "imbecilla hominum natio," and brings together the two strains of idealistic and pessimistic rhetoric which have been contrasted throughout the *De mundi*.

The work ends with two distichs which express the positive side of the human condition:

> Membra quibus mundus non indiget, illa necesse
> Physis in humana conditione daret:
> Excubias, capitis oculos, modulaminis aures,
> ductoresque pedes, omnificasque manus.

In creating man Physis had to bestow limbs of which the universe has no need: eyes to keep watch in the head, ears for sound, feet to bear him, and all-capable hands.

The lines imply both necessity and capacity: on the one hand the need for man of ways to fend for himself in a universe from whose perpetual self-sufficiency he is to be excluded; on the other, the capacity for self-determination implied by his "ductores pedes" and the creativity of his all-capable hands. What man is all too soon to lose he can in some measure regain. The heroic struggle of which the *De mundi* as a whole is the foreshadowing is symbolized by this final comparison of macrocosm and microcosm.

The *De mundi universitate* begins and ends by emphasizing the will of created life to resist the tyranny of necessity and physical weakness, but makes plain the very definite limits which the nature of things imposes on human aspiration. As in the *Mathematicus* the dignity of man is powerfully asserted, but in both works we are

185

given only a tentative version of human fulfillment and one, moreover, which becomes most meaningful only when viewed in terms of its analogy with the completely fulfilling heroism of Christ. This dual perspective may be seen also in Bernardus' handling of Chartrian philosophy. His allegory is built around the *Timaeus*, and does full justice to the spiritual implications of Plato's cosmology, at the same time exploiting the Neoplatonist quasi-mysticism of Martianus and fusing it with notions drawn from the pseudo-Dionysius in the manner of Alain and Garnier in the sermons quoted above. But it is made clear in countless ways that the ideal significance of the cosmos demands a more than philosophical understanding, and that the rhetoric of astrology and physics serves finally to illustrate the confinement of understanding rather than defining the higher meaning of perceived reality. There is no facile association between *theologia mundana* and genuine illumination, as there is no single doctrine or formula to account for the divine meaning which is somehow present at the heart of the mystery of generation. Bernardus is consciously and precisely the poet of the *opus conditionis*, and goes beyond his Chartrian predecessors in making poetic capital out of the exigencies, as well as the positive values, which the term implies.

CHAPTER FIVE

NATURE AND GRACE: THE ALLEGORIES OF ALAIN DE LILLE

In the work of Alain de Lille the implications of Bernardus' cosmogony are elaborated in such a way as to clearly define its relation to sacred history. The analogy between creation and *restauratio*, suggested chiefly in negative ways in the *De mundi*, is systematized, and the disruption of man's relations with Nature is analyzed in such a way as to define both the Fall and the restoration it makes necessary.

This work of literary synthesis is only one aspect of Alain's role in late twelfth-century thought. He is a special combination of Chartrian philosopher, preacher and author of devotional works, Porretan theologian and pedagogue in the tradition of Hugh of St. Victor. Like Hugh in the *De sacramentis, Didascalicon,* and commentary on the *Celestial Hierarchy*, he employs Platonist cosmology and the resources of the Arts with a humanist's appreciation of their value, but rigorously subordinates them to a view of man and history of which the primary reality is sacramental. Like Hugh he is deeply concerned with the incarnation of sacramental meanings in *naturalia*—with what Huizinga, in his fine study, calls "the central miracle of the creation of form."[1] He lacks the delicacy which enables Bernardus, for example, to compare the manifestation of the World Soul to the play of light on the surface of water, and his elaborate formulations of the relations between *naturalia* and *gratuita* seem at times to involve no more than an exaggeration of the implications of analogy,[2] but he possesses some-

[1] Johan Huizinga, "Über die Verknüpfung des Poetischen mit dem Theologischen bei Alanus de Insulis," in *Mededeelingen der Koninklijke Akademie van Wetenschappen, Amsterdam* 74B (1932), p. 153; repr. in his *Verzamelde Werken* (Amsterdam, 1949), IV, 51.
[2] See Chenu, *La théologie*, pp. 185-87 (Taylor-Little, pp. 137-41).

187

thing like Hugh's deep sense of the sapiential reality which distinguishes true sacramental meaning from the "anagogie manquée" of the natural order.[3]

In the *De planctu naturae* and *Anticlaudianus* a major concern is the relation of poetry to this larger synthesis. The conventions of *courtoisie*, erotic as well as heroic, find a place in the complex fabric of these poems, and the *De planctu* incorporates as a major theme the historical view of mythology tentatively formulated in Bernardus' commentary on Martianus. Both the *De planctu* and the *Anticlaudianus* explore the effect of the Fall on the linguistic and metaphorical resources of poetry in a way which serves to define the scope and limitations of the *integumentum* with a new clarity.

1. The *De planctu naturae*[4]

Like Bernardus, Alain places the goddess Nature at the center of his allegories, and his use of her shows how far his purpose is from the cosmological concerns of the Chartrians. Though Bernardus' Nature has rich moral and psychological associations, her relations with Silva, Noys, and Urania are also developed. In the *De planctu naturae* such relationships are largely ignored. Alain's Nature is not simply the "mater generationis" of the *De mundi*, vessel and nurse of becoming, but also Bernardus' Endelechia and Imarmene, "similia de similibus procreans," and Urania, through whom divine *ratio* is expressed; she is, in short, God's deputy, and her most important function in the *De planctu* is as a source of moral law.[5]

---

[3] See de Lubac, *Exégèse* II.i, pp. 93-97, and below, pp. 218-19.

[4] The discussion of the *De planctu* which follows is based in large part on my article, "The Function of Poetry in the *De planctu naturae* of Alain de Lille," *Traditio* 25 (1969), 87-125.

[5] "Me igitur tanquam sui vicariam, rerum generibus sigillandis monetariam destinavit. . ." (*De planctu naturae*, ed. Thomas Wright, in *Anglo-Latin Satirical Poets of the Twelfth Century*, London, 1872, II, 469; PL 210.-453D). All references will be to page in Wright and column in the *Patrologia*. Quotations will be from Wright, though I have occasionally adopted an obviously superior reading from the PL text.

On the evolution of the figure of *Natura* and her moral role see Gregory, *Platonismo medievale*, pp. 122-50.

The subject of the *De planctu* and the burden of Nature's complaint is man's abandonment of her law. His lapse is characterized by a number of sustained metaphors, of which the most prominent are the abuse of language and sexual perversion. The two are linked in the opening *metrum*:[6]

> Se negat esse virum, Naturae factus in arte
> Barbarus; ars illi non placet, immo tropus.
> Non tamen ista tropus poterit 'translatio' dici;
> In vitium melius ista figura cadit.

Man denies himself to be man, become a blemish on the art of Nature; art has no appeal for him, only metaphor. And yet such metaphor cannot be called "translation"; this figure tends too readily to the corruption of meaning.

Man's actions have lost their proper *significatio*. They no longer express a *homo interior* of primordial perfection, but instead illustrate man's loss of the power to realize his true nature. Sexual perversion is the most vivid illustration of this failure, and with a boldness and clarity which reveal his schooling in Chartrian humanism, Alain accepts the logical consequence, and makes healthy sexuality his central metaphor for human perfection. Thus the proem includes, together with learned references to grammatical, logical, rhetorical, and mythological perversion,[7] the following expression of yearning for a state of simple, direct, and fulfilling communion:[8]

> Virginis in labiis cur basia tanta quiescunt,
> Cum reditus in eis sumere nemo velit?
> Quae mihi pressa semel mellirent oscula succo,
> Quae mellita darent mellis in ore favum.
> Spiritus exiret ad basia, deditus ori
> Totus, et in labiis luderet ipse sibi.
> Ut dum sic moriar, in me defunctus, in illa
> Felici vita perfruar, alter ego.

[6] Wright, pp. 429-30; PL 210.431B.

[7] On these see R. H. Green, "Alan of Lille's *De planctu naturae*," *Speculum* 31 (1956), 649-74.

[8] Wright, p. 449; PL 210.442B.

189

Why do such kisses languish on virgin lips, and none seek to claim
them as reward? These lips pressed to mine would sweeten with
their moisture kisses which, thus honeyed, would bestow upon my
mouth the honey-comb itself. My spirit, wholly committed to my
mouth, would pass forth in response to such kisses, and amuse itself
in playing about her lips; hence, though I should thus die, once
dead unto myself I should enjoy a happy life in her, a new being.

The "felix vita" of the final line is both a conventional hyperbole
for sexual fulfillment and an allusion to the primal state in which
rhetoric and experience were harmonious. As the De planctu devel-
ops its picture of the primordial condition of man in nature, the
relations of divine ratio and earthly nature are treated in a similarly
allusive way. The deeply fulfilling basia of the passage are recalled
in Alain's account of the loving impress of creative form on pliant
matter, and brought into implicit association with the archetypal
osculum of the Song of Songs.

But the erotic element in the proem can be justified on other
grounds as well. Alain has substituted the milder stirrings of fin
amors for the violent Ovidian passion of Bernardus' Nature, but
his purpose is similar. In effect, he provides a "historical" context
for something like the troubadour amor de lonh: what separates
the poet from realization of his love is what separates all men from
the lost joys of Paradise. The dignity of the feeling is preserved
even as the possibility of fulfillment is denied.

The establishment of a standard of behavior which incorporates
sexuality is an important development of the view of human life
presented by Bernardus, who never brings the perfection of Patri-
cida, the passion of Natura, and the heroic labor of generation into
precise relation. The sexual emphasis of Alain's treatment of man
is complemented by his depiction of Nature, which provides a cos-
mic context for the theme of the De planctu. The framework of
his portrait is the conventional descriptio of feminine beauty. The
description includes, together with the goddess's face and form, a
long account of her diadem, set with stones representing the zodiac
and planets, and of her garments, inscribed with all the varieties of
natural life, and the pageant thus created recalls in its scope and

effect the catalogue poem of the *De mundi*. But Alain makes clear that these externals serve only to set off the beauty of the goddess herself. It is this that is stressed and to this that the poet-hero of the poem, whose condition is that of fallen man, responds as Nature presents herself before him. The rest of nature greets the goddess with a joyful burst of fertility and sexuality, but the poet cannot express himself. He falls on his face in a sort of coma, "nec vivens nec mortuus." In this "neutered" state he is taken up by the goddess, whose motherly caresses and chaste kisses recall him to himself.

To account for this failure of nerve it is necessary to look back to the prior *descriptio*. This presents Nature in her pristine state; unlike Bernardus' catalogue Alain's makes no reference to human history. Man appears on Nature's robe only in his proper role as lord of creation: "homo, sensualitatis deponens segnitiem, directa rationis aurigatione, coeli penetrabat arcana."[9] But a flaw has marred the dignity which this image conveys: Nature's robe has been torn at just this point. The implications of this fact emerge when the poet is confronted with the ideal exemplar of the "aurigatio rationis," the divine *ratio* which guides Nature's chariot:[10]

Homo vero virginis capiti curruique supereminens, cuius vultus non terrenitatis vilitatem, sed potius deitatis redolebat arcanum, impotentiam sexus supplendo feminæi, modesto directionis ordine currus aurigabat incessum. Ad cuius pulcritudinis dignitatem investigandam, dum tamquam manipulos oculorum radios conligarem visibiles, ipsi tantae non audentes majestatis obviare decori, splendoris hebetati verberibus, nimis meticulosi ad palpebrarum contubernia refugerunt.

The figure of a man, towering above the maiden and her chariot, his countenance bespeaking not the meanness of mortality but the mysterious quality of godhead, guided the approaching chariot, sustaining her feminine weakness by a gentle firmness of control. Albeit I drew together the beams of my eyesight in military order that I might gaze on his comeliness and dignity,

9 Wright, p. 441; PL 210.437D. 10 Wright, p. 445; PL 210.439-40.

191

they dared not encounter the glory of such majesty: stricken by the darting beams of his radiance they became too fearful and fled to the shelter of their lashes.

Man exists "in extasis alienatione sepultus," and all virtue is "incarcerated" in the murky depths of his nature.[11] His inability to deal with the vision of *ratio* and *Natura* in their full majesty corresponds to the inability of the conventions of his rhetoric to express the nobility of love and heroism, the "inversion" which distorts and corrupts his language and syntax. His fall is thus a failure of poetry and also of something like *courtoisie*. The remainder of the *De planctu* is concerned with tracing the history of this failure, and arrives in the end at a vision of human nature in which the lineaments of man's original nature may still be perceived, thus providing a tentative vindication of both man and poetry. First, however, Nature and the poet must reach a common understanding of the problem of man's depravity. The long central portion of the work is a dialogue in which Nature explains, by a series of elaborate and repetitive descriptions of the order of creation, how man lost his position at the center of things. She first describes for the poet (who has not yet recognized her) her establishment of human life in the universe. Though she appropriates the terms in which Bernardus had described the work of Noys and Urania to illustrate her own handiwork,[12] she concludes by carefully defining

[11] On the use of the term "exstasis" see Alain's *Regulae caelestis iuris*, art. 99 (PL 210.673CD): "Nota quod aliud est thesis humanae naturae, aliud apotheosis, aliud hypothesis. Thesis dicitur proprius status hominis, quem servare dicitur quando ratione utitur ad considerandum quid bonum, quid malum, quid agendum, quid cavendum. Sed aliquando excedit homo istum statum, vel descendendo in vitia, vel ascendendo in coelestium contemplationem; et talis excessus dicitur exstasis, sive metamorphosis, quia per hujus modi excessum excedit statum propriae mentis vel formam." See also *Anticlaudianus* 6.3-8, quoted below, p. 215; Dronke, "Boethius, Alanus and Dante," *Romanische Forschungen* 78 (1968), pp. 119-25; and ch. 2, n. 58 above.

[12] Describing her joining of soul to matter Nature says (Wright, p. 450; PL 210.442CD): "Cujus vultum miserata deformem, quasi ad me crebrius declamantem, humanae speciei signaculo sigillavi. . ." And a little later,

the limits of her power, acknowledging that her work is only a "trace" of God's, and that the life she creates is to be transcended by a higher life, a new order. When at last she reveals her identity, the poet immediately feels restored to himself, and responds "as though to divine majesty." In a beautiful hymn he dwells on the cosmic role of the goddess and shows a renewed insight into the higher reality to which her creation conforms:[13]

> Quae noys puras recolens ideas
> Singulas rerum species monetas,
> Rem togans forma, chlamidemque formae
> Pollice formas.

Considering the pure ideas of Noys, you stamp their likeness on the individual species of creatures, clothing substance with form, and forming the cloak of form with your own hand.

The dreamer is vouchsafed his reintegrating vision primarily as poet, and the problems of literary expression are a major theme of the dialogue which ensues. The poet is enabled to understand imaginatively the condition of man at his creation only because Nature has caused him to "vomit forth all fantasy" and restored him to the position of her "secretary."[14] The account which she gives of human nature and its history has at best a poetic consistency, and conforms to no precise theological or philosophical conception. Indeed Nature is unable to explain her own *fabula* at certain points. Poetry, then, is the language in which Nature communicates with man, and thus the limits of poetic expression become an index to the limits of man's ability to realign his life with the natural order.

"Tuum etiam spiritum vitalibus insignivi potentiis, ne corpore pauperior, ejus successibus invideret."

[13] Wright, p. 458; PL 210.447C.

[14] Wright, p. 457; PL 210.446C. Alain is recalling the preparation of Philology for immortality in Martianus, *De nuptiis* 2.135-36, p. 59. "Secretarius" or "secretarium" seems to mean "repository" or "keeper" of a sacred trust. Nature descends "a supernis coelestis regiae secretariis" to commune "quasi cum familiari et secretario meo" (Wright, p. 464; PL 210.450CD). Cp. the prologue to Alain's *Summa* "*Quoniam homines*" (ed. P. Glorieux, *Archives d'histoire* 28, 1953, p. 119): "sicut olim philosophia cum familiari et secretario suo Boetio. . ."; also Augustine, *De libero arbitrio* 2.16.42.

To explain her coming Nature recurs to the analogy between sexuality and verbal expression. A perverse Venus has led man "Naturae naturalia denaturare" by perverting the Arts. A false orthography promulgates pseudo-authoritative precepts which teach a corrupt grammar, a prostitute logic, and a bizarre rhetoric studded with reminiscences of mythical perversions. It is this state of affairs which has led her to appeal to the poet. He responds to the honor by asking how he may learn to tell true from false among the "figmenta poetarum"; for it would seem that gods as well as men have succumbed to the perverse Venus, and should be included accordingly under the terms of Nature's censure.[15]

Nature's reply has been cited as the last word on Alain's poetic practice, and on the conception of poetic allegory which he shared with his contemporaries. The documentary value of its unequivocal repudiation of any "pagan" conception of poetry has distracted critics from the more immediate question of its relevance to the *De planctu*. In this context it seems to me to raise more problems than it solves, and to leave wholly unexplained certain ambiguities which grow increasingly important as the allegory proceeds.

Nature's countenance, hitherto bright with the "authentica serenitas" of true doctrine, becomes clouded. Some poets, she says, use fiction to titillate their readers, some to insinuate immorality into their minds. Others devote their art to creating the vehicle for a "secretum altioris intelligentiae" so that "when the husk of outer falsehood is cast aside, the reader may discover within the sweeter kernel of hidden truth."[16] But a certain falseness is in the nature of poetry. When poets present a plurality of gods, and especially if these gods are shown behaving indecently, all is falsehood. For that God is one "ratio probat, mundus eloquitur, fides credit, Scriptura testatur." He is the source of all true understanding, "seminale vitae seminarium, sapientiae principale principium."

Nature offers the typical twelfth-century view of poetry as *in-*

194

volucrum, but does not really answer the poet's question about the use and abuse of mythology. There are human problems to which poetic fable and its mythological apparatus lend themselves naturally. Nature has herself employed these resources to illustrate the corruption of human nature. That her account of poetry does not explain how true and false myths are to be distinguished is thus a crucial omission, and assumes a thematic function almost at once, in her review of the origin and corruption of human nature.

By way of preface to this new departure, Nature, following Boethius' Philosophy,[17] harks back to the cosmogony itself. Her account, she says, will demand a highly sensitive response from the poet, for she must adapt the deformity of language to the *informitas* of pre-existence,[18] and trace the process whereby the Word first expressed itself in the "materiale verbum" of cosmic order. From this, the archetypal source of allegorical expression, she proceeds to the formation of the natural world, and the establishment of those laws which are, she says, her Scriptures, inscribed "supremi suppositoris digito" to ensure the orderly continuance of existence.[19] To aid in administering these laws, Nature, "vicaria Dei," has appointed Venus as "subvicaria," to regulate, with her husband Hymen and their son Cupid, the renewal of the human species by generation.

The poet is aroused by the name of Cupid, and demands that he be defined, since all *auctores* have treated him very obscurely, "sub integumentali involucro aenigmatum." As at the poet's previous request, Nature pauses. The subject is of labyrinthine complexity, and can only be approached in a negative way, but at length she

---

[17] Cp. *De consolatione* 4, pr. 6, where Philosophy prepares to deal with the problems of fate and providence by a "new beginning" from the initial generation of things by the divine mind.

[18] *Informitas,* like *exstasis,* can refer to any state other than the condition of rational-formal "thesis" described in the passage from Alain's *Regulae* quoted in n. 11 above. Alain uses it in the *De planctu* of the pre-creation, of the disintegration effected by sin, and of the super-formal reality of God.

[19] In the *De mundi* the mind of *Noys* is said to contain all that is to come about in the universe "exarata supremi digito dispunctoris" (*De mundi* 1.2, line 160, p. 13). On the image cp. Augustine *De spiritu et littera* 16 (PL 42.218); *Luke* 11:20.

grudgingly agrees to abandon constructive discourse and explain as best she can what is inexplicable: "haec de ignoto habeatur notitia, haec de non scibili paretur scientia . . ."

The long poem which follows describes the influence of Cupid in terms of the corruption of language and metaphor. He is foolish reason, mad judgment, a soothing hell, a sorrowful paradise. He operates by *antiphrasis* and robs all words of their normal associations. As Nature hastens to explain, it is not the original nature of Cupid that her poem depicts, but what he has become. His influence would be good if he were restrained by "the bridle of modesty" and "the harness of temperance." But she takes the matter no further, and instead returns to her historical account of the establishment of Venus' administration in human life. The goddess was entrusted with a "calamus praepotens" and taught the principles of sexual orthography, grammar, and logic, with due stress on the relation of subject to predicate, and careful strictures against the excesses of rhetoric. But after bearing Cupid to Hymen, Venus has fallen into adultery with *Antigamus* and spawned Cupid's perverse counterpart *Jocus*, thus diverting the whole meaning of her activity *in malum*: "suam artem in figuram, figuramque in vitium transferebat."[20] This *Jocus* is in effect the perverting Cupid described in Nature's poem, and thus the living demonstration of how the poetry of life has been corrupted.

Nature's influence, it seems, does not extend to the will of man. Ideally this is subject to an innate *ratio* like Nature's own charioteer, but man has subverted reason, cut himself off from Nature, and in the process lost touch with his own divine archetype. Nature can offer him only negative assistance. Her poem on Cupid ends by prescribing total abstinence:[21]

> Ipse tamen poteris istum frenare furorem
> Si fugias; potior potio nulla datur.

[20] Wright, p. 480; PL 210.459CD.
[21] Wright, p. 474; PL 210.456C. Cp. these lines from the coda of the "Parce continuis" (cited above, ch. 2, n. 68): "Fuga tantum/fallitur amantum."

You yourself can restrain this madness if you flee; there is no more effective remedy.

In terms of the literary theme of the poem, the problem is Nature's inability to interpret fully the myths which veil her principles from the human mind. Her only interpretative model is the "divinum opus mundi," and she is powerless to account for deviations from the divine plan. Her feminine appeal once refused, Nature is bankrupt. The arts of the Trivium and the *integumenta* of the poets, once stepping-stones to the higher truths of philosophy, have become instruments of corruption, insinuating a perverse significance into mythology and rhetoric—enhancing, that is, just the antiphilosophical aspects of the poetic figment which they ought rather to illuminate and transcend. Nature is not only unable to deal with the contradictions of the poets, who are properly her clerks, but she compounds the dilemma by coining myths of her own in an attempt to augment the deficiencies of her understanding. In fact this does serve to define the problem, but only by making it clearer than ever that the natural order, with its fixed laws and archetypal metaphorical associations, is no longer congruent with the understanding of man.

Nature's dilemma brings to a head a number of themes which we have seen partly developed in earlier works. It is the realization of the doubts expressed by Boethius' prisoner, and Alain emphasizes this by innumerable echoes of the *De consolatione*. It is also a definitive formulation of the historical view of mythology present in Bernardus' commentary on Martianus, and it dramatizes in a number of ways the limited vision of man which is implied by so many details of the *De mundi universitate*. Though a long account of the vices which stem from corrupted love follows the denunciation of Cupid, the dialogue of Nature and the poet ends indecisively. In the highly complex denouement of the *De planctu*, the *goddess* appeals directly to the higher powers which had once ensured right relations between man and cosmos. On this higher allegorical plane a tentative resolution is suggested: a resolution in principle only, but one which suggests the survival in human nature of the lineaments of its original dignity and so, in a very oblique way, the possibility of a renewal of that dignity.

The nature of this renewal, the ways in which the very deficiencies of Nature are made to define the *opus restaurationis*, will be discussed farther on. It is necessary first to see how the *De planctu* illustrates and defines the elements in nature at large and in human nature which will contribute to this renewal. One such factor, clearly present, though hard to define systematically, is the series of oblique references to *courtoisie* which occur in the earlier portions of the allegory. The "basia" passage of the proem, the long *descriptio* of Nature's beauty, her rebuke to man for having offended the majesty of his *domina*,[22] her reference to the "courtly precepts" by which Venus' grammar is inculcated[23]—all of these imply a standard of right relations which is drawn neither from religion nor from nature, and yet has deep affinities with both. This standard is reinforced by frequent references to magnanimity and largesse, aspects of a liberality of spirit which is both an essential element of *courtoisie* and a sort of natural analogue to charity, and which is finally personified in the figure of *Largitas*.[24]

A more coherent pattern of allusion develops the idea of Nature as a type of the Church. Her descent into the world, charioteered by divine *ratio*, closely conforms to the mission of *Ecclesia* as described by Alain in a gloss on the *equitatus* of *Canticles* 1:8, guided by Christ and bearing the *dulcedo* of salvation.[25] Nature has her scriptures, canons, sacraments and hierarchy; she is "mater et domina," the "temple" of Genius, her priest, wherein man, fulfilling his office in the universal hierarchy, celebrates the "mystery of regeneration"[26]—one of several allusions to the quasi-sacramental significance of sexual reproduction.

[22] Wright, p. 460; PL 210.448C.

[23] Wright, p. 476; PL 210.457B. On *curialitas* in the system of values of the *De planctu* see Huizinga, "Über die Verknüpfung," pp. 154-59 (*Verz. Werken* IV, 52-56).

[24] See below, pp. 200-01, and *Metamorphosis Goliae* (cited above, ch. 3, n. 6), lines 133-36.

[25] *Elucidatio in Canticum Canticorum* I; PL 210.59.

[26] The proem concludes with the warning "In Genii templo tales anathema

More broadly, man's "divorce" from Nature corresponds to a common view of the Fall as an abrogation by man of his place in the celestial hierarchy, which was to have been restored to its original integrity by his creation. This theme appears in a number of Alain's works, and offers a framework for the cosmic parallel of creation and Incarnation in the *De planctu*.[27] We may perhaps see in Nature's mission to man a recollection of the parabolic figures of *Luke* 15, especially the woman in search of her lost tithe, who were conventionally associated with this view of the Fall.[28] In themselves, of course, such correspondences only point up the inadequacy of Nature to perform the sacramental office of restoration, an inadequacy which she herself makes plain in her initial address to man. But they assume a more positive meaning when brought together and set in relation to the work of Genius in the concluding episodes of the *De planctu*.

The action of the later portions of the allegory may be summarized briefly: Hymen appears with a cluster of attendant Virtues, and bears Nature's summons to Genius, who presents himself and pronounces excommunication on all servants of the *Venus scelesta*. Then the Virtues cast down their torches, and as they slowly die the poet passes from vision into sleep. There is no very deep message in these events as such. Their meaning is in the character of the principles involved and the terms in which Alain describes their interrelations. For what takes place is the imaginatve reconstruction of man's sexual nature as it had existed before the Fall.

The transition to a new and more arcane level is effected by the sudden introduction of Hymen, a power at once natural and sup-

---

merentur/Qui Genio decimas et sua jura negant" (Wright, p. 431; PL 210.-432). On tithing as a prescriptural sacrament see Hugh, *De Sacramentis* 1.11.1-4 (PL 176.343-45). Nature defines the role of procreation in the hierarchy of the natural order in her opening speech (Wright, p. 453; PL 210.444B): "Deus imperat auctoritatis magisterio, angelus operatur actionis ministerio, homo obtemperat regenerationis mysterio."

[27] See the *Expositio prosae de angelis*, ed. d'Alverny, *Alain de Lille: Textes inédits*, p. 215; *Anticlaudianus* 2.45-46 (Bossuat, p. 74), on the "new Lucifer" who will not fall.

[28] See d'Alverny, *Textes inédits*, p. 215, n. 61.

plementary to Nature. Human marriage is analogous to the mysterious concord which exists among the elements of cosmic life, but is not merely a natural relationship. It solemnizes a natural process by the "sacramentalis matrimonii fides."[29] Hence Hymen is attended by the Virtues, rather than the merely natural Venus and Cupid. No reference is made to his betrayal by Venus, but it is clear that his powers are in a state of suspension. He appears on the verge of tears, and the musicians who follow him are silent. Only when Nature has called him by name and greeted him warmly does any sign of *festivitas* appear.

Hymen's office is the reconciliation of opposites, the balancing of potentially discordant forces. Thus the Virtues who attend him, *Castitas, Temperantia, Humilitas,* are devoted to restraint and discipline. An exception is *Largitas,* whose description contrasts sharply with those of her companions. While the others are described primarily in terms of minute details of dress and expression, Largitas gives off only a general radiance, and it is said of her garment that the material is finer than any subtlety of adornment. The imposing figure is strikingly similar to Nature herself as described in the opening *prosa,* and it is evident that a specal bond exists between the two. After Hymen has been dispatched to summon Genius, Nature apostrophizes Largitas in glowing terms:[30]

O virgo, cuius architectatione praesigni humana mens virtutum destinatur palatium, per quam homines favorabilis gratiae praemia consequuntur, per quam aetatis aureae antiquata saecula reviviscunt, per quam homines sese glutino amicitiae praecordialis astringunt, quam aeterna usia aeternali suae noys osculo generando producens, mihi sororem largita est uterinam . . . . Tanta enim unio conformitatis, immo conformitas unionis fideli pace mentes nostras conciliat, ut non solum illa unio similatoria unitatis vestiatur imagine, verum etiam, unitionis phantasia deposita, ad identitatis aspiret essentiam.

[29] Wright, p. 503; PL 210.472B. On the sacramental status of marriage before the fall see Hugh, *De Sacramentis* 1.8.12-13 (PL 176.313-18); Augustine, *De civitate Dei* 14.21-22.

[30] Wright, p. 515; PL 210.478BC.

O maiden through whose noble architecture the human mind is made a palace for the Virtues, through whom men pursue the rewards of gracious favor, through whom the far off times of the Golden Age live anew, through whom men align themselves by the bond of heartfelt affection, thou whom the eternal *Usia* brought into being by the timeless kiss of his *Noys*, distending the womb of his bounty with my sister. . . . Such a conforming bond, nay, such a binding conformity unites our minds in trusting peace that not only does our love seek to vest itself with the appearance of unity but indeed, casting aside all spurious uniting, it aspires to an identity of essence.

The allusion to the Golden Age and the association of Largitas with the pristine purity of Nature herself set her in a special relation to the other virtues. Though too easily confused with prodigality by frail mankind, Largitas is in the deepest sense a natural virtue, an emulation of the plenitude of the goddess herself, and a quality essential to human fulfillment.[31] I have suggested that the description of Largitas, "through whom men pursue the rewards of gracious favor," is the culmination of the theme of *courtoisie* in the *De planctu*, and the allusions to nobility, magnanimity, and sumptuousness help to make this clear. The poet's reference to her kinship with Nature, and her birth through the impregnation of the divine bounty by the generative kiss of Noys shows how these attributes stand for a capacity of will and spirit which is godlike, and which man has lost. It is the most striking instance of the bond which joins Hymen and all the Virtues to Nature and it contributes also to the development of the theme of Nature as *ecclesia*. The Virtues are a "sacramental synod,"[32] and as Nature

---

[31] *Largitas* becomes prodigality when it ceases to emulate the bounty of Nature, as the Arts are corrupted when a sense of their higher rationale is lost. Thus in Alain's discussion of the use and abuse of wealth the wisdom which frees the mind from the love of money is compared to philosophy and the Arts, and the image of the divine charioteer is opposed to meaningless prodigality (Wright, pp. 489-90, 493-94; PL 210.464-65, 466-67).

[32] The imagery of the robe of *Humilitas* shows "qualiter in virtutum catalogo Humilitas insignitatis praefulgeret vexillo; superbia vero a *sacramentali*

tells them, their charge is to ratify the excommunication of man which her priest Genius is to pronounce, "abominationis filios a sacramentali nostrae ecclesiae communione sejungens."[33]

The unfolding of this pattern of quasi-sacramental relationships is the most elaborate of the means whereby the stage is set for Genius' decisive entry into the poem, and it is from the priestly office of this figure that his action derives much of its meaning. But Genius is Nature's scribe and lover as well as her priest, and their relationship exists on several levels of meaning. She can refer to him as one whose office is ancillary to hers, but on another level he stands forth as capable of wholly comprehending and governing the goddess and her world.[34] In all of these roles Genius is an ideal representation of the inner nature of man, and it is in him that the sexual, literary, and chivalric, as well as the sacramental theme of the *De planctu* are resolved.

When we first see Genius he is engaged in decorating a parchment—the bare hide of a dead beast, as Alain reminds us—with images of human life. Helen, the type of a quasi-divine beauty is shown surrounded by masculine figures whose attitudes seem to constitute responses to her powerful but ambiguous stimulus: Turnus' reckless courage, the strength of Hercules, Ulysses' cunning, Plato's vision, Cicero's eloquence, Aristotle's subtlety, even Cato's passion for abstinence. These, says Alain, are the *solemnia*, the sanctioned channels of human activity. But at times, weary from unceasing labor, Genius allows his left hand to take over the task of inscription. Then appear the baseness of Thersites, the voluptuary Paris, Sinon's treachery, the crude and outlandish art of an Ennius. For the fortunes of Genius' productions depend on the conflict of *Veritas*, who assists Genius like a dutiful daughter, and

---

virtutum synodo, excommunicationis suspensa charactere, extremo relegationis damnaretur excidio." (Wright, p. 509; PL 210.475B).

[33] Wright, p. 512; PL 210.477A.

[34] Nature speaks of Genius as a chaplain "qui mihi in sacerdotali ancillatur officio" (Wright, p. 510; PL 210.476A), but also acknowledges the dependence of her life on his "ut omnino tecum sim, aut in tuo profecto proficiens, aut in tuo defectu aequa lance deficiens" (Wright, p. 511; PL 210.476C).

a perverting *Falsitas* who preys on her creations: "quicquid illa conformiter informabat, ista informiter deformabat."[35] This *Falsitas* corresponds to that failure of human art which has been analyzed in the course of the poem, and points to the source of this failure in the corruption of man. What Genius' art represents is suggested more fully by Alain's account of the birth of *Veritas*:[36]

Quae non ex pruritu Aphrodites promiscuo propagata, sed ex solo Naturae natique geniali osculo fuerat derivata, cum Ylem formarum speculum meditantem aeternalis salutavit idea, eandem iconiae interpretis interventu vicario osculata. Huius in facie divinae pulchritudinis deitas legebatur, nostrae mortalitatis aspernata naturam.

She had not been spawned by the lecherous itch of Aphrodite, but had sprung from the pure genial kiss of Nature and the Son, when the eternal idea presented itself to Hyle as she meditated upon the mirror of the forms, and impressed itself upon her through the mediary agency of the interpretative ikon. In the countenance of this maiden the divine beauty of godhead was revealed, repudiating the condition of our mortality.

The description recalls the opening scene of the *De mundi*, where Noys hails Nature as "uteri mei beata fecunditas." From this hinted comparison of Nature to the Virgin, Alain develops a natural analogue to the Annunciation.[37] Every true creation is an incarnation of ideal reality, a type of this higher union in which God and

[35] Wright, p. 519; PL 210.480CD.

[36] Wright, p. 518; PL 210.480B. Cp. Alain's account of the "palace" of the divine *ychones* in the *Sermo de sphaera intelligibili* (ed. d'Alverny, *Textes inédits*, p. 300): "In hoc palatio celebrantur nuptie Nature et nati, forme et forme nati, proprietatis et subiecti. Forma etenim geniali inherentie osculo subiectum osculatur, ex quo varie prolis fecunditas propagatur." Cp. also *Anticlaudianus* 1.457, 459 (Bossuat, p. 70).

[37] See Huizinga, "Über die Verknüpfung," pp. 136-38 (*Verz. Werken* IV, 38-39); J.A.W. Bennett, *The Parlement of Foules* (Oxford, 1957), p. 108. On correspondences between Nature and the Virgin developed in later medieval poetry, largely inspired by Alain, see Rudolf Krayer, *Frauenlob und die Natur-Allegorese* (Heidelberg, 1960).

Nature meet through their subordinate principles Genius and matter. Genius is at once the angelic herald and the natural agent of this union: his *calamus* and his concern with sexuality ally him with the original office of Venus, while his relationship to the higher *ratio*, the *aeternalis idea* of creation gives a virtually eucharistic significance to the conceptions he effects. It is true that Genius, like Nature and Largitas, has been betrayed by the *falsitas* which perverts human life. He has lost the orientation which a clear awareness on the part of man of his origin and destiny would provide. But the constant allusion in this part of the work to the original pure union of form and substance, and the mystical love which expresses itself in Nature, Largitas, and Genius as they re-encounter one another, suggest that a link survives between man's present degenerate condition and his original state. Thus when Nature greets Genius with kisses wholly untainted by Venus, but rather "mystici signantia Cupidinis amplexus," and "figural of the concord of a mystic love," the effect is to revive Genius' memory of paradise lost:[38]

> Quamvis enim mens mea hominum vitiis angustiata deformibus, in infernum tristitiae peregrinans, laetitiae nesciat paradisum, in hoc tamen amoenantis gaudii odorat primordia, quod te mecum video ad debitae vindictae suspirare suspiria. Nec mirum, si in nostrarum voluntatum unione conformi concordiae reperio melodiam, cum unius ideae exemplaris notio nos conformet, . . . cum mentes nostras non superficiali dilectionis vinculo amor jungat hypocrita, sed penitiora animorum nostrorum latibula casti amoris pudor inhabitet.

> Though my mind, straitened by the hideous vices of men, and strayed into a hell of sorrow, no longer knows the paradise of delight, yet here it scents the first beginnings of a renewal of joy, in that I behold you sharing my grief at the judgment which must be imposed. Nor is it strange that I should discover the melody of concord in the intimate union of our wills, since the exemplary notion of a single idea conforms

[38] Wright, p. 520; PL 210.481AB.

us, . . . since no false love binds our spirits with the spurious bond of pleasure, but the purity of chaste affection dwells in the innermost vaults of our souls.

The words reveal Genius' reviving awareness of his intrinsic dignity. He sees behind the veil of *falsitas*, realizes once more his kinship with the *exemplaris notio* of created life, and reassumes something of his true masculine authority. In response to his words Nature, too, undergoes a transformation, described in terms delicately suggestive of the response of a courtly *midons* to her lover: as Genius "plies the reins" of his discourse, "suae exclamationis quasi aurora nascente, tristitiae tenebras paulisper abstractans, salvo suae dignitatis honore, Natura Genio gratiarum iura persolvit."[39]

With this reassertion of Genius' "manhood," and the cosmic reestablishment of right relations between male and female, the poem reaches a tentative resolution. But like Bernardus' Patricida, Alain's abstracted hero exists finally on a transcendent level which merely natural restoration cannot attain, a level above and beyond the cosmos defined by the aesthetic structure of the poem. Thus, after this earthly affirmation of his authority, Genius steps outside the allegorical universe. He removes those robes which testify to his involvement with mortality, and, dressed in his priestly vestments, issues a decree of excommunication which is sanctioned, in terms appropriate to this higher dignity, "auctoritate superessentialis usiae, eiusque notionis aeternae."

Thus the *De planctu*, like the *De mundi universitate*, comes to a climax in the affirmation of those qualities of heroism and dignity which Genius embodies. But like Bernardus, Alain is well aware of the ironic implications of this view. Genius in his final role speaks from the timeless elevation of the ideal, but the excommunication and penalties he imposes only perpetuate conditions which we have already seen realized in the course of Nature's complaint. Like Vulcan's capture of Venus and Mars, Genius' censure only defines in authoritative terms the "tristis consuetudo" into which man has been drawn. In literary and psychological

[39] Wright, p. 520; PL 210.481B.

terms, Genius' exile in the "inferno of sorrow" and the liability of his productions to the attacks of *falsitas* are only the most profound demonstration of the impossible complexity of the maze of *phantasia* and corrupted impulse which has interposed itself between Genius' guiding influence and the consciousness of man.

But the very existence of Genius and the attributes with which Alain endows him set the problem in a different perspective. Though Alain has virtually refuted Nature's claim to be a guide and standard for man, I think that a recognition of the full complexity of Genius' role in the poem makes it possible to detect a more positive implication in the natural order. To demonstrate this will involve a brief digression into the philosophical and theological concerns which lie behind the allegory of the *De planctu*.

I have already mentioned Alain's involvement with the thought of Gilbert de la Porrée and his followers. A major concern of their thought was the doctrine of "secondary forms," intermediary between the eternal ideas and their substantial embodiments, and the union of these *formae nativae, imagines*, or *ikones* with the *subiecta materia* or *hyle*.[40] It is apparently to a version of this doctrine that Bernardus alludes in describing the *Oyarses* who assigns each creature its proper form, and it is obviously the basis of Alain's account of the birth of *Veritas*, fruit of that union of "ikon" and *hyle* through which the "genial kiss of Nature and the Son" is effected. Genius is this intermediary, and his role is the transmission of the divine wisdom to the sphere of Nature. He is Nature's alter ego, an expression of the same "exemplaris notio," and Nature beholds in him "velut in speculo" a higher reflection of herself.[41] But Genius is also specifically present in human nature, where he has the special function of ensuring right relations between the rational and physical principles, and where he oversees the transmission of form from one generation to another.[42] In this he re-

---

[40] See above, ch. 1, pp. 62-63; d'Alverny, *Textes inédits*, pp. 166-80; Huizinga, "Über die Verknüpfung," pp. 119-23 (*Verz. Werken* IV, 26-28).

[41] Wright, p. 511; PL 210.476C.

[42] Thus Genius' delineation of human figures is described as follows (Wright, p. 517; PL 210.479D): ". . . styli subsequentis subsidio imagines rerum sub umbra picturae ad veritatem suae essentiae transmigrantes, vita sui

calls the sexual *genii* of the *De mundi,* and the conventional asso-
ciation of the genius figure with "naturalis concupiscentia."[43] The
range of his activity is as broad as that of Nature herself, and the
comparison must be emphasized. As Nature is ideally a guide and
standard for man, so Genius, seeking to preserve man in his ideal
relationship with Nature, is the innate principle of rational dignity
and vision, as well as the regulator of the process of generation.
And as Nature, properly understood, is a type of *Mater Ecclesia,*
so Genius, the priest, the lover, and ideally the lord of Nature, is
a type of the divine wisdom, the Word, through whom man ex-
presses the likeness of the godhead within himself and to that ex-
tent assumes the power and majesty of the divine charioteer.

The significance of such comparisons may be seen more clearly
in the light of a passage in Alain's commentary on the angelic hier-
archy, in which he attempts to explain the difference between the
philosophical and the spiritual approach to the divine in terms of
the difference between the substantial and the "symbolic" mode of
existence of created life:[44]

"Through the substantifying genii," that is, through the sub-
stantial natures (of things). For the genius (of a thing) is its
nature or the god of its nature. Now this kind of manifestation
is the object of natural philosophy, which deals with the na-
tures of things. However, knowledge of God is not gained
from the substantial natures of things. . . , but from signs is-
suing forth, that is, from the effects of the Supreme Cause.
. . . Thus the difference between philosophy and theophany
is clear; they differ in this, that natural philosophy arises from

---

generis munerabat. Quibus deletionis morte sopitis, novae nativitatis ortu
aliae revocabantur in vitam."

[43] In addition to the *genii* of Bernardus and Guillaume discussed above,
see the references gathered by Raynaud de Lage, *Alain de Lille,* pp. 89-90.

[44] *Hierarchia Alani,* ed. d'Alverny, *Alain de Lille: Textes inédits,* p. 228;
see also *Expositio prosae de angelis* (*ibid.,* pp. 203-06) and Mlle. d'Alverny's
commentary, p. 95. Like *Theologia* in the *Anticlaudianus, Theophania* seems
to be partly an aspect of human understanding, partly a mode of existence of
the divine.

the intellect and descends to sensory experience of things . . . .
Theophany begins with the senses and tends toward under-
standing. For as was said above, when we behold the beauty,
grandeur, and order of things, we understand God not fully,
but in a half-complete fashion: yet what is now imperfect in
our understanding will be made perfect hereafter.

To consider the "genius" here described, the principle of individu-
ation and inner coherence in natural existence, as analogous to the
informing presence discerned by inspired, "theophanic" vision is
to open a large field for speculation, for it suggests the further
analogy, and at the same time, of course, the complete difference,
between the "deus nature" and the Logos. At its extreme, this
amounts to conceiving the *opus restaurationis* as precisely a return
to the condition of man before the Fall, and as Chenu has shown,[45]
this is exactly the view adopted by much of the thought of the
later twelfth century. The recreation of fallen man becomes a re-
turn "au regime paradisiaque, état idéal et vrai 'nature' de l'homme,
point de départ du mouvement cosmique autant que lieu où a été
commis le péché; au terme, c'est la réintégration de tout le genre
humain dans l'unité primordiale."[46] Grace is present in man ahis-
torically "comme une nature, selon laquelle l'homme est *imago
dei*. Suivre cette nature, c'est s'assimiler à Dieu." Restoration thus
involves a double movement, a rediscovery of the divine likeness
within and a renewal of participation in the cosmic harmony.

This process of restoration is precisely the object of the dual ap-
peal of Nature and Genius in the *De planctu*, and the natural con-
sequence of a half-century of speculation in the tradition of the
pseudo-Dionysius. The true significance of Nature and of the di-
vine likeness in man abides behind those *integumenta* which con-
found the poet-hero; the vision of Nature's original integrity and
of her relations with Genius foreshadows the effect of renewing
grace and in so doing suggests the subtlety of the sacramental trans-
formation which distinguishes one condition from the other. It is

[45] *La théologie*, pp. 289-308.   [46] *Ibid.*, p. 295.

the same fine line which differentiates the "substantifying" from the "theophanic" mode of existence, and it reappears in other writings of Alain. Commenting on a sequence celebrating the angelic hierarchy, he observes that man was created in God's image by virtue of his natural attributes, and is recreated in this same image through grace; the virtues of reason and understanding which were man's original endowment are recreated as fortitude, piety, patience.[47] For all virtue which is now infused into man by grace was originally present *per naturam*; and as Alain explains in the treatise *De virtutibus et vitiis*, if Adam had not succumbed to temptation, these natural virtues would have been sufficient by themselves to gain him eternal life.[48]

All of this may help us to appreciate the full significance of the revival which Genius undergoes in the concluding episode of the *De planctu*, his recollection of the "paradisum laetitiae," and his resumption of authority. For Genius is man's link with Paradise, the element in his nature which, albeit subliminally, recalls and seeks to regain his original perfection. But it is essential to recognize also that Genius has been deeply involved in the special situation of fallen man as well. He has known, like all lovers, the "infernum tristitiae," and thus his experience constitutes an illuminating gloss on that of the figures of thwarted *ingenium*, Orpheus and Vulcan, in the commentaries of Guillaume and Bernardus. It constitutes a profound vindication of the lyric impulse of Orpheus, the definitive art of Vulcan, and the heroism of the *genii* of the *De mundi*. Alain has in effect identified the creativity of these figures with the natural impulse they seek to control by tracing the latter to its origin in man's original nature. It is in Genius that the power and office of Venus and Cupid, as well as man's rational and visionary capacities, have their source, and it is he whose complex role as priest, lover, and artist contains and somehow coordinates the desires and rebellious tendencies of human *ingenium*, guiding

[47] *Expositio prosae de angelis*, ed. d'Alverny, *Textes inédits*, p. 200.
[48] *Tractatus de virtutibus et vitiis et de donibus Spiritus Sancti*, ed. O. Lottin, *Psychologie et morale aux XIIe et XIIIe siècles* (Gembloux, 1960), VI, 59, 65-66.

it onward by the dim light of his recollection of man's original destiny.

Thus by conflating the cosmic *Oyarses* and the sexual *genii* of Bernardus, and elaborating the analogies implicit in Bernardus' hinted comparisons of Nature with the Virgin, and of generation with redemptive sacrifice, in the light of his own Neoplatonist theology, Alain brings new illumination to the shadowy human world of the *De mundi*. He conveys a sense of the presence of the divine in the structure of perceived reality in ways beyond the reach of Chartrian philosophy as such. His achievement is one of sheer poetic inventiveness, but it is nonetheless remarkable. His ultimate vindication of Nature and Genius does not, of course, obviate the need for the sanctions of Scripture and the Church; these are clearly enough acknowledged in the allusions of his poetic typology. But Alain creates a context in which these sanctions may be seen to extend to the whole of human experience, and to confirm man's intellectual, moral, and sexual participation in cosmic life. This poetic context, in which rationalism and sacramentalism collaborate, where *largitas* and *humilitas* are invoked together and Venus and Cupid can reassume their natural roles, devoid of ambiguity, is itself a powerful symbol of redemption.

But when all this has been said, certain questions remain unanswered. Despite Alain's vivid and complete alignment of Nature and grace, the restoration he presents is *only* symbolic, for Genius and Nature are by definition incapable of bringing it to pass. "Ego Natura," says the goddess, "huius nativitatis naturam ignoro." Moreover, it is a necessary condition of the structure of Alain's allegory that all human activity not condemned as vicious should be figurative of spiritual excellence, so that its intrinsic meaning remains deceptively difficult to gauge. No attention is given to the "battle against formlessness" on the earthly level in which Genius and his allies in human nature must engage.[49]

The second of these problems is tentatively addressed in the *Architrenius* of Jean de Hanville, and later, in a more rough and ready way, by Jean de Meun. The first is the theme of the work

[49] The phrase is Dronke's, "L'amor che move," p. 414.

which Alain seems to have considered his masterpiece, the *Anti-claudianus*.

2. The *Anticlaudianus*

Though it has been called a sequel, the *Anticlaudianus* is really a restatement of the theme of the *De planctu*. The corruption of man and Nature's dissatisfaction are again the *donnée*, but this time Nature does not attempt to deal with the problem directly. Instead she decides to create a single man in whom all the flaws of fallen man will be eliminated. She summons the Virtues to a council, and it is resolved that *Prudentia* will be sent to ask God to create a soul for the new being. A chariot is made by the seven Arts, and Prudentia sets out, drawn by the five senses and guided by Reason. She comes at length to the seat of *Theologia*, with whom, after abandoning all of her equipage except the sense of hearing, she ascends still further, beholding the Virgin and Christ, and finally entering the palace of the "arbiter celestis aulae." God agrees to make the necessary soul, and Prudentia returns to earth. Nature prepares a body, Concord unites it to the soul, and all the Virtues bestow their gifts on the new man. Meanwhile Allecto and the Furies, having heard of the new creation, muster an army of vices to overthrow him. These are encountered by the Virtues in a *psychomachia*, the happy outcome of which leads to a restoration of the Golden Age.

The *Anticlaudianus* is also a "super-Bernardus," a Christian counterpart to the cosmogony of the *De mundi*.[50] Nature's handiwork must be renovated, for the chaos, the *germana bella* of the pre-creation have reappeared in the contradictions of human life. *Prudentia*, a passive quality capable of accepting the limitations of natural reason and seeking recourse to faith,[51] undertakes a journey

---

[50] The two authors are compared by de Lubac, *Exégèse* ii.i, pp. 201-07.

[51] On *Prudentia* see R. H. Green, "Alan of Lille's *Anticlaudianus*: Ascensus mentis ad Deum," *Annuale Medievale* 8 (1967), pp. 14-15. As a gloss Green aptly cites John of Salisbury, *Metalogicon* 4.17 (Webb, p. 183): "cum prudentia, que de terrenis est et rationis amor, ad incorrupte ueritatis diuinorumque archana consurgit, in sapientiam transiens, quodammodo a mortalium conditione eximitur."

closely analogous to Nature's ascent to the seat of Urania. The differences between Alain's *novus homo* and Bernardus' *microcosmus* will be discussed below. Here it need only be said that in general the *Anticlaudianus* emphasizes the negative, rather than the positive aspects of the relations of man and Nature. Thus in the opening description of the abode of Nature, the pictures on the walls form a panorama of the history of human corruption which recalls both Bernardus' catalogue poem and the proem of the *De planctu*, and Alain remarks of the effect, "Naturam peccasse putes," a thought unthinkable in the world of the *De planctu*. Human sin becomes a reflection of the limitation of Nature in general. The goddess of the *De planctu* had absorbed the roles of Bernardus' Endelechia and Imarmene, and to a certain extent that of his Urania. Having in that work narrowed the focus of Chartrian allegory from cosmology to psychology, Alain here effects a further refinement, abandoning detailed treatment of the scope and power of Nature to concentrate on her limitations as a guide for man's spiritual experience. Thus Nature does little more than state the human problem, which is then taken up by *Ratio, Concordia,* and *Prudentia* (whose speech is prefaced by an elaborate description of her form and garment which suggests that she is to play the normative role played by Nature in the *De planctu*). These figures define the problem philosophically, and in a negative way theologically, for they define the limits of Nature's creative power and its contingency on the operations of a higher mind. Thus Alain stresses the divine origin of animating form in a passage which both recalls Bernardus' vision of birth into earthly life as a *descensus ad inferos* and anticipates the later description of how *Theologia* gives definition to the vastness of God. The subject is the activity of *Ratio*, and the mirror in which she perceives[52]

> Quomodo terrestrem formam celestis ydea
> Gignit et in nostram sobolem transcribit abissum,
> Mittit in exilium formas quas destinet orbi,
> A patre degenerat proles faciemque paternam
> Exuit antiqui uultus oblita parentis;

[52] *Anticlaudianus* 1.495-503 (Bossuat, p. 71).

Qualiter in mundo fantasma resultat ydee,
Cuius inoffensus splendor sentitur in umbra;
Qualiter a fonte formarum riuus aberrans
Ingenitum perdit subiecti labe nitorem. . .

how divine idea begets terrestrial form, transcribes formlessness into
human progeny, and sends into exile those forms which it destines
for the world; how the offspring become degenerate and put off the
likeness of the father, grown forgetful of the countenance of their
ancient parent; how in the universe a "phantasm" of the idea is re-
flected, and its unsullied splendor is perceptible in this shadowy
reflection; how the stream which descends from the fountain of
forms loses its original radiance in the tide of material existence. . . .

Concordia, too, stresses the dependency on a higher power of the
nexus, the "unus amor" which binds form and subject together.[53]
These themes had been treated in the *De planctu*, but in the *Anti-
claudianus* they are subsumed by the larger question of how nat-
ural existence transcends itself, what "forma melior" is necessary
to purge it of its taints and inconsistencies. Ratio, having gazed
long into the *specula* which contain all rational knowledge con-
cerning the origins of form and matter and the nature of their
"unio nativa," confesses herself powerless to explain the problem,
and Concordia can offer no other advice than prayer.

The limitations confessed by these two powers precisely define
the attitude of Prudentia, in whom the exigencies of natural un-
derstanding are to be augmented by faith. In its preliminary stages
her undertaking still demands the assistance of all the resources of
human nature and human knowledge; Prudentia must know the
limits of the natural world in order to see beyond them, and her
voyage is in the Chartrain tradition, an ascent "per creaturas ad
creatorem."[54] But the account of the Arts who fashion her chariot,

[53] *Anticlaudianus* 2.293-309 (Bossuat, p. 81). Cp. *Anticl.* 1.363-71 (Bos-
suat, pp. 67-68) which closely echo the lines on *res* and *forma* in *De mundi*
2.8 (quoted above, pp. 178-79), but shift the emphasis from the "endurance"
of matter to the divinity of form. For Alain the Porretan theologian form is
always a manifestation of the Logos, the "osculum" of God, rather than a
mere static shape.

[54] Alain gives classic expression to this theme, and at the same time indi-
cates his intention to transcend philosophy, in the prologue to the *Anticlaudi-*

insofar as it is more than a stage set, seems to look forward to the unfolding of the poem's spiritual theme, rather than dwelling on the humanistic significance of the Arts themselves. Alain's representation of the humble and pallid *Grammatica*, a virgin yet nursing a host of infant scholars at her breasts, is perhaps intended to anticipate Prudentia's encounter with the Virgin Mary.[55] The Virgin is clearly present in the description of the robe of *Arithmetica*, on which is set forth[56]

> Quomodo principium numeri, fons, mater, origo
> Est monas, et de se numeri parit unica turbam;
> Quomodo Virgo parit, gignens manet integra, simplex
> Sese multiplicat, de sese gignit et in se
> Incorrupta manet, partus imitata parentis. . .

in what manner unity is the beginning, fount, mother, source of number, and alone conceives of itself all the host of numbers; how a Virgin gives birth, and remains unsullied, makes manifold her own simplicity, brings forth life from herself, yet remains inviolate within herself, imitating the parturition of her progenitor. . .

There is an aptness in the association of these two elementary disciplines with the creativity of a virgin nature, and by contrast the elaborate strategies of logic and rhetoric, the presumption of geometry and astronomy, seem like a confusion and violation of something which only the pristine simplicity of language and number can adequately express.

After Concord has joined the parts of the chariot together and Ratio has harnessed the senses, the ascent begins. Charioteered by

---

anus (Bossuat, p. 56). See also the sermon "de clericis ad theologiam non accedentibus," ed. d'Alverny, *Textes inédits*, p. 275: "salutande liberales artes a limine, id est, postquam nos perduxerint ad limen theologie, ad ianuam celestis regine, relinquende sunt in pace, non ut ibi figamus pedem, sed ut faciamus pontem."

[55] *Anticlaudianus* 2.387-98 (Bossuat, p. 84). See also the reference to the *partes dissutas* of grammar which were synthesized by Dindimus (*Anticl.* 2.498-99). The words recall that language, like the *opus Naturae* as a whole, was once a *tunica inconsutilis* like the *opus Dei matris* (see John 19:23; Krayer, *Frauenlob und die Natur-Allegorese*, pp. 31-42).

[56] *Anticlaudianus* 3.311-15 (Bossuat, p. 98).

Ratio and surrounded by the wonders of creation, Prudentia is reversing the journey of Nature in the *De planctu*.[57] But it is the poet of the *De planctu* rather than the goddess whom she recalls when, approaching the heavens, she begins to undergo a psychic disintegration. At the threshold of Paradise, the senses rebel against Ratio, and Prudentia is left powerless until Theology appears to guide her.[58] Still more strongly reminiscent of the *De planctu* is her swoon as she enters the palace of God:[59]

> Offendit splendor oculos mentemque stupore
> Percussit rerum nouitas, defecit in illis
> Visus et interior mens caligauit ad illas.
> Sic sopor inuasit uigilem, sic somnus adulter
> Oppressit Fronesis animum, sompnoque soporans
> Extasis ipsa suo, mentem dormire coegit.

The splendor troubles her sight; the wonder of these holy things dazes her mind; her sight fails in beholding them and her inner thoughts become clouded. Thus a drowsiness overcomes her active faculties, sleep comes unbidden to overpower her will, and her very exaltation, infusing a slumber of its own, forces her mind to sleep.

And as the poet of the former poem is revived and instructed by Nature, so Prudentia is recreated by Faith. Having passed through the state of *extasis*, she is confronted by Theology with paradoxes which represent a positive counterpart to those presented by the perverse *Cupido* of the former poem:[60]

> . . . assensus discors, discordia concors,
> Pax inimica, fides fantastica, falsus amoris
> Nexus, amicicia fallax, umbratile fedus. . . .

[57] Alain is perhaps recalling a standard gloss on *Timaeus* 41E which explained the *currus animarum* as *ratio* and *intellegentia*; see Gregory, *Platonismo medievale*, pp. 9-10, 100. See also Green, "Alan of Lille's *Anticlaudianus*," pp. 12-13, who cites the *Sermo de sphaera intelligibili* (p. 302) on the chariot of the soul, propelled by *sensus*, *imaginatio*, *ratio*, and *intellectualitas*, "qua ascendens nobilis auriga philosophus recte aurigationis ductu ad eterna deducitur."

[58] *Anticlaudianus* 5.51-82 (Bossuat, pp. 124-25).

[59] *Anticlaudianus* 6.3-8 (Bossuat, p. 141).

[60] *Anticlaudianus* 5.316-18 (Bossuat, p. 132). Cp. the opening lines of the poem on Cupid in the *De planctu* (Wright, p. 472; PL 210.455BC).

... discordant agreement, concordant discord, hostile peace, incredible belief, the union of a false love, a treacherous friendship, an insubstantial compact ...

The basis for these lines, with their bizarre exploitation of the fact that normal relationships between substance and accident have been transcended, is Alain's splendid account of the activity of Theology. This occurs symbolically at the exact midpoint of the poem and marks the transformation of the allegory from naturalistic to anagogical terms. Alain explains the inability of the figural and philosophical resources of the human mind to express divine truth, and describes how Theology, rejecting any attempt to impose a specious continuity on ultimate reality, abandons reason and analogy altogether, and uses words in a new, wholly mystical way. Recalling Bernardus' vivid portrayal of the resistance of *hyle* to the discipline of form, he describes the repudiation by language itself of any pretense to adequacy. At this point the relations of formal continuity and anagogical impulse are radically transformed. The profound moral significance attributed to the integrity of the natural order in the *De planctu* is left behind, and the Platonic cosmos becomes a negative image of the divine infinitude:[61]

> Quomodo nature subiectus sermo stupescit
> Dum temptat diuina loqui, uiresque loquendi
> Perdit et ad ueterem cupit ille recurrere sensum,
> Mutescuntque soni, uix barbutire ualentes,
> Deque suo sensu deponunt uerba querelam;
> Qualiter ipse Deus in se capit omnia rerum
> Nomina, que non ipsa Dei natura recusat,
> Cuncta tamen, mediante tropo, dictante figura
> Concipit, et uoces puras sine rebus adoptat.

Albeit speech, subject to nature, is stultified when it seeks to express the divine, loses its powers and seeks to lapse back into its old deno-

[61] *Anticlaudianus* 5.119-27 (Bossuat, pp. 126-27). With lines 119-21 cp. "Quoniam homines" (Glorieux, p. 119): "Cum enim termini a naturalibus ad theologica transferuntur, novas significationes admirantur et antiquas exposcere videntur. Hoc ignorantes plerique iuxta naturalium semitam de divinis sumentes iudicium celestia terrenis conformant, quasi in terris bestialiter viventes, et non ad veram intelligentiam ingenii fastigium attollere valeant."

tations; though its sounds are altered, and the crudest utterance becomes difficult, until our words cast off all pretence to meaning; however it is that God comprehends in himself the names of all things, and even his divine nature suffers itself to be expressed by them—all of these things, by the agency of tropes and figures (Theology) conceptualizes, and employs pure names, divorced from their natural reference.

It is in the light of this total transformation that we must understand the action of the last three books, the chivalry of the *novus homo* and the "triumph of Nature" which is the result of his conquest of vice.[62] But once the transformation has taken place these later events are wholly redundant. The real resolution of Alain's theme, in the *De planctu* and in the *Anticlaudianus*, takes place in heaven, as Prudentia is guided by Theology and informed by Faith to the point at which she can stand forth in the dignity of man's original nature and appeal directly to God:[63]

> Erigitur, mentemque regit, partimque retardat
> Virgo metum; stat mens cum corpore, corporis equat
> Mens erecta situm. Sic mens submissa resumit
> Vires, et erectam mentem sua uerba sequuntur.

The maiden is drawn erect, gains control of her mind, and partly allays her fear. Her mind stands firm with her body, her erect mind responds to the stance of her body. Thus her mind, having been bowed down, regains its powers, and her words conform to her erect mind.

This recovery of "erectness," of the dignity of the *imago dei*, and the psychological integration to which it testifies are the necessary climax of the allegory, and the "Iliad" of the final books is a concession to artistic pretensions which almost betray Alain's sure re-

[62] As Huizinga notes, the virtues and vices who participate in the *psychomachia* are themselves transformed, so that we see, e.g., a conflict of spiritual fortitude and poverty of spirit; "Über die Verknüpfung," pp. 80-81; *Verz. Werken* IV, 63-64. This accounts for the role played by courtly attributes like *favor*, *risus*, and *juventus*, whose presence led Lewis to conclude that Alain was describing "not the perfect man, but the perfect gentleman" (*Allegory of Love*, p. 104). See also the passage from the *Expositio prosae de angelis* cited in n. 47 above.

[63] *Anticlaudianus* 6.291-94 (Bossuat, p. 149).

ligious instinct. The *homo novus* exists in Prudentia herself once mind, will, and speech have become congruent again with the dignity implied by man's upright carriage. This is the fulfillment of the profound and subtle relationship between the natural and the sacramental which is Alain's constant theme.

The *Anticlaudianus* brings "worldly" and divine theology into confrontation, and demonstrates the unique and total transformation which distinguishes the latter. Its character is Neoplatonic, and it is only imperfectly linked with the idea of a single, pivotal intervention of the divine in human history, but it is a remarkably full expression of the great attempt of twelfth-century theology to reconcile structure and anagogy, cosmological and sacramental Platonism. The vision it seeks to realize has been characterized by Henri de Lubac, in words which might almost have been taken from one of Alain's more reflective theological writings:[64]

> The first impulse of the spirit emerging in the bosom of nature was meant to be anagogical; but since the Fall, this anagogy is flawed. All around, everything has become turbid, obscure. Not through any fault of the world, or of its Creator, but through the fault of man, "the world conceals God." . . . but it always remains, in itself, capable of revealing Him.

For the mind fully alive to the meaning of sacred history and the signs and patterns which manifest this meaning, he goes on,

> This first book, the great "fabrica mundana," will be made clear once again; anagogy will be revived. Its impetus will carry it even higher, making it penetrate deeper into the mystery of the Trinity, which is the mystery of Love. Then the circle will be perfect, or if one may say it, more than perfect. *Felix culpa!*

The poems of Alain make a significant contribution to the poetic elaboration of this vision, which demands a mode of allegory both cosmological and sacramental. The work here begun is completed

[64] *Exégèse* ii.ii, p. 174.

in the *Commedia* of Dante, where the relations of Platonist cosmology and the "itinerarium mentis ad Deum" are magnificently resolved.[65]

[65] See John Freccero, "Dante's Pilgrim in a Gyre," *Publications of the Modern Language Association* 76 (1961), pp. 168-81; "The Final Image: *Paradiso* XXXIII.144," *Modern Language Notes* 79 (1964), 14-27; Andrea Ciotti, "Alano e Dante," *Convivium* 28 (1960), 257-67.

CHAPTER SIX

THE POETRY OF THE SCHOOLS
AND THE RISE OF ROMANCE

The courtly poetry of the later twelfth century is social rather than
philosophical, and its primary emphasis is on concrete emotional
situations and *avanture*, rather than the abstract dialogues and
tableaux of Chartrian allegory and mythographical lyric. But the
major vernacular poets possessed the same grounding in classical
poetry and rhetoric as their contemporaries writing in Latin, and
an important development of the latter half of the century is the
adaptation of the materials of school-poetry to the uses of *cour-
toisie* and romance.

The famous *Altercatio Phyllidis et Florae*, prototype of a host
of debates between *miles* and *clericus*, is also a veritable anthology
of themes and motifs of "learned" verse. Based largely on the *Me-
tamorphosis Goliae*,[1] it incorporates the mythography, the theme of
intellectual vision, and the heightened sense of the implications of
rhetoric typical of such poetry, but adapts these resources to a bas-
ically social theme. The poem begins as a debate, in which Phyllis
argues for the superiority of the knight as lover, while Flora speaks
for the clerk. In general Flora has the better of the argument, but
they resolve to present the case for judgment in the court of Cupid.
After a long description of their equipage, and another of the set-
ting of Cupid's court, they present their claims, and the case is
decided in favor of the clerk.

Much of the poem's humor is derived from the translation of the
vices to which the life of the clerk is liable into positive qualities.
Thus material comfort becomes an image of the clerk's lordly rela-
tion to the plenitude of nature,[2] and his *otium* becomes a state of

---

[1] On the chronology of the two poems see Karl Strecker, "Die Metamor-
phosis Goliae und das Streitgedicht Phyllis und Flora," *Zeitschrift für
deutsches Altertum* 62 (1925), p. 180.

[2] On this theme see Giuseppe Tavani, "Il dibattito sul chierico e il

tranquillity superior to knighthood as the contemplative life is to
the active:[3]

> Otiosum clericum semper esse iuras:
> viles spernit operas, fateor, et duras;
> sed cum eius animus evolat ad curas,
> celi vias dividit, et rerum naturas. . .
> Quid Dione valeat, et amoris deus,
> primus novit clericus et instruxit meus. . .

You claim that the clerk is always given to idleness: I grant that he
spurns demeaning and exhausting work. But when his mind flies
forth to seek its true object, he embarks on celestial journeys and
sees into the natures of things. . . . It was my clerk who first came
to know, and taught mankind, the power of Dione and the god of
love. . .

These lines conclude the debate as such. Most of the rest of the
poem is taken up by sumptuous descriptions, first of the damsels'
cavalcade, then of the situation and activity of the court of Cupid.
The suggestion that Flora has won the argument is strengthened
by the fact that she travels on a magnificent horse, while Phyllis
rides a mule. The latter is a handsome beast, originally given by
Neptune to Venus, to console her for the loss of her young knight
Adonis, but its beauty pales beside the pride and rich adornment
of Flora's stallion. The poet dwells at length on the ways in which
this steed expresses the *studium Naturae* at its most intense, and
then proceeds to an even fuller description of the throne-like sad-
dle, made out of ivory, gold, and precious stones by Vulcan, and
adorned by Minerva with richly colored fabrics:

---

cavaliere nella tradizione mediolatina e volgare," *Romanistisches Jahrbuch*
15 (1964), pp. 53-55. See also Robert S. Haller, "The Altercatio Phyllidis et
Florae as an Ovidian Satire," *Medieval Studies* 30 (1968), 123-24. On the
relation of clerical *otium* to love cp. Andreas Capellanus, *De amore* 1.7 (ed.
E. Trojel, Copenhagen, 1892, p. 221): "Quia vix tamen unquam aliquis
sine carnis crimine vivit, et clericorum sit vita propter otia multa continua
et ciborum abundantiam copiosam prae aliis hominibus universis naturaliter
corporis tentationi supposita, si aliquis clericus amoris voluerit subire certa-
mina . . . suo sermone utatur et amoris studeat applicari militiae."

[3] *Altercatio Phyllidis et Florae*, st. 39 and 41; ed. A. Bömer, *Zeitschrift
für deutsches Altertum* 56 (1918), p. 231.

Multa de preteritis rebus et ignotis
erant mirabilibus ibi sculpta notis;
nuptie Mercurii superis admotis,
fedus, matrimonium, plenitudo dotis.

Nullus ibi locus est vacuus aut planus;
habet plus quam animus capiat humanus.
solus illa sculpserat, que spectans Vulcanus
vix hoc suas credidit potuisse manus.

Many things were carved there in wondrous detail, concerning events long past and little known: the marriage of Mercury, with the gods in attendance; the compact, the wedding celebration, the bountiful dowry.

No area was left blank or smooth; more was set forth there than the human mind can grasp. Vulcan alone was the carver, and looking upon his work he could scarcely believe that his hands had achieved it.

The significance of the sequence of descriptions is ambiguous. The mule of Phyllis, which the poet associates with a dynasty of ardent women, seems to embody a comment on the humble quality of passionate love, by comparison with the magnificent stallion, surmounted by the still more magnificent saddle, suggesting the greater dignity of a love associated with knowledge and vision. As in the *Metamorphosis*, the art of Vulcan seeks to assert the primacy of order by establishing a bond between sensual nature and an idea of harmony. This is further suggested by the poet's declaration that to fashion the saddle, bit, and shoes for this steed Vulcan set aside the shield of Achilles, in which we may perhaps recognize a definitive image of the function of military prowess in the order of things, in order to create this testimony to the greater dignity of a love according to the refined and intellectual standards of *clergie*.

The maidens journey to the paradise of love, a place so beautiful that they are almost distracted from their mission. "If he remained there, a man would become immortal," says the poet; "one could guess the identity of the lord from his domain." The paradise resembles the grove of Apollo appropriated from Martianus by the author of the *Metamorphosis*. But at its center, rather than the cosmic trinity of Jove, Juno, and Pallas, sits Cupid, adorned with flowers, scents, and his own "venerabilis iuventus," surrounded by Silenus and a mob of drunken satyrs, and attended by the Graces, who administer his drinking cup. The girls do homage and present their case, and Cupid, after some deliberation, refers the matter to *usus* and *natura*, who decide in favor of the cleric.

Simple and humorous in itself, this resolution becomes more meaningful when set in relation to the vision of order expressed by the artistry of Vulcan. That his handiwork and that of Pallas should provide the bridge to a transcendent level of meaning is appropriate, but it is plain that the paradise of the *Altercatio* is a debased version of the "locus universitatis" of the *Metamorphosis*. Both divinities, moreover, have abandoned other, and perhaps nobler pursuits in order to create Flora's saddle. Pallas' embroidery reminds us of her contest with Arachne, one of the less admirable episodes in her career, and Vulcan's laying aside of the shield of Achilles may be intended to suggest an abandonment of that larger vision with which his art at its most profound is associated, in which order and violence cooperate to define the course of human life.[4]

Such a reading would help to account for the corrupt state of the *paradisus amoris*, for it would suggest a view of love possessing neither the serious sense of a relationship with the celestial order proper to the study of the cleric nor the direct commitment to fulfillment in action which is the defining quality of the knight. Both *usus* and *natura* (or *mores* and *scientia*) are compromised,[5] and this obviously clerical exercise seems finally to suggest a moment of ironic reflection on the part of a *litteratus* aware of a tendency to become overabsorbed in the intricacies of belles-lettres and Ovidian dialectic and so to neglect higher things.

The *Altercatio* provides a convenient means of transition from

[4] Vulcan's role as governor of sensuality is recalled in st. 56 (Bömer, p. 234), where he is said to have fashioned reins for Flora's stallion "de sponse capillis."

[5] The poem's parody of the conventional roles of knight and cleric is noted by Haller (see above, n. 2) who, however, seems to me to overemphasize the moralistic purpose of the parody.

the philosophical poetry we have been considering to the generally
freer and less systematic use of Chartrian literary resources in ver-
nacular poetry. The note of compromise on which it concludes is
appropriate to its comparatively realistic focus, and to the fact that
it is concerned more with social *mores* (and from an ironic perspec-
tive) than with ideas. These qualities it possesses in common with
vernacular French poetry of the third quarter of the twelfth cen-
tury. That the authors of this poetry were in close contact with the
classical studies of the schools was long ago demonstrated by Faral.[6]
More recently Bezzola has provided an excellent survey of the bril-
liant literary society which developed around the figure of Henry II
of England,[7] in his youth the pupil of Adelhard of Bath and pos-
sibly Guillaume de Conches, and later the patron of authors so
distinguished and diverse as John of Salisbury, Walter of Chatillon,
Walter Map, Wace, and very possibly Marie de France and the
anonymous authors of the *Roman de Thebes* and *Eneas.*[8] In such
a milieu, intellectual and social ideals inevitably took on similar
characteristics. Literary articulation of the ideals of *curialitas* often
corresponds strikingly to the allegorizing of philosophical *sapientia*
in school-poetry.[9] Indeed, as in the case of the Latin poets and
rhetoricians discussed above, much of the creative energy of the
early romancers seems to have been devoted to the creation of a
poetic world, unified by rhetorical convention and the ideals of
courtoisie, a world with its own cosmology, its own quasi-sapiential

[6] Faral's pioneering *Recherches sur les sources latines des contes et romans
courtois* (Paris, 1913), gives ample discussion of sources and analogues of
the French debates of clerk and knight, of *Eneas* and *Thebes*, and of the
many poems based on Ovid's *Metamorphoses*, but says relatively little about
the specific literary activities of the schools.

[7] Reto R. Bezzola, *Les origines et la formation de la littérature courtoise
en occident* (Paris, 1944-63) III.i.

[8] Bezzola, pp. 269-306. On the possible relation of the early work of
Chrétien to the court of Henry see pp. 306-11.

[9] On the intellectual backgrounds of the ideal of *courtoisie* or *curialitas*
and its relation to the attribute of "clergie," see Antonio Viscardi, "Le ori-
gine della letteratura cortese," *Zeitschrift für romanische Philologie* 78
(1962), pp. 272-84; Jean Frappier, "Vues sur les conceptions courtoises dans
les littératures d'oc et d'oïl au XIIᵉ siècle," *Cahiers de civilization médié-
vale* 2 (1959), pp. 146-49.

hierarchies of meaning and value, its own mythic equivalents for the religious exaltations and historical dilemmas of twelfth-century man. As Alfred Adler remarks, there is a real correspondence between the effort of twelfth-century *litterati* to order and refine the conventions of rhetoric, the pervasive concern with the graces and emotional subtleties of *courtoisie*, and the great appeal of Bernardus' yet-to-be-born *Natura* "ut mundus pulchrius expoliatur."[10]

Courtoisie itself was an intellectual as well as a social ideal, and was treated with widely varying degrees of seriousness as the true property of the learned cleric in the Latin poetry of the period. Andreas Capellanus sees it as the law of love, "per quem universus regitur mundus, et sine ipso nihil boni aliquis operatur in orbe."[11] In the *Altercatio* it is the cleric, whose love is intimately, if ambiguously, bound up with a knowledge of the *arcana* of nature and the gods, who prevails, and in the famous "Love-Council of Remiremont" the beneficiaries of clerkly *curialitas* tell of a state in which their whole being is governed by the wisdom of those clerics[12]

> quorum sapientia   disponuntur omnia,
> totum quicquid agimus,   vel cum nos desipimus.

What these authors treat facetiously takes a more serious form in the early vernacular romances, where *courtoisie* often functions in ways analogous, on the level of society and the *vita activa*, to the role of philosophical wisdom on the intellectual plane. Such correspondences are not limited to those romances which take their *matiere* from classical sources. In fact it was in connection with more strictly medieval themes, and above all in the evolution of the great controlling ideal of the court of Arthur, that the world of romance assumed its characteristic form. Vinaver has explained this evolution as an original exploitation of the poetics and rhetorical theory set forth in the *artes poeticae*,[13] but other links with the

---

[10] "The *Roman de Thebes*, a 'Consolatio Philosophiae,'" *Romanische Forschungen* 72 (1960), pp. 257-58.

[11] *De amore* 1.6 (Trojel, p. 98).

[12] "Das Liebesconcil in Remiremont," ed. Wilhelm Meyer, *Nachrichten von der kgl. Gesellschaft der Wissenschaften zu Göttingen* (1914), p. 15.

[13] Eugene Vinaver, "From Epic to Romance," *Bulletin of the John*

Latin humanism of the twelfth century seem to me equally signifi-
cant. The court of Arthur or Mark may be seen as analogous in its
function to the court of Jove, the "locus universitatis" in the mytho-
graphical poetry of the schools, like the Platonic cosmos, the cen-
tral image of the court imposes thematic coherence and a system
of values on the fictional world in which it functions, and enables
us to analyze the tensions which beset the heroes of romance. For
the theme of the great romances, as of Chartrian allegory, is the
situation of man, and the processes by which the full significance of
his nature and destiny are realized. The cosmic doubts of Boethius
and the anguish of Abelard's *planctus* have their counterpart in the
alienation of Tristan, the continually frustrated idealism of Chré-
tien's Lancelot, the madness of his Yvain. The order of the court,
like that of the cosmos, is threatened by disruption: the formality
of *courtoisie* is a defense against formlessness, and to stray from its
precepts and obligations is to become involved in the encroaching
silva, the dark wood where civilization is tested, and the ordering
power of the mind menaced by psychological chaos.[14]

But the comparison between the Platonic and the courtly uni-
verse is complete only when it is recognized that both stand for
unattainable ideals. The perfect society is as inaccessible as perfect
participation in the natural order. Neither is capable of providing
the human will with a place of rest; each romance hero must meet
the challenge of the *silva* for himself, whether to emerge, like Perce-
val, on a level which transcends mere *avanture*, and where the way
lies open to *sapientia*,[15] or to seek a symbolic triumph, as in Tris-
tan's "Hall of Statues," or the Edenic fantasy of the *Minnegrotte*.

The contrasting careers of Perceval and Tristan illustrate what

---

Rylands Library, Manchester 46 (1964), 488-503; introduction to *The
Works of Sir Thomas Malory*, 2nd edn. (Oxford, 1967), I, lxiv-lxxxii.

[14] See Jean Györy, "Le cosmos, un songe" (cited above, ch. 2, n. 9),
pp. 95-108; Leo Pollman, *Das Epos in den romanischen Literaturen* (Stutt-
gart, 1966), pp. 78-88.

[15] The relation of the *Perceval* of Chrétien to the allegorical treatment of
the *silva* in Chartrian allegory is discussed by Leo Pollman, *Chrétien von
Troyes und der Conte del Graal* (Tübingen, 1965), pp. 86-99; *Das Epos*,
pp. 87-88.

may be called the "epic" and "lyric" tendencies of the romance hero's experience,[16] but they are similar in that their full meaning is accessible only when both heroes pass, like Bernardus' Patricida, beyond the limits of normal experience. The love of Tristan and Isolt seeks continually for perfect expression, and this is achieved only when the lovers complete their tragedy through death. For the *extases* of visionary exaltation and sensual degradation it substitutes, finally, the crystallization of passion through art. Perceval achieves consciousness and purpose insofar as the pursuit and significance of the Grail come to define his existence. This common emphasis on symbolism and on the workings of the imagination is fundamental to serious twelfth-century romance. The discovery that there is a "logic of the will and passions," and the development of literary forms capable of expressing this insight, is one of the great achievements of the twelfth century,[17] and it led writers like Chrétien, Marie de France, Thomas, and later Gottfried to place a special emphasis on the power of the mind to give symbolic expression to its affections. This psychological concern corresponds strikingly to the preoccupation with structure and scientific analysis which we have seen as characteristic of the treatment of symbols in the theology and exegesis of the period.[18] It gave rise to a certain obscurantism: how can we assess the true significance of the dead bird in Marie's *Laustic*, or do justice to the inner feelings of Chrétien's Perceval, as he leans on his lance and contemplates the drops of blood on the snow? But it had as well the function of calling attention to the intricacy and richness of that human nature in which all higher impulses must find their expression. And like Abelard in the *Planctus*, though rarely with such directness, these authors often seem to be suggesting that a certain spiritual significance is intrinsically present in human love.

[16] See Paul Zumthor, *Langue et techniques poétiques à l'époque romane* (Paris, 1963), p. 13.

[17] See the suggestive discussion of the context in which romance developed in R. W. Southern, *The Making of the Middle Ages* (New Haven, 1953), pp. 221-46, and his magnificent account of the growth of the study of logic, pp. 174-84.

[18] See Chenu, *La théologie*, pp. 185-90 (Taylor-Little, pp. 137-45).

Without pursuing such speculations any further, it is worth noting the sense of a complex artistic intention which is conveyed by the occasional reflections of vernacular poets on their own work. The most famous of these is the subtle and enigmatic prologue to the *Lais* of Marie de France, to which Leo Spitzer devoted a commentary which remains a valuable survey of medieval poetics.[19] Though the author cited in the following passage is Priscian, Marie's words are also reminiscent of Macrobius' discussion of the *involucrum*:[20]

> Custume fu as ancïens,
> Ceo testimoine Precïens,
> Es livres ke jadis feseient,
> Assez oscurement diseient
> Pur ceus ki a venir esteient
> E ki aprendre les deveient,
> K'i peüssent gloser la lettre
> E de lur sen le surplus mettre.
> Li philesophe le saveient,
> Par eus meïsmes entendeient,
> Cum plus trespassereit li tens,
> Plus serreient sutil de sens
> E plus se savreient garder
> De ceo k'i ert a trespasser.

It was the custom of the ancient authors, as Priscian testifies, to speak in a somewhat obscure manner in their writings, so that those who were to come after them and study their works might gloss the texts, and so augment them with their own knowledge. For the sages knew [that this would be done] and they themselves realized that the more time passed the more subtle men's understanding

---

[19] "The Prologue to the *Lais* of Marie de France and Medieval Poetics," *Modern Philology* 41 (1943–44), 96-102.

[20] Prologue, lines 9-22, ed. Jean Rychner, *Les Lais de Marie de France* (Paris, 1966), p. 1. The sources and meaning of the passage are discussed in Rychner's excellent notes, pp. 235-38. Marie alludes to the preface of Priscian's *Institutiones grammaticae* (ed. Martin Hertz in *Grammatici latini*, ed. Heinrich Keil, Leipzig, 1857–80, II, 1), where he speaks of the errors which come to light in the course of the transmission of the art of grammar "cuius auctores, quanto sunt iuniores, tanto perspicaciores, et ingeniis floruisse et diligentia valuisse omnium iudicio confirmantur eruditissimorum."

would be, and that they would be better able to avoid passing over what was [contained in these writings].

The precise emphasis of these lines, and of the allusion to Priscian, is difficult to determine, for the formula *quanto iuniores, tanto perspicaciores*, like the equally famous comparison of the *moderni* to dwarfs perched on the shoulders of the giants of antiquity,[21] may be read as affirming at once the greater perspective and accumulated knowledge of the modern, and his utter dependence on the ancients for authoritative confirmation of his new insights.[22] Moreover, the obscurity of the ancients is both a consequence of the dim age in which they lived and a matter of deliberate artistic intention.[23]

I think both kinds of emphasis are present in Marie's prologue; she exploits Priscian's figure as a way of alluding to the delicacy and acuteness with which she herself has refined the traditional material of her *Lais*, and at the same time invites the reader, not altogether frivolously, to treat them as in some way comparable to the *integumenta* of the Latin authors.[24] The fulfillment of this promise, it seems to me, is the love-world of the *Lais*, where, with a certain fine irony, Marie grants fulfillment to the fantasies of a Lanval, a miraculous resolution to the involved affairs of Eliduc, an artistic reincarnation to the love described in the *Laustic*. It is a world whose values are neither worldly nor spiritual, where biblical paral-

[21] The image is usually attributed to Bernard of Chartres on the authority of John of Salisbury, *Metalogicon* 3.4 (Webb, p. 136).

[22] See Edouard Jeauneau, " 'Nani gigantium humeris insidentes.' Essai d'interpretation de Bernard de Chartres," *Vivarium* 5 (1967-68), 79-99.

[23] Here my reading differs from that of Mortimer J. Donovan, "Priscian and the Obscurity of the Ancients," *Speculum* 36 (1961), 79, who mentions Macrobius, but denies that Marie has any such notion as the *involucrum* in mind.

[24] See D. W. Robertson, "Marie de France, *Lais*, Prologue, 13-16," *Modern Language Notes* 64 (1949), 336-38. He finds Marie's words suggestive of the terms commonly used to characterize the exegesis of Scripture. The emphasis on hard work in lines 23-30 of the Prologue seems to me to refer to the task of Marie herself, but may also be taken as a reference to the interpretative effort demanded of her reader, the sort of *labor* enjoined upon the would-be exegete by Augustine, *De doctrina christiana* 2.6.7. Augustine's words are quoted in connection with the Macrobian notion of the *involucrum* by Abelard, *Introductio* 1.20 (PL 178.1021-22).

lels and reminiscences of the Celtic otherworld form and disperse, whose point is precisely in the delicacy with which it balances the demands of spiritual and social reality, and invites us to see in her sketches of romantic love the lineaments of higher or harder truths without committing ourselves to either.

The *integumenta* to which Marie seems to allude are thus a very different thing from the mythical and cosmological motifs of the school-poets. Where these appear at all in vernacular romance they seem, like the bizarre versions of biblical history and liturgical symbolism in the thirteenth-century cycles, to have undergone a "sea-change," and their reference to the moral and cosmic contexts of mythographic tradition is almost always oblique. The following examples, however, together with the more general correspondences discussed above, seem to me to indicate a keen awareness of this tradition.

On the face of it the *Roman d'Eneas* seems wholly free of the philosophical associations with which Bernardus and the mythographic tradition had encumbered Vergil's epic. Passing references to Cupid as the "freres charnaus" of Eneas,[25] and to the Sibyl as having knowledge of the Liberal Arts, suggest a familiarity with Bernardus' *Commentum*, but there is a marked absence, even a deliberate avoidance of the philosophical,[26] and certainly nothing approaching a consistent allegorical intention.

At the same time there are underlying themes. Adler has called attention to the *topos* of the *puer senex*, which illustrates the compatibility of Eneas and Lavine, and contrasts the latter, young yet self-aware, with the aging and recklessly passionate Dido,[27] while

[25] *Eneas*, lines 8630-33, 8922-24. All references are to the edition of J. J. Salverda de Grave (2 vols., Paris, 1925–31). Cp. Bernardus' account of the parallel genealogies of Cupid and Aeneas, *Commentum*, p. 10.

[26] See Peter R. Grillo, "The Courtly Background in the Roman d'Eneas," *Neuphilologische Mitteilungen* 69 (1968), pp. 688-89.

[27] "Eneas and Lavine: *Puer et Puella Senes*," *Romanische Forschungen* 71 (1959), pp. 73-91. Adler seems, however, to go too far in denying the presence of allegory; see, e.g., his declaration that we must not look for a figural intention in *topoi* like the *puella senex*, but must rather show how these help to evoke "a classically sumptuous setting for the display of erotic Ovidian

Helen Laurie finds in Lavine's lively and articulate response to falling in love the expression of a kind of naturalism, a rhetorical counterpart to the physical theories of Calcidius and ultimately Aristotle, and an affirmation of the goodness of earthly love.[28] Another broad theme, at once central and hard to define, might be called the theme of necessity, and consists in a variety of recurrent allusions to the interplay of historical and psychological forces which form a backdrop for the poem. For the legacy of Troy and of Paris, of Eneas' thwarted search for sustained love and friendship, of endless responsibility and endless longing, shapes the action of the *Eneas* as of the *Aeneid*, and urges it forward in a variety of ways. From the opening lines revenge is a major theme. The Trojan War is emphatically Menelaus' war, his revenge, and on a deeper level that of Pallas and Juno, against Paris,[29] and the effects of these primordial causes are almost literally handed on as the poem proceeds. The giving of gifts is a recurring motif, and provides a pattern of allusions which enables us to set the different aspects of necessity in their proper perspective. On the most direct level, Eneas gives Dido the sword with which she eventually kills herself;[30] love and betrayal are the only factors here. On his arrival in Italy, Eneas sends to King Latin a crown and mantle which Dido had given him and a golden vessel presented to him by Menelaus during an ambassadorial encounter in the course of the Trojan War.[31] The effect here is more complex, for it recalls the chaos which love has brought to two kingdoms, and the contradictory roles that Eneas has been forced to play by his peculiar destiny, and suggests how his present role as lover, destroyer of one kingdom and founder of another brings the forces of the past to bear on the action of the present. A similar cluster of associations accompanies

---

dialectic." The two intentions do not seem to me altogether mutually exclusive.

[28] " 'Eneas' and the Doctrine of Courtly Love," *Modern Language Review* 64 (1969), 283-94.

[29] On Menelaus, see *Eneas*, lines 1, 22, 863, 879. On Pallas and Juno, lines 93-182.

[30] *Ibid.*, lines 2025-32.　　　　[31] *Ibid.*, lines 3133-42, 3216-20.

the two beautiful cloths, gifts of Paris and Dido, which Eneas places on the bier of the Arcadian prince Pallas,[32] and which provide a vivid image of the contrast between Pallas' pure and incorruptible goodness and beauty and the world of passion and betrayal in which Eneas is forced to act. For Pallas, like the Italian warriormaiden Camile, exists in an essentially abstract relation to the action of the *Eneas*: both are images of an ideal balance of youth, vitality, beauty, and chivalric excellence which, as the *Eneas* poet recognizes with Vergilian clarity, cannot endure in the world of necessity. Pallas is cut down, like Camile, in his youthful perfection, and symbolically enshrined, like Tristan and Isolt, as the image of an unrealizable love.[33] His memory is at once a solace and a goad to the frustrated hero from whom he is cut off.

The deepest meanings naturally adhere to the gifts of the gods, from Venus' requital of the judgment of Paris to the favor of Juno which is at once the reward and the emblem of Dido's fatal *desmesure*,[34] and the arms forged for Eneas by Vulcan at the instigation of Venus. The latter episode is developed at length and includes a number of details not found in Vergil. As in the *Aeneid*, Venus gains her request by sexual means, but the *Eneas* poet adds that Vulcan is seduced the more easily because Venus, angered at his exposure of her relations with Mars, has denied herself to him for seven years.[35] After a brief digression to explain this episode, the poet gives a long description of the arms themselves. The great shield of the *Aeneid*, with its panorama of Roman history, is omitted, and is replaced by this account of a standard suspended from the hero's lance:[36]

[32] *Ibid.*, lines 6117-24.

[33] Among the many verbal and imagistic parallels between the accounts of the two figures, one may mention their common virginity (note especially the Diana-like response of the "demoisel" Pallas to his first sight of the Trojans, *ibid.*, lines 4654-60), and the elaborate descriptions of their tombs (e.g., lines 6510-18, 7673-81).

[34] See *ibid.*, lines 515-27.

[35] *Ibid.*, lines 4349-54. Do these correspond to the seven years during which Aeneas' destiny has been suspended?

[36] *Ibid.*, lines 4523-42. With 4525-26 cp. 3137-38.

Venus i ferma une ansoigne;
longuement l'ot Mars en domaine,
il li dona par drüerie,
quant el devint primes s'amie;
bien fu tissu et bien ovree
et par listes fu d'or broudee;
cent torsels valut d'altres dras.
Par anvie l'ot fet Pallas:
ele l'ovra par grant mestrie,
quant Arannes l'ot aatie. . . .
Por ce qu'el fist meillor ovraigne,
Aranne mua an iraigne,
qui contre li s'ert aatie;
s'entente ot mis tote sa vie
en tailes faire et an filer,
por ce ne puet ancor finer:
toz tens file iraigne et tist,
sa filace de son vantre ist.

[To the lance] Venus affixed an ensign; it had long been in the possession of Mars, and he had given it to her as a token when first she became his mistress. It was finely woven and finely worked, and was embroidered with bands of gold. It was worth a hundred pieces of any other kind of cloth. Pallas had made it in a spirit of rivalry: she worked it, with great skill, when Arachne had provoked her. . . . And because Arachne produced a superior piece of work, she changed her to a spider. She had devoted all her life to making cloth and spinning; because of this she can never again complete her task. The spider spins and weaves through all time. Her flax issues from her own belly.

The Ovidian digressions which bracket the account of Vulcan's work illustrate the ambiguous relation of the divinities involved to the action of the poem. If we keep in mind the common interpretation of Vulcan's exposure of Venus and Mars as the fettering of *virtus* by *consuetudo*, and recall that Arachne was punished by Pallas for having depicted the amours of the gods in all their complexity, we may see the two episodes as pointing to parallel subversions of the qualities ideally associated with Vulcan and Pallas. Vulcan, responding to the *losengerie* of Venus, succumbs to the sensuality he had once exposed and controlled. Pallas, provoked to

233

reply in kind to the *anvie* of Arachne, becomes involved herself in Arachne's web.[37] The ordering function of the two divinities, and its subversion, bring into focus the broad theme of divine rivalry and animosity, and define the way in which Eneas' own heroic mission is affected by passion and revenge. For the implications of this description extend to the very conclusion of the Vergilian action, where the death of Turnus is described in non-Vergilian terms which again bring the names of Vulcan and Pallas into conjunction, and so allude, quietly but distinctly, to the psychological complexities with which the two are now linked. As Eneas beholds the ring of the dead prince Pallas on the hand of Turnus[38]

> . . . sailli avant,
> se l'a feru de maintenant,
> o le branc que Vulcans forja
> an prist lo chief: Pallas vanja.

He moved forward and struck him down at once. With the sword which Vulcan had forged he cut off his head: thus he avenged Pallas.

Thus the image of the standard woven by Pallas plays an important role in preserving something of the Vergilian psychological complexity in the generally simpler and more optimistic *Eneas*. The function of the image is essentially that played by the image of Flora's saddle in the *Altercatio*, which may very well have inspired it. There too, though in a less serious context, the task of the forging of a great shield is, so to speak, laid aside, in favor of a more strictly psychological image.[39] In both cases the image has a broad

---

[37] An ironic parallel to the moralization of the Vulcan-Venus-Mars episode is provided by Arnulf's interpretation of the fate of Arachne as illustrating how "insipientia seipsam seducit" (Ghisalberti, "Arnolfo d'Orléans," p. 215), a moral which might here be applied to Sapientia herself.

[38] *Eneas*, lines 9811-14. My reading of course assumes a play on the name of the Arcadian prince Pallas.

[39] As Helen Laurie observes, "Virgil's contemporaries might thrill at the words 'tantae molis erat Romanam condere gentem,' but for a man of the eleventh or twelfth centuries, whatever reverence or admiration he felt for the past, the old civilization had passed away, the life of the individual as

controlling function and defines the limits within which the human subject pursues his goals.

There is, as I have said, little trace of Fulgentius' and Bernardus' conception of the *Aeneid* as *Bildungsroman* in the *Eneas*, but the role of Vulcan and Pallas suggests the possibility that this is a deliberate adjustment. For Pallas in the Eneas is hardly the figure of divine wisdom we have seen before; she is hostile and self-interested, both in relation to the Trojans and in her treatment of Arachne. Venus' appropriation of Pallas' handiwork suggests a further compromising of her authority, and brings her activity into an intimate relation with that of Vulcan.

What has happened, I think, is that Pallas, reason in the highest sense, has ceased to exercise her traditional function under the pressure of human sinfulness and the stern limitations of necessity. In the hard world of the *Aeneid* and *Eneas* continuity is maintained only through such complex manipulations of impulse and motivation as that suggested by the history of Pallas' embroidery, and the allusive terms in which Eneas' final decisive action is described. Pallas' motives and actions are emblematic and indirectly illuminating as reflections of the human situation, but authority has passed into the hands of Vulcan. It is he who forges Eneas' arms, and so provides the means through which necessity is kept at bay and destiny fulfilled.

Thus this image, so central to the *Eneas*, is central also to the mythographical tradition we have considered. Bearing in mind the difficulty of determining chronology and precise influence, we may perhaps see in it a shrewd comment on the image of the saddle in the *Altercatio*; as illuminating retrospectively the issue of the battle of the gods as described in the "Dant ad veris honorem," where Vulcan's intervention saves the day when Pallas has been put to flight; and, tracing the development of this same theme, as providing a gloss on the "novercation" of Pallas in the *Metamor-*

---

an embodied soul with a high destiny was the most important thing on earth." ("'Eneas' and the Doctrine of Courtly Love," p. 290.)

235

phosis Goliae.[40] We may, finally, discern in the arms forged by Vulcan a striking analogy, if not indeed a deliberate allusion to the *genialibus armis* with which the *genii* of procreation, operating at a similar remove from rational awareness, battle the Fates and preserve the continuity of human life in the *De mundi universitate.* In that work, too, as I have suggested, the lineaments of the *Aeneid* as a characterization of the *vita activa* are preserved.

An elaborate pattern of allusion to the "philosophical" *Aeneid* appears in the *Erec et Enide* of Chrétien de Troyes.[41] The *Erec* is by far the most bookish of Chrétien's works, with its many allusions to Arthurian and other traditional heroes, to the story of Tristan, and, most significantly for our purposes, in its use of Vergil and "Macrobius." Two passages define the role of these *auctores* in the poem. The first occurs immediately after the curing of Erec and the reaffirmation of his love for Enide, and helps to introduce the adventure of the "Joie de la Cort." Enide has been presented with a handsome palfrey, and the poet, after describing its remarkably colored head and rich trappings, lingers over the saddle bows, on which is depicted[42]

comant Eneas vint de Troye,	comant ele por lui s'ocist,
comant a Cartaige a grant joie	comant Eneas puis conquist
Dido an son leu le reçut,	Laurente et tote Lonbardie,
comant Eneas la deçut,	dom il fu rois tote sa vie.

> How Aeneas came from Troy, how at Carthage with great joy Dido received him to her bed, how Aeneas deceived her, and how for him she killed herself, how Aeneas conquered Laurentum and all Lombardy, of which he was king all his life.

The summary is terse and straightforward, and the sharp repetitions of "comant," interrupted only by the brief interlude of Aeneas' sojourn with Dido, serve to mark the stages of his long *via laborum.*

[40] See above, ch. 3, pp. 130, 134-37.

[41] The following discussion of the *Erec* owes a great deal to the study of my friend Joseph S. Wittig, "The Aeneas-Dido Allusion in Chrétien's *Erec et Enide,*" *Comparative Literature* 22 (1970), 237-53.

[42] *Erec et Enide,* lines 5291-98. The text is that of Mario Roques (Paris, 1966), the translation by W. W. Comfort, *Arthurian Romances by Chrétien de Troyes* (London, 1914), p. 69.

We are obviously intended to ponder the relevance of the story of
Aeneas to that of Erec, and it is clear that there are a number of
correspondences. In the early stages of the *Erec* the hero moves
swiftly to the plateau of erotic fulfillment, only to be exposed as
having lost all self-awareness, even as Aeneas is rebuked by Mer-
cury and induced to abandon Dido. But Enide is, in a sense, the
Lavinia as well as the Dido of Erec's career, and his reunion with
her is an equally important point in his career. For the discovery
of her true importance in his life involves a coming to terms with
himself. This new self-control is confirmed by the adventure of the
"Joie de la Cort," and leads logically to his coronation.[43] He has
achieved a capacity for fruitful activity and so both attains his own
Laurentum and becomes a king, like Dante, "sovra se."

From the beginning Enide seems part of some such larger pat-
tern of meaning. When she first appears, Chrétien remarks of her
shabby dress,[44]

> povre estoit la robe dehors,
> mes desoz estoit biax li cors.

Shortly thereafter her father assures Erec[45]

> Molt est bele, mes mialz asez
> vaut ses savoirs que sa biautez.

These linked references lead inward in a way which suggests not
only a truer worth in Enide than Erec at first discovers, but also
the possibility that she is herself only a stage in a figural pattern,
that Erec's love of her must lead to something higher. The promise
of these couplets is largely fulfilled by the account of her saddle,
which, like the description of the saddle of Flora and that of the
standard in the *Eneas*, projects the action of the poem against a
larger background. We are shown in the full realization of Erec's
love for Enide all that separates the transitory sensuality of Aeneas'
experience with Dido from the *certa requies* offered by Laurentum
and (though she is not mentioned at this point) Lavinia.[46]

[43] See Jean Frappier, *Chrétien de Troyes* (Paris, 1957), pp. 92-94.
[44] *Erec*, lines 409-10.   [45] *Ibid.*, lines 537-38.
[46] That Chrétien has the conventional associations of Dido and (such as

With this pattern in mind one may well wonder why, when the name of Lavinia is finally introduced, it is connected, not with Enide, but with her cousin, the prisoner of the *Joie,* who is said to be four times fairer than Lavinia.[47] The seemingly misplaced allusion and the loose hyperbole call attention to themselves and seem to blemish the resolution of Erec's personal Aeneid. The point here, I think, is that the "Joie de la Cort" not only completes the love story, but marks a new departure. Erec is about to go beyond such success as marriage implies and assume higher responsibilities. The values hinted at in the early allusions to Enide's inner beauty and wisdom, and the associations of the carved saddle, are finally more than the earthly ideal of mature marriage is adequate to convey. Hence in the coronation scene the controlling images center not on Enide, but on Erec himself.

The most important of these images occur in the description of Erec's coronation robes and of the scepter which Arthur bestows upon him. The account of the robe is too long to quote but its main emphasis is on images of the four sciences of the *quadrivium,* in the description of which Chrétien professes to follow the account of "Macrobe." The emphasis of his characterizations of the individual arts is more on their relation to the physical world than on their philosophical significance; arithmetic "numbers the leaves of the forest," and music is primarily a source of "deduit."[48] But this is appropriate to the quasi-philosophical tone of the episode as a whole, and typical of the oblique and half-playful manner of so many of Chrétien's uses of portentious imagery.[49] In any case Chré-

---

they are) of Lavinia in mind is argued convincingly by Wittig (see above, n. 41).

[47] *Erec,* lines 5828-43.   [48] *Ibid.,* lines 6903-14.

[49] See, e.g., the description of Enide's palfrey (lines 5275-81) and the account of the beasts whose fur forms the lining of Erec's mantle (lines 6732-41). In such passages Chrétien seems to play off his audience's high susceptibility to the appeal of the marvellous against their capacity to seek out his deeper meaning—a test to which his heroes are continually being subjected. But at times the bizarre and lavish detail of such passages seems to allude to a symbolism far more obscure and profound than the conventional poetic *integumentum,* something with the richness and variety of biblical imagery.

tien's rhetorical account of the *quadrivium* seems to me to recall the earlier references to the *Aeneid*, and with them to define the sense in which Erec's destiny both parallels and finally transcends that of Aeneas. With the introduction of the *quadrivium* all worldly activity is set in a new perspective, and he becomes a philosopher-king, for whom earthly dominion is only a stage in the realization of a higher objective. This divergence from the heroic model may be compared with Bernardus' allegorization of the *Aeneid* itself, in which the odyssey of the early books becomes a prelude to the study of philosophy. Chrétien, by incorporating the whole *Aeneid*, sets off his transcendent emphasis all the more strikingly.

The stress on transcendence is confirmed, I think, by the description of Erec's scepter, made of a single emerald and carved with the images of all creatures:[50]

> La verité dire vos os
> qu'an tot le monde n'a meniere
> de poisson, ne de beste fiere,
> ne d'ome, ne d'oisel volage,
> que chascuns lonc sa propre ymage
> n'i fust ovrez et antailliez.

I dare to tell you in very truth that in all the world there is no manner of fish or wild beast, or of man, or of flying bird, that was not worked and chiselled on it with its proper figure.

It is significant that each creature appears in "sa propre ymage." The scepter represents an Edenic vision in which things are seen in their true natures and as a unity, as they were once beheld by man before the fall.[51] This vision and its setting recall the climactic visions of Patricida and Alain's Genius, and constitute a particularly appropriate image for the final position of Erec. His progress through the poem has been parallelled by the penetration of a series of *integumenta*: the beauty of Enide, the heroic story of the

---

[50] *Erec*, lines 6814-19; tr. Comfort, p. 89.

[51] "Proper" attributes or *propria* are those which adhere to a thing by definition or as originally created. Thus Alain de Lille refers to the condition of *thesis* in which man existed before the fall as "proprius status hominis," "status propriae mentis, vel forma" (*Regulae*, art. 99, quoted above, ch. 5, n. 11).

Aeneid, poetry and rhetoric have performed their proper role as "introducers to philosophy," culminating in the image of a philosophical kingship which comprehends and transcends the natural order itself, governing by right of dignity the universe represented by the scepter.

The *Erec* is, as I have suggested, atypical in the literary character of its allusions, but it is closely related to the later romances of Chrétien in theme and narrative pattern. Without going so far as Leo Pollman, who finds the archetypal pattern of Chrétien's narratives in Bernardus' account of the evolution of created life from chaos,[52] I would suggest that the thematic complexity which Chrétien achieved in the *Erec* by bringing the "active" and "philosophical" versions of the *Aeneid* into confrontation continued to interest him in his creation of later romances, and may be seen as his equivalent to the Chartrian theme of intellectual pilgrimage. The *Perceval*, in which the meaning of the hero's quest is shown to transcend the limits of earthly life, and to demand an intuitive penetration to the inner meaning of experience, is the most obvious instance. But both the *Yvain* and the *Lancelot*, which deal, like *Erec*, with a love which is formed, disrupted, and finally reestablished, suggest a certain dissatisfaction on the part of Chrétien with this kind of resolution. The almost Christ-like character of Lancelot's heroism and suffering in liberating Guinevere from her captivity in Gorre is hardly requited by his arbitrary and belittling treatment at her hands, and it is perhaps significant that Chrétien breaks off the story with his hero imprisoned in a tower, for it illustrates effectively the self-defeating tendencies of Lancelot's idolatrous love. The *Yvain*, again, derives its deepest meaning from the experience of the hero during the years of exile which separate his marriage with Laudine from the reunion with her which concludes the poem. But here too we are given a sense of the largeness of the hero's nature and the superiority of his heroism to that of mere textbook chivalry which makes his reentry into conventional relations with his legalistically minded lady seem very constraining. One feels that there will always be a level on which Yvain and his

[52] See above, n. 15.

lion commune apart. All three poems suggest in their various ways that full self-realization demands the transcendence of even the noblest of merely social ideals, and set heroic endeavor in the larger context of spiritual pilgrimage.

The dialogue between the active and the philosophical conception of heroic experience as formulated by Chrétien is a major contribution to the resources of medieval narrative poetry, and was exploited by poets so diverse as Dante and Jean de Meun. It is important to recognize that this theme is already implicit in the *Eneas* and even the *De mundi,* and that Chrétien is consciously working in a classical tradition of thought and expression. The structure of his romances, like the imagery of the scene of Erec's coronation and the account of the arming of Eneas, shows the themes and motifs of Chartrian poetry finding vernacular equivalents. As Faral clearly saw,[53] Chrétien and his anonymous predecessor drew their very conception of the poet from the literary activity of the schools, and the motifs which we have considered illustrate their recognition of the new responsibilities and significances which were being assigned to imaginative expression, metaphor and symbol, in the intellectual centers of their day. Chrétien's achievement involves much more than this, for in his romances a complete and distinctive literary world is created. But whether or not we see this world as a deliberately conceived equivalent for the Platonic cosmos of the Chartrian poets, it shows him susceptible to a fascination like that of the authors of the *Altercatio* and the *Metamorphosis Goliae* with the idea of the poem as a cosmos, ordered and charged with meaning by its own autonomous imagery. And with a remarkable sureness and delicacy Chrétien uses his imagery to show the necessity, for the Christian hero, of passing beyond the state of rapport with this cosmos which happy and fulfilling marriage implies. In this his vision is at one with that of the great Chartrian allegorists.

[53] *Recherches sur les sources,* pp. 194-95, 398-99; Pollman, *Das Epos,* pp. 64-67.

CHAPTER SEVEN

CHARTRIAN ALLEGORY AND THE WORLD

1. The *Architrenius*

Though Chrétien deals with man's life in the world, analyzes concrete moral problems, and goes far beyond Alain in exploiting the moral and spiritual suggestions implicit in the conventions and rituals of *courtoisie*, his emphasis is finally on transcendent values. His work resolves itself in the world-transforming experience of Perceval, and the actions and sufferings of all his heroes are most meaningful when seen as images of spiritual discipline, or as stages in the attainment of transcendent wisdom. Other poets of the later twelfth century, however, were coming to terms with the *silva* of experience in other ways. Even among the most conservative of the clergy and nobility, courtly values, political and social, were an object of increasing interest, and the humanism of the schools nourished an intense interest in ancient moral philosophy. I have already alluded to the growth of the "intellectual proletariat,"[1] the new class of educated men living in the world. In general, clerical and courtly society were attaining a new degree of self-awareness, and it was perhaps inevitable that there should arise a tendency to justify worldly existence wholly in worldly terms. This tendency, exploited for purposes of comedy in the *Altercatio*, is perceptible in romance to the extent that the court displaces more abstract and spiritual ideals as the "locus universitatis." In the poetry of the schools its fullest expression is the *Architrenius* of Jean de Hanville, a remarkable blend of Chartrian allegory and social satire which seems to have been written at least partly to challenge the view of the relations between man and Nature presented by Alain. The poem has fundamental defects, due partly to the fact that it is in many ways a transitional work. It differs from previous Char-

---

[1] See above, ch. 3, pp. 126-27.

trian poems on the grand scale in its wholly conventional, almost casual use of natural philosophy, the more or less topical nature of many of its allusions, and its reliance on sheer rhetoric to perform the function of Alain's carefully constructed cosmic-sacramental universe. The narrative is extremely unwieldy, and mingles realistic description with abstract allegorical tableaux in a confusing way, but these defects and the often absurd length of Jean's descriptions and declamations coexist with real merits. Jean had mastered the techniques of Bernardus and Alain, and made a careful study of Horace and Juvenal. His blending of the allegorical and the realistic is at its most successful an important step in the direction of Jean de Meun and Chaucer, and he has also something of their ability to incarnate vice in recognizable human form.

The theme of the *Architrenius*, as summarized in its opening lines, is the "furor ingenii" of the modern world and its distorting effects. An elaborate denunciation of the sins of the age stresses the contamination of all life by human artifice, the perversion of will and purpose by dissipation, and the decline of mankind into a general *segnities* and impotence. The situation is that with which Alain's allegories begin, but here the *planctus* which follows is uttered not by Nature, but by her human offspring Architrenius, the "Arch-Weeper," a young man on the threshold of maturity who is horrified at what seems to him the corruption of all life. Shocked to discover that all his thoughts and impulses tend to vice, he accuses Nature of having brought him into the world defenseless. The Nature he depicts is a terrifying power, scarcely compatible with the beautiful and benevolent goddess of Alain:[2]

> Natura est quodcumque vides, incudibus illa
> Fabricat omniparis quidvis operaria nutu
> Construit, eventusque novi miracula spargit.
> Illa potest rerum solitos avertere cursus;
> Enormesque serit monstrorum prodiga formas,
> Gignendique stylum variat, partuque timendo
> Lineat anomalos larvosa puerpera vultus.

[2] *Architrenius*, ed. Wright, *Anglo-Latin Satirical Poets* I, 248. With the opening words cp. Lucan, *De bello civili* 9.580.

243

Whatever you behold is Nature: she labors at her forge, an omnifarious artisan, and creates anything at a nod, and spreads abroad a miraculous array of new events. She has power to alter the normal course of events; prodigal, she litters the world with huge and monstrous shapes. She is ever changing the manner of her conception, and with fantastic fertility gives shape to abnormal beings by a fearful labor.

As in the *Anticlaudianus*, Nature in general seems to be assigned responsibility for those "left-handed" creations which the *De planctu* had attributed to man's betrayal of Genius. The difference is that these seem to characterize the goddess for Architrenius, and there is no hint in his words of her traditionally providential role. He presents a long catalogue of the freaks and atrocities she has produced, its fantastic detail interspersed with hints of the fears which have colored his view of reality:[3]

> Non est passa levi Crassum mollescere risu,
> Antoniam Drusi sordente madescere sputo,
> Fumida Pomponii solvi ructatibus ora,
> Fulmine fortunae Socratis pallescere vultus,
> Aut miseris lethos rigidum flexisse tenorem.

She (i.e., Nature) did not allow Crassus to relax in a gentle smile, nor Antonia, wife of Drusus, to issue a shower of spittle, nor the steaming face of Pomponius to find relief in belching, nor the countenance of Socrates to grow pale at the menace of his fate—nor has death relaxed its hold on wretched mortals.

At this point Architrenius resolves to go forth into the world and seek out Nature "wheresoever she may have hidden her Lares," in the hope that his hapless situation may arouse her motherly compassion.

The distortion of the hero's vision is analyzed in the description of the Court of Venus, the first way station on his journey and allegorically the most illuminating. Here he is charmed by the sight of a maiden whose grace and beauty are all but divine, and

---

[3] Wright, p. 250. The four exempla are taken from Solinus, *Collectanea rerum memorabilium* 1.72-74 (ed. T. Mommsen, Berlin, 1864, p. 21).

require a *descriptio* of some three hundred lines. This occasions the
mention of the "authentic" Nature of Chartrian allegory:[4]

> Consuluit Natura modum, cum sedula tantum
> Desudaret opus, ne qua delinqueret, utque
> Artificis digitos exemplar duceret . . .

Nature pondered long over her plan, eager though she was to per-
form so great a work, lest anything be lacking, and so that the
exemplar might guide her shaping fingers . . .

But Architrenius' reaction is more lustful than aesthetic, an exag-
gerated version of that sought by Matthew of Vendome in address-
ing his sumptuous description of the female body to the "lector
deliciosus."[5] This response is in sharp contrast to Jean's own de-
scription, which is remarkably free of the standard erotic *blanditiae*,
and makes it clear that whatever feelings of lust the maiden arouses
originate in the mind of the beholder. Particularly striking is the
account of the *hortus secretior*, frankly but delicately described in
terms which recall Bernardus' description of the earthly Paradise
and the *muscosi fontes* of classical pastoral:[6]

> Invius exclusae Veneri secretior hortus
> Flore pudicitiae tenero pubescit, ubique
> Vernat inattritus, nec adulto saucius aevo.
> Nondum praeda pudor vacua qui regnat in aula,
> Solus habens thalamos ubi non admittitur hospes.
> Temperat innocuas juvenilis flamma favillas,
> Nec Venus intrudit quo mores pruriat ignem;
> Nec divertit amor ad inhospita tecta pudoris. . . .
> Pro foribus lanugo sedet, primoque iuventae
> Vellere mollescit, nec multa in limine serpit,
> Sed summo tenuem praecludit margine muscum.

Inaccessible, to the exclusion of Venus herself, a hidden garden
flourishes with the tender bloom of chastity. Here blooms unsul-
lied, not yet disturbed by maturity, a modesty still unravaged, rul-

[4] Wright, p. 258.
[5] With the opening portion of Book Two (Wright, pp. 258ff.) cp. *Ars versificatoria* 1.57 (ed. Faral, *Les arts poétiques*, p. 130).
[6] Wright, p. 259.

ing over an empty court, and possessing alone that couch to which no guest is admitted. Her youthful flame tempers its harmless spark, and Venus does not intrude her ways to give a wantonness to its glow, nor does love steer his course to this unfriendly refuge of modesty. . . . Soft down lies about the portals, soft with the first fleeciness of youth; it strays not in profusion but confines its mossy carpet to the outermost edge.

The beauty of this passage is enhanced by subtler allusions as well: to the womb of Silva in the *De mundi universitate,* and to Claudian's "Cave of Nature," matrix of all medieval descriptions of the figures of Nature and Genius.[7] Such allusions reveal a sureness of touch, a Chartrian sense of the larger life implicit in budding sexuality which the excesses of the description as a whole tend to obscure.

Architrenius cannot see this hidden beauty, though his thoughts are on things unseen, "nudaque pro speculo velatae gratia servit." What stimulates his imagination is not so much the natural sexual attractiveness of the girl as a certain more ambiguous quality. "It is just this tender and girlish budding that lures the eye to boys of tender years as well," says Jean,[8] and he develops this point by following the description of the maiden with an equally elaborate description of Cupid, in which the emphasis is on Cupid's loose, light garments and provocative attitude; these wholly divert Architrenius' attention, for they are, in effect, superimposed on the actual beauty of the maiden, and correspond to the false "texts" described in the *De planctu.* The description of the maiden herself is a genuine *integumentum,* in which physical purity suggests a state of primal innocence and vitality. The *descriptio Cupidinis* is mere titillating *blanditia,* the trope which never resolves itself in allegory, but instead exploits the resources of true poetry to suggest pseudonatural processes and reveal how "levitas occulta forensi/Scribitur in cultu."[9] Through the cooperation of his own imagination with the corrupt trappings of his environment, Architrenius has created

---

[7] With the fourth line of the passage quoted cp. *De mundi* 1.1, line 56, p. 8; with the ninth line cp. Claudian, *De consulatu Stilichonis* 2.432.

[8] Wright, p. 255.   [9] *Ibid.,* p. 263.

a "monster" of his own, wholly independent of the agency of Nature, and has allowed it to divert his feelings from the channels of natural fulfillment.

This passage sets a general tone for the scenes which follow, and which describe the ways in which man labors to undo the work of Nature by subjecting her to his own perverted will, or tries to rival her with new productions of his own. Thus the devotés of gluttony, whom Architrenius visits next, after transforming substance into accident, reduce created life to chaos again in their tormented bellies, "Naturae vile sepulcrum." In a powerful tirade against the state of affairs in the schools of Paris, the truly fulfilling labors of the hungry scholars in whose minds the "mundus intellectualis" is realized anew are contrasted with their social situation, the poverty which works to create a condition of primeval squalor around them.[10]

The evils of the court are summarized in Jean's account of the Palace of Ambition, a magnificent structure whose towers overtop Olympus, but whose lower passages descend imperceptibly to the Styx and Tartarus. The palace is a monument of worldly glory, a new universe, "sole suo contenta," created by man in defiance of time, and in a vain attempt to preserve the illusion of control over the workings of the real universe. The centerpiece of Jean's description is a magnificent tapestry, the work of Arachne, on which are described the creation, the Trojan War, and a catalogue of famous lovers which is climaxed by a picture of Hercules, driven by his love for Omphale to take up the work of a handmaid. These are surrounded by representations of the bounty and philanthropy of Nature, but the description concludes with the image of Fortune; we are reminded that what is being described is an artifice, and an image of false security:[11]

> ibi laeta et tristia spargit
> Ambigua Fortuna manu, fati exitus omnis
> Texitur et tenui dependent omnia filo.

Here Fortune's equivocating hand scatters joy and sadness; all the course of fate is woven, and all hangs by a slender thread.

[10] Ibid., pp. 275-91.   [11] Ibid., p. 301.

The image of the tapestry, together with the references to the sub-
jection of Hercules and the operation of Fortune, recalls the elab-
orate history of the standard affixed to Aeneas' spear in the *Roman
d'Eneas*. But there it was the gods whose activities impinged upon
human life, shaping the course of events, while here human *in-
genium* has projected itself upon the universe, "that a second Na-
ture may equal Nature in the fruits of her industry, a new Minerva
rival Minerva."[12] The result is a bizarre and distorted version of
the ideal of the court as the controlling center of life. By such rhe-
torical means Jean de Hanville suggests the absence of any norm
in Nature capable of stabilizing human conduct. As the *Largitas*
of the *De planctu* had become confounded with prodigality by a
seemingly inevitable perversion, so here Nature herself seems to
feed the dissipation of Architrenius and his fellow sinners. This is
the burden of Architrenius' complaint against her, and the ironic
moral of one scene after another in the poem. As for Fulgentius,
plenitude seems here to be the mother of lust.

After surveying the works of the presumptuous, the avaricious,
and the warlike, Architrenius comes to Thule, home of the ancient
philosophers, and there receives a long lesson in the vanity of
worldly things and the need of discipline. The lesson runs to well
over a thousand lines, and falls into four more or less clearly defina-
ble stages. The first deals with self-governance and the scorning of
worldly values: Cato and Diogenes lecture Architrenius on the
evils of wealth, Democritus on the folly of hoarding and Cicero on
that of squandering, Seneca and Boethius on the uncertainties of
the courtier's life.[13] The second stage begins with a diatribe against
Venus by Xenocrates. The tone is shrill and the rhetoric hyperboli-
cal, building to the point at which lust seems to menace the entire
universe:[14]

> Ha! Venus, ad nutum trahis omnia numina coeli,
> Astra moves, alioque rotas errore planetas,
> Accendis gelidam sine fratris lampade Phoeben
> Mutato coetu. . . .

[12] *Ibid.*, p. 302.   [13] *Ibid.*, pp. 326-44.
[14] *Ibid.*, p. 347.

> . . . ecce supernae
> Relligio sedis caveat sibi siquis utrisque
> Axibus ulterior latuit deus, imminet hostis
> Quem vix afficiat omnis satis impetus, in quem
> Fulminis et tonitrus omnis natura laboret.

Venus, at thy will thou drawest all the powers of heaven, sendest the planets whirling on strange journeys, set Phoebe afire, she who is so cold when her brother's lamp is absent, by a new conjunction. . . . Yea, let the sacred power of the heavenly region be watchful, and any lesser god who lurks between the two poles, for an enemy is at hand whom all your power can scarcely affect, against whom a universe of thunder and lightning might be spent (in vain).

There is something slightly ridiculous in the extravagance of this denunciation. Like Architrenius' own cataloguing of "natural" monsters it seems to confuse the literal and the figurative, and to reflect an unnaturally strong reaction to the potentially denaturing effect of Venus. Xenocrates' speech is one of several hints in the long philosophical section of the poem that Nature must have the last word if Architrenius is to be cured.

Xenocrates is followed by Pythagoras, who exhorts man to recreate the Golden Age by a life of blessed poverty, inveighs against the depravity of the fashions of the day, and paints a grim picture of the judgment to come after death. Architrenius is reduced to fear and trembling at the contrast between man's potential dignity and his present state.[15] Thales appears, followed by Bias and Periander, who instruct the hero on the worship of God, but the conflict of emotions aroused within him is too strong to allow him to take their counsel. In the final phase of his instruction an attempt is made to strike a happy medium. Pittacus appears to urge mildness and restraint; Cleobolus discourses on the need to meet whatever may come with fortitude, and to dare much: "felicia numquam/ Magnanimo desunt."[16] Solon then concludes the lesson with a speech in praise of *prudentia*, balancing Cleobolus' arguments with the reminder that forewarned is forearmed, and those of Pittacus with the admonition that one must see through to the end what-

[15] *Ibid.*, p. 351.   [16] *Ibid.*, p. 363.

ever one undertakes. Solon's main emphasis is on the choice of good habits, good examples on which to model one's self, and the pursuit of wisdom through philosophy. To one truly prudent, the good appears most beautiful, while voluptuousness seems as dross:[17]

> Succedente mora succedit gratia morum,
> Inque dies cedet Venus, accedente venusto,
> Rectificatque virum declivem regula, virtus,
> Philosophumque facit facundia philosophantis,
> Socraticosque bibit Xenocratis alumnulus imbres.

> As dalliance gives way the charm of morality takes its place, and Venus yields at the coming of day; as its charm gains sway, right conduct rectifies fallen man, and virtue; the charm of philosophizing makes him a philosopher, and the protégé of Xenocrates imbibes draughts of Socratic wisdom.

Solon's speech leaves certain problems unresolved. Venus will yield to philosophy, but whether she is to be flatly rejected or in some way disciplined is left uncertain. Solon seems uncertain about the possibility of accepting Nature whole, and the catalogue concludes with Architrenius suspended between the extremes of depravity on the one hand and the fanatical austerity of Xenocrates on the other.

As Solon concludes, Architrenius becomes aware of Nature, dazzlingly bright and surrounded by an aura of fertility, but with a dignity which dispells any hint of wantonness. In a passage which seems to recall the famous image of Bernard of Chartres, "dwarfs perched upon the shoulders of giants," Jean describes how the philosophers encircle the goddess so that the poet and his reader, following in their footsteps, can approach her more closely.[18] But Architrenius can respond at first only to the strangeness and the sensual impact of her appearance: "he burns to know the goddess, her novel appearance beguiles him, and he grows hot with desire."

[17] *Ibid.*, p. 368.
[18] The lines are somewhat obscure (*ibid.*, pp. 369-70):
> Illasciva sedet [i.e., Natura], quovis reverenda corusco
> Imperiosa throno, quem lactea crine coronat
> Turba senum, dominae genibus minor ardua sedes
> Est illos aequasse pedes, plenaque licemur
> Nobilitate deae summum contingere calcem.

When he learns her identity he rushes toward her in a burst of conflicting emotions. But the goddess ignores him and launches directly into a long description of the order of the universe intended to show how all of its harmonious and unceasing activity centers on man. After one hundred and fifty lines Architrenius breaks in to voice a doubt which has existed in undertone throughout the poem: whether the order of Nature can in fact have meaning for the lives of men.[19] And yet, he adds, there is something compelling in the spectacle which Nature presents: *ignotis delector et aure libenti/Sollicitor.*" Nature does not linger to discuss the matter, but resumes her description of the universe, descending at last to conclude by emphasizing the bounteous gifts of the universe to man. Once allowed to speak, however, Architrenius contradicts the whole tenor of Nature's argument, accusing her of denying herself to man:[20]

> Pace tua, Natura, queror; tibi supplicat omnis
> Majestatis apex, et nobis semper avarum
> Obliquas oculum . . .
>   . . . homo praeda doloribus aevum
> Tristibus immergit, nec amicis utitur annis,
> Nec fruitur laetis nec verna vescitur aura.

By thy leave, O Nature, my complaint is of thee; the very crown of thy majesty entreats thee, and always thou turnest away thy covetous eye. . . . Man, prey to grim sorrows, floods the world with tears, knows no favorable years, enjoys no delights, feels not the breeze of spring.

The passage echoes Nature's appeal to Noys in the *De mundi*, and the mild irony of the former scene, in which nonexistence reproaches absolute being for its lack of compassion, is recalled here by a fundamental contradiction in Architrenius' charge, to which Nature adverts in her rebuttal:[21]

> Sollicitis hominem studiis limavit, et orbem
> Officiosa dedit, cumulato larga favore,

[19] *Ibid.*, p. 376.
[20] *Ibid.*, p. 383. (With the opening words cp. *De mundi* 1.1, line 55, p. 8.)
[21] *Ibid.*, p. 383.

251

Nostra Jovi bonitas cognata, et cognita; numquam
Plenior exhibuit veram dilectio matrem.

Our goodness, near kin to Jove and sanctioned by him, fashioned
man with wearisome labor, and unstintingly gave the universe into
his hands, with lavish generosity. Never did a more loving act reveal
the true mother.

At this point the dialogue ceases. Nature goes on to analyze Architrenius' condition, and prescribes procreation as the cure for his distemper:[22]

Sanctio nostra virum sterili marcescere ramo
Et fructum sepilire vetat, prolemque negantes
Obstruxisse vias. Commissi viribus uti
Seminis et longam generis producere pompam
Relligio nativa iubet. . .

Our commission forbids man to wither on the barren bough, or let
his fruit fall upon the earth, or block up the proper channels to
prevent generation. Nature's religion bids a man exercise the powers
of the seed entrusted to him, and give rise to a long procession of
offspring. . . .

Elaborating her metaphor Nature gives a vivid characterization of
vice as an old whore, and analyzes in graphic terms the effects of
adultery with her, the unhousing of the twin brothers, and the removal of the distaff wielded so heroically by Bernardus' Mentula.[23]
As an alternative to this fate Nature offers marriage with the beautiful and chaste maiden *Moderantia*, and gives a full account of
her attractions. She then describes the "girdle of Venus" which
Moderation will present to her husband, and which Vulcan
wrought for his wife when their love was at its height.

Inscribed on this girdle are two catalogues of *exempla* of chastity, one of philosophers renowned for their resistance to Venus,
the other of prodigiously faithful wives. In both cases the examples
given range from the conventional (Hippolytus, Lucretia) to the
grotesque. The account of Democritus' self-mutilation sounds curiously like Alain's discussion of perversion in the opening lines of
the *De planctu*:[24]

[22] *Ibid.*, pp. 384-85.   [23] *Ibid.*, p. 385.   [24] *Ibid.*, p. 387.

... sexumque virilem
Exuit et neutrum recipit, fratresque togatos
Detogat, et Veneris geminum depellit avito
Mancipium tecto, lumbique incendia ferro
Ingelat, et nervi succisus apocopat usum.

He forsook the male sex and became neuter; he divested the brothers of their cloaks, banished Venus' twin servants from their ancestral home, quelled with cold steel the fire in the loins, abridged, by the severing of a sinew, the work of that organ.

The lines also resemble closely Nature's own description of the effects of vice a few lines earlier, and suggest, like Xenocrates' terror of Venus, the substitution of one excess for another. At the opposite extreme is the concluding example of Artemisia, who mixed her husband's ashes with honey and drank them; it is couched in the bizarre rhetoric usually reserved for "miracles" like the hermaphrodite, and suggests a similarly distorted image of the synthesizing power of Nature:[25]

Connubium servat, uteri torus alter, et una
Conjugis est coniunx, tumulus, pyra, pyramis, urna.

She preserves unbroken the bond of marriage, her belly a second nuptial bed, and is at once the wife, tomb, pyre, monument, urn of her husband.

In relation to these extremes of virtuous behavior, the frankly sexual associations of the girdle and the sexually inspired artistry of Vulcan assume a normative function, urging passionate feminine fidelity and intense masculine control into a constructive relationship, away from the self-defeating and potentially self-destructive extremes represented by the figures described above. The girdle thus provides that image of natural control and fulfillment which has been strikingly absent from the poem until now, and sets the excesses of all sorts which have been illustrated in a natural perspective. This artistic resolution stands for the resolution of Architrenius' dilemma: he rejoices at the prospect of marriage with Moderation, and the poem concludes with their wedding.

[25] *Ibid.*, p. 389.

It is obvious that Jean de Hanville has made no serious attempt to resolve the situation he depicts through the actual argument of Nature's appeal to the hero. To attempt to explain his purpose is to risk taking the will for the deed, and romanticizing what is in fact a tour de force of sheer rhetoric. He has sought, I think, to convey the effect of a broad emotional and psychological experience. The influence of Nature on a mind riven by vice and *timor mortis*, he seems to suggest, is as imperceptible and gradual as that of time on the mind of one bereaved. The "consolatio Naturae" involves no complex intellectual exchange, only a reimpression on Architrenius' mind of the face of Nature as she is in reality. There is, Jean suggests, something intrinsically beneficial in the very act of contemplating the order of the universe, in an awareness of the unceasing labor of Nature and in the conscious acceptance of her gifts. The recognition of these truths is enough to restore Architrenius to health—though only after he has purged himself emotionally by an excess of wrath and grief. What had seemed an uncontrollable depravity now appears a willful self-denial, and the disturbing absence of a natural norm is revealed as a refusal to trace Nature's gifts to their source. The result is paradoxical: viewed in the light of Nature indulgence becomes repression, and prodigality is barrenness. But Nature does not explain these paradoxes. Her argument is majestic in its indifference to the poverty of human reason, and wholly ignores moral distinctions in its overpowering affirmation.

Viewed in this way, Jean may be seen to have avoided a difficulty of the *De planctu Naturae*: for Alain, as for Jean, there are natural laws which conduce to moderation; but in allying herself with the cause of Hymen, and invoking the imagery of church and chivalry, Alain's Nature is always on the verge of upholding laws not strictly natural, and transgressing boundaries which she herself has defined. But Jean does not indulge in the imaginative typology by which Alain's allegory is redeemed; he carefully excludes any standard more formal than Nature's own "native religion," and by marrying his hero to "Moderantia" (rather than the "real" maiden of the Court of Venus, or Chastity, or Fidelity) he suggests the sweet reasonableness of something like marriage without violating the integrity of his Nature. Thus it is really he, more truly than Alain, who has created, in the fine phrase of Raynaud de Lage, "une nature à la mesure de son humanisme."

Of course Jean's resolution presents problems of its own. Whether or not we consider his introduction of Moderation as the great panacea to be begging the question, there are clearly certain awkwardnesses involved in the unqualified affirmation of the religion of Nature, as Jean de Meun and the Wife of Bath will cheerfully point out. And as an allegorist Jean has none of the philosophical subtlety of Bernardus and Alain, though he is perhaps their equal as an intuitive psychologist. He is forced to rely on sheer rhetoric to establish those relationships between Nature and man which the structure of his poem is inadequate to convey. But the material thus ordered is the substance of actual human experience, and much of the awkwardness in its disposition is a consequence of the great innovation which is Jean's chief contribution to the Chartrian tradition: in the *Architrenius*, for the first time, the Nature of the Chartrians is given a local habitation, and the challenge of seeking her out is presented in terms of life as lived.

2. Jean de Meun and the Chartrians[26]

The works of Bernardus, Alain, and Jean de Hanville were widely circulated and copiously annotated. Their verse was increasingly used in place of classical examples of style in the *artes poeticae*. Gervaise of Melkley declared that a careful study of the *Architrenius* was "sufficient by itself to inform the untrained mind."[27] and John of Garland found Alain "greater than Vergil and truer than Homer."[28] But no Latin poet of comparable stature appeared to continue their work. By the turn of the thirteenth century the shift

[26] The discussion which follows is based on my article, "The Literal and the Allegorical: Jean de Meun and the *De planctu Naturae*," *Medieval Studies* 33 (1971), pp. 264-91.

[27] *Ars poetica*, ed. Hans Jürgen Gräbener (Münster Westfalen, 1965), p. 3.

[28] *De triumphis Ecclesiae* 6.13 (ed. Wright, London, 1856, p. 74).

of scholarly activity from the cathedral schools to the rising universities, the increasing specialization in individual disciplines, and the discrediting of mere "literature" as a legitimate concern of the scholar were in full swing, and the themes and ideals of Chartres were reduced to a marginal existence. The destruction of the old intellectual milieu is described in the *Bataille des vii ars* of Henri d'Andeli, in which an array of humanists and poets, classical and modern, is routed by the forces of logic. Donatus battles Plato; Boethius and Bernardus (who is wistfully extolled as master of "toz les langages/Des esciences et des ars") fight on opposite sides, and "mon seignor Architraine" is slain by Aristotle *On Interpretation*, as grammar abandons poetry and leaves the field to the logicians.[29]

The decline of Chartrian philosophical idealism and literary culture is of course only a symptom of deeper changes. In the thirteenth century the symbolic, anagogical vision of nature which had coexisted with and gradually displaced the rationalist view of the Chartrians came into contact with a materialist view in which the beauty and fertility of nature were accepted with increasing frankness as goods in themselves, gifts which God had intended for man's enjoyment. A purely religious fusion of the two views can be seen in the Franciscans' gratitude for the beauty of nature and their use of it as a stimulus to the mystical love of God. Elsewhere science, commercialism, and a general reaction to the idealistic assumptions of feudalism and the outmoded Platonism of the twelfth century induced a more skeptical, even cynical attitude, in which the relations of nature and God were considered in terms, not of the visible expression of a divine order which man might rationally apprehend, but of end and means, the duties and pleasures of this life becoming in themselves an avenue to the attainment of religious fulfillment, if, indeed, such fulfillment could be gained by man. The implications of this sort of materialism are easy to exaggerate, and it would be difficult to demonstrate, for instance, that there existed any widespread religion of sexuality, but there is no doubt that the thought and expression of the thir-

[29] *La Bataille des vii ars*, lines 187-95, 282-84, 328-30; ed. Paetow (see above, ch. 1, n. 6), pp. 49-55.

teenth century, outside of strictly religious circles, reflect what we have already seen foreshadowed in the experience of Architrenius, "the shifting of the whole scale of values a little earthward."[30]

Jean de Meun's portion of the *Roman de la Rose* is in many respects a striking illustration of the effect of these complex changes. Like the Chartrian poets, he is concerned to explore the relations of man and Nature, and illustrates his theme with a series of elaborate sexual metaphors. But unlike the heroes of Alain and Jean de Hanville, the Lover of the *Roman* remains willfully ignorant of his plight to the end. Nature and Genius interest themselves in his situation, and play a major role in his final sexual conquest, but they evoke no perceptible moral awakening, and indeed their positive implications are as nearly as possible repudiated. Sexual fulfillment, not as a metaphor for rational self-awareness, but as an end in itself, is the Lover's goal, and it is hard to see his success as affirming anything more positive. There is evidently something amiss in the world of the *Roman* which has no clear precedent in the allegories of the Chartrians.

At the same time comparison with Chartrian allegory can do a great deal to clarify Jean's special attitude. The late Rosemond Tuve demonstrated brilliantly the important role played in Jean's poetic technique by the manipulation of the traditional associations of allegorical figures and patterns;[31] the *De planctu naturae* is the work most often used in this way, and the technique itself has much in common with, for example, the exploitation of the *Metamorphosis Goliae* in the *Altercatio*, or the use of traditional mythography in the "Profuit ignaris." The broad structure of the *Roman* has much in common with that of the *Architrenius*: both poems combine social criticism and realistic detail with moral and philosophical allegory, thereby enriching the associations of their basic sexual and naturalistic theme. In both works the hero progresses from an initial state of sinful "disfiguration" to a capacity

---

[30] Charles Muscatine, *Chaucer and the French Tradition* (Berkeley, 1956), p. 76.

[31] *Allegorical Imagery: Some Medieval Books and Their Posterity* (Princeton, 1966), pp. 239-83.

for sexual fulfillment which is gained through a renewal of contact with Nature. But in the *Roman* the works of artifice and corrupted will which had thwarted Architrenius' search for fulfillment conspire to help the Lover achieve his goal, thus making it all the harder to see a moral significance in his success.

The sharp contrast between the final effect of Jean's poem and that of the *Architrenius* or the *De planctu* is all the more striking in view of the care with which he preserves certain basic relationships. His Nature, *Raison*, and Genius play essentially the roles of Nature and Genius in the earlier allegories, and define essentially the same relationships between the natural and sacramental orders of reality. Thus Raison, in a long appeal to the Lover which is the first important event of Jean's continuation, describes his problem in terms borrowed directly from Alain and Bernardus. She contrasts natural generation with the barren pursuit of *delit*, linking the former with a *largice* which emulates the bounty of God.[32] The same appeal is made by Nature and Genius, and it is obeyed, although unconsciously, by the Lover. But like Alain's Nature, Raison cannot understand the full implications of human depravity, the contradiction between the fact of a powerful *Amors* for which the only remedy is flight,[33] on the one hand, and the necessity of procreation in obedience to Nature on the other. Like the Nature of the *De planctu*, Raison cannot think in theological terms,[34] and

[32] *Le Roman de la Rose*, ed. Felix Lecoy (3 vols., Paris, 1965–70), lines 4373-98, 4655-84, 5207-18.

[33] See *ibid.*, lines 4321-28, which are almost literally translated from the *descriptio Cupidinis* of the *De planctu* (Wright, p. 472; PL 210.455).

[34] See line 4373, where Raison introduces her speech on procreation with what seems to me a pun on *deviner*, meaning "guess," "prognosticate," or "engage in theological speculation," and her repeated references to the will of Nature, her high court of authority. Raison's limitations are those defined by Alain's Nature in comparing God's power and her own (Wright, pp. 455-56; PL 210.445-46): "Auctoritatem theologicae consule facultatis, cujus fidelitati, potius quam mearum rationum firmitati, dare debes assensum," and of the Incarnation, "ego Natura hujus nativitatis naturam ignoro; et ad haec intelligenda mei intellectus hebet acumen, meae rationis confunditur lumen."

D. W. Robertson (*Preface to Chaucer*, p. 199) notes the divine origin of Raison (lines 5783-87) and professes to find in her words "the voice of

the account she gives of man's lapse from participation in the all-embracing *joutice* of his original condition rests in unresolved contradiction to her confident feeling that *joutice, largice,* and she herself can still claim his affection. Like Nature in Alain's poem, she tries to explain her position by reference to myth, in this case the myth of the castration of Saturn, and the *integumanz* by which the inner significance of this myth is concealed,[35] but she is incapable of glossing her own allusions, and the Lover, in any case, cannot understand her "Latin."[36] Like Alain's Nature, she can think only in terms of an allegorically coherent universe where the *integumenta* of human behavior are reflective of a harmony with cosmic processes, a harmony which man has now lost; her rejection by the Lover only underscores the effects of this loss.

It is essential to recognize how faithfully Jean follows Alain in such matters, for it is the same basic view of the limitations of man's natural faculties that accounts for the extraordinary speech of Genius which brings the action of the *Roman* to its climax. It is Genius who provides a full allegorical context for the laws of conduct which Raison had offered to the Lover. It is he who elaborates on the myth of the castration of Saturn, showing how Jupiter's violent act ushered in the world of necessity, yet did so in the name of a false, willful *delit*.[37] It is he, finally, who proffers the vision of Paradise, the "beau parc" which is to the garden of Deduit as substance to accident, and cites largesse, cleanness, compassion, and fidelity, together with obedience to Nature, as the means of gaining entry and possessing eternal life in the company of the

---

patristic authority," and the same points are emphasized by John V. Fleming, *The Roman de la Rose* (Princeton, 1969), pp. 112-37. But insofar as Jean is allegorizing the effects of the fall, there is no inconsistency in Raison's being God's daughter and at the same time ignorant of grace, divine in origin yet limited to strictly rational comprehension. With her inability to dissuade the Lover cp. the powerlessness of the *sapientia* of Orpheus as glossed by Guillaume de Conches (above, ch. 2, pp. 96-98), and the declaration of Andreas, *De amore* 3 (Trojel, p. 337): "sapientia propter amorem suum in sapiente perdit officium."

[35] *Roman*, line 7138.   [36] *Ibid.*, lines 5809-10.
[37] *Ibid.*, lines 20053-190.

Lamb. And in all of this he is only acting out the implications of his role in the works of Bernardus and Alain, as a link between fallen man and his original state of psycho-physical integration, when the dictates of Raison and the impulses of physical desire were harmonious.

The great difference between Jean's handling of these traditional figures and that of the Chartrians is his insistence on following out their literal as well as their allegorical implications. Thus it is at least as important to our understanding of the *Roman* that we follow out the effects of Genius' exhortation to the point at which they result in the conception of a child as that we see in Genius' providential role a type of the office of the Good Shepherd, or in his exhortation an allusion to the spiritual multiplication of the Word. And the literal event is emphasized by contrast in every allusion Jean makes to the highly abstract conclusion of the *De planctu*. For Genius comes forth from his communion with Nature to address, not Hymen and the Virtues, but *l'homme moyen sensuel* in full armor, and submits his authority to the will of Venus and Amors. And the obstacles which have interposed themselves between the Lover's sexual nature and any conscious fulfillment of a divine duty are made plain in the pageantry which surrounds Genius' appeal to the barons. The renewed sense of dignity and authority which had been the direct result of Genius' reunion with Nature in the *De planctu* emerges in the *Roman* only after Amors has clad him in priestly vestments of his own, and Venus has armed him with her "ardent cierge."[38] Only then is he moved to recall in their full significance the duty of procreation and the Paradise lost by man through unnatural conduct. As he concludes, Venus augments his eloquence with the stimulus of her torch; the action moves beyond the context of the *De planctu* altogether—though in a manner precisely the opposite of the world-transcending gestures of Patricida, Erec, and the Genius of the *De planctu*—and forward to the pell-mell, anticlimactic events of the poem's conclusion, on a wave of sexual impulse inspired by a virtually inextricable combination of nature and deception.

[38] *Ibid.*, lines 19447-60.

Jean's treatment of Nature herself corresponds to this deliberate shift of emphasis from the positive aspects of Raison and Genius to their limitations. Like these faculties, the goddess is carefully established in her Chartrian dignity; Jean gives a brief, vivid panorama of the struggle between her powers of renewal and the forces of death,[39] dwells on her indescribable beauty, and assigns to her a long account of the divine rationale and harmony of the universe at large. She then turns to the irregularities of human life, the unnatural follies and accidents which disrupt its natural course.[40] She extols Raison as a means of liberation from the burden of necessity and rebukes man for refusing to recognize his freedom of will, and his power to achieve self-knowledge.[41] All of this is in keeping with the decorum of the *De planctu*; but at this point, where Alain's Nature had tacitly acknowledged her limitations and referred the problem of man's aberration to Genius, Jean's goddess embarks on a long digression, and analyzes in minute detail the various aspects of the cosmic paradigm she has constructed. In the process she provides her own quite unconscious illustration of the very denaturing forces which have aroused her anger.[42]

To show man's superiority to physical necessity and chance, Nature gives a long discussion of divine foreknowledge, destiny, and free will. Her arguments are for the most part conventional and stringent, but as she proceeds she is increasingly sidetracked by hypothetical considerations: what if *man* had foreknowledge, and could anticipate natural disasters? what if animals were endowed with reason? Nature seems oddly sympathetic to the pictures she conjures up, of man mocking the elements and engaging in feasts and orgies while famine and tempest rage, or of the animal king-

---

[39] *Ibid.*, lines 15861-982.   [40] *Ibid.*, lines 16925-17008.
[41] *Ibid.*, lines 17029-70.
[42] The elaborate rhetorical structure of Nature's discourse and its importance to the "Grand Debate" on the nature of love which the *Roman* presents are stressed by A.M.F. Gunn, *The Mirror of Love* (Lubbock, Texas, 1952), pp. 125-32, 396-406. But it seems to me that the careful disposition of her speech serves mainly as a foil to the headlong course of her thoughts and feelings, and that what she reveals unconsciously is more important than any "argument" she presents. See Tuve, *Allegorical Imagery*, pp. 267-75.

dom rising up to overthrow tyrant man. She returns to her argument long enough to reassert the primacy of Raison, but as she goes on to other topics the curiously centrifugal tendency of her thoughts becomes dominant. She dilates on the theme of the obedient cosmos, but is soon involved in describing the ravages of a flood, which lays waste fields and towns, and sweeps the very images from shrines and altars. From the happy return of fair weather she passes to the optical phenomenon of the rainbow, and thence to the properties of magnifying glasses: had Venus and Mars had such a glass they would have seen Vulcan's fine net and escaped the shame of exposure. This coarse allusion, evocative of the atmosphere of Faus Semblant and La Vieille, is followed by a discussion of the tricks of perspective played by mirrors and lenses, in which we may perhaps detect a hint at the quasi-narcissistic preoccupations which have characterized so much of the Lover's experience since his initial encounter with the fountain of Narcissus in the garden of Deduit:[43]

> uns hom, ce dit, malades iere,
> si li avoit la maladie
> sa veüe mout afoiblie,
> et li airs iert occurs et troubles,
> et dit que par ces resons doubles
> vit il en l'air, de place en place,
> aler par devant soi sa face.

A man, says [Aristotle], was ill, to the point at which his sight was greatly weakened and saw the light only in an obscure and distorted way; and he says that for these reasons he saw, wherever he went, his own countenance, hovering in the air before him.

By the extraordinary cavortings of Nature's imagination Jean intends, I think, to mirror the real and illusory attractions, the complex of impulses and the many misleading paths by which the quest of the Rose has proceeded. Jean's Nature seems scarcely to know herself. She defines the order of the universe only to seek to evade its sterner implications, divesting it of its Chartrian Platonic veil and subjecting it to a degrading materialistic analysis which reflects all the corruptions of rationality and desire that have been drama-

[43] *Roman*, lines 18170-76.

tized in the earthly context of Deduit and Faus Semblant.[44] Fascinated by the ceaseless conflict within her dominions to the point of forgetting the rationale which contains it, sympathetic with men's attempts to evade necessity in pursuit of pleasure or expand the limits of their earthbound vision by technology, Nature views herself, as it were, through human eyes, in an empirical manner. This is a devastating elaboration on Alain's critique of the Chartrian faith in Nature as source and standard of moral law. The ideal cooperation of Nature and Raison has become impossible, and the "face of Nature," which the Chartrians had seen as obscured by human artifice, is shown by Jean to be itself largely the product of such artifice.

The parallels between Jean's cosmos and the human world within it are compounded by the personality of Nature. She is more woman than divine power, garrulous, subjective, and easily distracted, and is seemingly led to confession primarily by the need to vent her righteous indignation:[45]

> Fame sui, si ne me puis tere,
> ainz veill des ja tout reveler,
> car fame ne peut riens celer;
> n'onques ne fu mieuz ledangiez.
> Mar s'est de moi tant estrangiez. . .

I am a woman, I cannot keep silent, but desire to reveal all at once; for a woman can keep nothing hidden. Never has [man] been more shamed [than he will be by me]. In an unlucky hour he deserted me. . .

By the end of her denunciation she has forgotten the question of procreation—though she taunts mankind as *sodomites*—and thinks, like La Vieille, only of devising a fit punishment for her betrayer.[46]

---

[44] With Nature's impulsive self-revelations in the *Roman* cp. the famous declaration of Macrobius (quoted above, ch. 1, pp. 37-38).

[45] *Ibid.*, lines 19188-92. The tone of these lines, which suggests a burlesque of the *Heroides*, is also, perhaps, a comic play on Nature's earlier appeals to Noys in the *De mundi* and to Genius in the *De planctu*.

[46] *Roman*, lines 19279-89; cp. lines 12846-52.

This larger-than-life femininity is set off by Jean's treatment of Nature's relations with Genius. The elaborate formality of the *De planctu* is abandoned. In the *Roman*, though Genius' priestly function is if anything more precisely indicated, his relationship with Nature is flawed, in ways which once again reflect the conditions of the world of the poem. Genius' contributions to the dialogue with Nature consist almost entirely of reflections on feminine duplicity, and though he concurs in Nature's general sense of wrong, he has evident reservations, as the poet implies in commenting on his ambivalent response to Nature's coarse allusion to Venus and Mars:[47]

> Ainsinc s'acordent, ce me samble,
> Nature et Genyus ansamble.
> Si dit Salemon toutevois,
> puis que par la verité vois,
> que beneürez hom seroit
> qui bone fame troveroit.

Thus it would seem that Nature and Genius reached agreement. But still, as Solomon says (and I go by the words of Truth), blessed would be the man who should find a good woman.

The spectacle of Genius sparring with his mistress—the emissary of Noys, as it were, declining to bestow the loving impress of the eternal idea—is at once the most brilliant and the most crucial of Jean's exploitations of the allegory of the *De planctu*, the final measure of the contamination of man's relations with the natural order, and leads directly into the profoundly ironical denouement of the *Roman*.

The relations of Nature and Genius thus largely reflect the confusion and duplicity of the world of human experience, the world of *cupido*, *deduit*, and *faus semblant*, where delusion and self-interest prevail. But Genius is not wholly betrayed by these disintegrative forces, and in fact the final event of the poem reveals his controlling influence in a crucially important way. For the conception of the Lover's child serves to illustrate, unobtrusively and, it

---

[47] *Ibid.*, lines 18117-22. Cp. *Ecclesiasticus* 26:1.

may well seem, almost accidentally, the ultimate contingency of the world of experience on the order of Nature. In this balancing of the literal and allegorical "worlds" of the *Roman*, Jean shows an unflinching acceptance of the challenge offered by Nature to Architrenius, and his conclusion both greatly enriches and radically complicates our view of the providential role of Nature in human life.

The two worlds come together in the final action of the poem and collaborate to bring about the vital act of conception, even as the passions of the gods and the passions of Eneas himself conspire in urging him to slay Turnus and complete the heroic action of the *Eneas*. The result in both cases is a vivid dramatization of the limited consciousness and relative helplessness of man, but it is more than this. For it is through such virtually fortuitous manipulations of will and native impulse that the world is stabilized and renewed, by powers which, operating in the depths of human nature, inseminate that nature with the impulse to fulfillment.

In the *Roman*, then, Jean destroys the allegorical world of the *De planctu* in order to create his own world out of the actual facts of experience. It seems hardly possible to see the natural order presented by Jean de Meun as the type or vehicle of grace, or, given this state of affairs, to place any great faith in such standards as the Moderation affirmed by Jean de Hanville.

Perhaps the impregnation of the Rose, fulfilling as it does the command of Genius and preserving the continuity of human life, must be accepted as an end in itself. But the terrific release of energy on the level of human action which results from Jean's subversion of the authority of the Chartrian Nature presents an awesome challenge to rationalization. The *Roman de la Rose* is brilliant comedy; it anticipates the irony of Erasmus, asserting the dignity and power of Folly, and Rabelais' rediscovery of the fecundity of chaos. The world it presents is as far from the ideal harmony of the Platonic cosmos of Alain and Bernardus as it is from the park of the Good Shepherd. But when the Lover, like Aeneas receiving his great shield from Vulcan and Venus, blindly assumes responsibility for the future of mankind, he is responding to a creative impulse which seeks to realize both of these lost ideals. And in understanding this we recognize the almost miraculous fertility of that human nature which, hidden beneath the proliferation of conflicting desires and false visions, is the rock and loam from which all such impulses must necessarily and perpetually spring.

APPENDIX

Selections from the Commentary of Bernardus
Silvestris on Martianus Capella
(Cambridge, University Library, MS, Mm 1.18, ff. 1r-28r)

1. (f. 1ra) Ecce habemus rationem circa formas in mathesi primo excitari oportere, ut consequenter causas in phisica rimari queat, nouissime uero in substantiis, theologie insistens, intuitum figat. Unde in secundo Arismetice commento de mathesi agens *Boethius* hoc inquit: "Est illud quadruuium quo his uiandum est quibus animus excellentior sensibus nobiscum procreatis ad cerciora intelligentie perducitur." Certiora namque intelligentie accipit certam in theologicis intelligentie comprehensionem. Addit etiam quia animi oculum orbatum illuminant rursus hee discipline.

2. (f. 1rb) Genus doctrine figura est. Figura autem est oratio quam inuolucrum dicere solent. Hec autem bipertita est: partimur namque eam in allegoriam et integumentum. Est autem allegoria oratio sub historica narratione uerum et ab exteriori diuersum inuoluens intellectum, ut de lucta Iacob. Integumentum uero est oratio sub fabulosa narratione uerum claudens intellectum, ut de Orpheo. Nam et ibi historia et hic fabula ministerium habent occultum, quod alias discutiendum erit. Allegoria quidem diuine pagine, integumentum uero philosophice competit.

3. (f. 1va) [Intentio] uero auctoris imitatio est, quia Maronem emulatur. Sicut enim apud illum ducitur Eneas per inferos, comite Sibilla, usque ad Anchisem, ita et hic Mercurius per mundi regiones, uirtute comite, ad Iouem. Ita quoque in libro de Consolatione scandit Boecius per falsa bona ad summum bonum duce Philosophia. Que quidem tres figure fere idem exprimunt. Imitatur ergo Marcianus Maronem, Boecius Marcianum.

4. Text: "Complexuque sacro dissona nexa foues" (*De nuptiis* 1.1, p. 3).

(f. 4ra) *nexa*, id est iuncta, *complexu*, proportione, *sacro* quia,

267

ad tempus, diuinum mortali ut, in eternum, mortale iungatur diuino; quod *tibi* illud de Polluce et Castore apte figurat. Pollux enim "perditio," Castor uero "extremum malum" interpretatur. "Perditio" dicitur spiritus humanus quia sicut semina terre mandata primo moriuntur ut post modum uiuant, sic anima corpori iuncta. Corpus autem "extremum malum" dicitur quia, ut super Virgilium diximus, parcientibus omne quod est nil inferius humano corpore occurrit . . . . Et Pollux quidem dicitur deus quia est spiritus substantia rationalis et immortalis, Castor mortalis quia corpus substantia hebes et dissolubilis. Deus mortalem mortem recipit ut suam deitatem ei conferat, quia spiritus ad tempus moritur ut corpus in eternum uiuat.

5. Text: "atque ita metamorphosi supera pulchriores per Geminos . . ." (*De nuptiis* 1.30, p. 20).

(f. 26rb) Vita contemplatiua Pollux, i.e., "perditio" dicitur quia bona hec relinquendo animam suam perdit ut eam inuenire mereatur. Actiua uita "extremum malum" dicitur quia terminus corporee uoluptatis esse perhibetur. Inter uoluptatem namque et contemplationem media est actio. Ille immortalis esse ex hoc monstratur, quia morte corporali non ita contemplatio ut actio terminatur. Unde dominus dicit Mariam eam elegisse, propterea quod ab ea non auferetur. Castori Pollux confert deitatem quia actio ad contemplationem transiens assequitur immortalitatem.

6. (f. 7va) Iouis nomen ad sex integumenta equiuocatum inuenimus: ad summum deum; ad superius *elementum*; ad planetam; ad animam mundi; ad animam *hominis*; ad ipsum mundum. Iunonis uero uocabulum ad quattuor: ad uoluntatem dei; ad aerem; ad terram; ad practicam uitam.

7. Text: "Entelechiae et Solis filiam . . ." (*De nuptiis* 1.7, p. 7).

(f. 13rb) Endelichia uero "intima aetas" nuncupatur, sapientia uero "dei aetas" quasi euitas, eo quod absque initio et fine et temporali successione existit. Si enim initium habuisset uel finem habitura esset, non semper deus esset sapiens. . . . Intima uero dicitur ideo quia ei absque doctrina innata est. Unde legimus Pallada sine matre a Ioue ortam. Endelechia ergo est mater Siches, i.e., dei sapientia est causa anime non materialis sed formalis.

8. Text: "Lemnius quoque faber illi insopibilis perennitatis igniculos, ne caligantibus tenebris nocteque caeca opprimeretur, incendit" (*De nuptiis* 1.7, p. 8).

(f. 15rb) Animus autem noster dicitur uulcanus quasi "uolitans candor," quia et pulcher est et mobilis. Filius Jouis et Junonis quia opus dei est et eius uoluntatis. Dextro pede claudus sinistro sustinetur, quia in consideratione eternorum debilis, considerationi temporalium totus innititur. Licentia data est ei a Joue ducendi Pallada quia naturalem potentiam habet a creatore qua iungatur ei sapientia. Habet enim *tibi* innatum ingenium, *quae* est uis naturalis omnia concipiendi; rationem, quae naturalis est potentia omnia discernendi; memoriam, quae est uis naturae omnia retinendi. His et si perfectam scientiam non assequitur, potest tamen assequi . . . nichil uidet sed potentia uidendi non caret.

8a. (f. 15rb) Quia claudus est a Pallade contempnitur, quia dum prefatam debilitatem habet, sapientiam non assequitur. In conflictu dum iste instat, illa fugit, quia in studio dum hic inuestigat, illa cedit. Quanto enim plura comprehendimus, tanto plura superesse perpendimus. Unde Psalmus: "Accedet homo ad cor altum, et exaltabitur Deus" [*Ps.* 63:7]. Ex intemperantia semen funditur dum presumptione doctrina emittitur. Arbitratur enim homo quod scire suum nihil est nisi se scire hic sciat altus. Semine recepto terra parit Erictonium dum, doctrina accepta, humanam sapientiam gignit cor nostrum.

8b. (f. 15va) Ingenium quoque Vulcanus, quasi "uolicanus," quia semper esse in discursu dicunt. Hic *faber* legitur quia iugiter aliquos rerum conceptus molitur et dum membra nostra sopiuntur ingenium nostrum aliquid machinatur. Hos ergo conceptus indeficientes dicit hic *igniculos insopibiles*, et hic est *Lemnius faber*.

Vides brucum . . . discurrentem, si aurum preciosum ut lapidem offendat, non ibi morantem; si uero stercora inuenerit, ibi potius sedem eligit. Sic ingenium nostrum, dum repentina meditatione discurrit, si forte honestum aliquod ei occurrerit, uix ibi stare poterit. Dum enim uerbi gratia in ecclesia orando meditationem meam celestibus affigere studeo, illam statim elapsam repente alicui immundicie inherentem inuenio.

9. Text: "omnes uero illecebras circa sensus cunctos apposuit Aphrodite . . ." (*De nuptiis* 1.7, p. 8).

(f. 15va) *Omnis uero illecebras* Hactenus ostendit quae data sint anime in prima creatione ad exornationem et decus. Nunc enumerat sordes quas contrahit ex originali delicto ad contaminationem. Prius quidem ostendit eam muneratam a Joue, Junone, Tritonia, Vulcano, unde innuit illa munera naturalia. Post uero ponit dona Afrodites tamquam aliena. . . . *Sed Afrodite*, id est uoluptas carnis, *apposuit*, quasi aduenticia et extranea superaddidit, *illecebras*, uicia. . .

9a. (f. 15va) Circa hunc [i.e., gustum] quidem quinque illecebras ponit Afrodite. Prima est statutum tempus prandendi (f. 15vb) preuenire, que arguitur ubi dicitur "Ve ciuitati cuius rex puer est et cuius princeps mane comedit." [*Eccles.* 10:16] Secunda est lautiores cibos querere quam *habuit*, ut Israel qui, reiecto manna, porros et cucumeres desiderabat. [*Num.* 11:5] Tertia est in accurato apparatu operam dare ut filii Heli qui a sacrificio carnes crudas mallebant accipere, ut accuratius coque*rent*. [*I Sam.* 2:12-17] Quarta est mensuram refectionis excedere, in quo peccauit Sodoma, ut dicitur: "Hec fuit iniquitas Sodome, saturitas panis." [*Ezek.* 16:49] Quinta est nimio appetitu iniare ut Esau in lenticulis. [*Gen.* 25:29] Qui nec statutam horam preuenit, nec lautiorem escam quesiuit, nec in apparatu operam dedit, nec mensuram refectionis excessit. Sed in nimio desiderio uisi leguminis *deliquit*.

9b. (f. 15vb) Sed dicit *omnes illecebras*, et non modo circa sensus, sed circa *cunctos sensus*. Unde consonat locus hic illi quo legis Venerem omnes quinque filias solis ad illicitum amorem accendisse, quia adulterii eius et Marcis sol index extitit. Mars enim Veneris complexibus polluitur dum uirtus uoluptatis illecebris corrumpitur. Testimonio solis accusantur dum indicio rationis rei conuincuntur. Vulcanus adamantino nexu Martem ligat dum ignis concupiscentie insolubili consuetudine uirtutem artat. Quinque filie solis sunt quinque sensus, famuli rationis; uel filie doctrine dicuntur quia per rationem corriguntur.

10. (f. 27ra) Talia quidem nomina [i.e., pater, filius, spiritus]

dininitati diuina pagina dedit, philosophica uero alia quedam. Quae cum modo aperto, modo mistico utatur sermone, in aperto quidem deum "patrem" ponit, ut diuina pagina; ut uero illa dicit sapientiam "filium," haec "noim," id est "mentem" . . . et ut illa "spiritum," haec "mundi animam" habet. Spiritu enim Dei uiuunt mundana, ut alias monstrabatur. . . . Hec ergo nomina trinitatis, pater, nois, anima mundi, ponit in aperto sermone philosophica pagina. In mistico autem "Jouis" est nomen diuine potencie, "Pallas" diuine sapiencie, "Juno" diuine uoluntatis. . . . In eo enim quod facturus est Jupiter querit assensum Junonis, consilium Palladis, nam et uoluntas mouet et sapientia disponit quod potentia in actum perducit.

The following summarial comments may serve to illustrate Bernardus' sense of the development of Martianus' allegory.

11. Text: *De nuptiis* 1.1, p. 3.

(f. 1va) Tractaturus namque philosophus de coniunctione sermonis et rationis incipit de causa coniunctionis, scilicet concordia utili, que naturas licet dissonas in unam sociat essentiam. Plato quoque de mundo sensili tractaturus ab eius causis orditur, cum enim tractatus materiam debet emulari. . .

12. Text: ". . . amplius deliberandum suggerit Virtus. Neque eum sine Apollinis consilio quicquam debere decernere . . ." (*De nuptiis* 1.8, p. 9).

(f. 17va) [Virtus] proponit adire primo Apollinem, id est scientiam de creaturis. Apolline autem comite deinde erit iter ad Jouem, id est agnitione creaturarum . . . ascensus erit ad creatorem.

13. Text: "talia conserentes ut procul Pythius aduentare conspexit . . ." (*De nuptiis* 1.20, p. 15).

(f. 22va) Ultima distinctio, scilicet conuentus illorum trium [i.e., Virtus, Mercury, Apollo]. *Talia conserentes*, id est predictas scientias coferendo perlustrantes, *aduentare*, ad se prouenire, *procul*, a longe uenerunt qui ab ignorantia naturali progressi scientiam iam contingunt. . .

14. Text: "petaso autem ac talaribus concitatis coepit praeire

Mercurius. sed scandente Phoebo Musarum pedisecus adhaerensque comitatus candenti canoraque alite uehebatur." (*De nuptiis* 1.26, p. 19.)

(f. 24va) Propositum philosophi fuit geminum Mercurii ascensum tractare, primum ad Apollinem per inferiorem regionem comite Virtute, secundum ab Apolline ad Jouem ipso Apolline comite, *et* Virtute numquam eum relinquente, et per etheream regionem. . . . In hoc ascensu cum Mercurio et Virtute Apollo incedit quia in itinere ad creatorem quod bonum est sapientia concipit, eloquentia aperit.

14a. Text: "tum uero conspiceres totius mundi gaudia convenire" (*De nuptiis* 1.27, p. 19).

(f. 25rb) *Totius mundi*, id est utriusque partis hominis, quem microcosmum dixerunt, *gaudia*, quia non est in humana uita *ullum* maius gaudium quam si sapientia et eloquentia et uirtus simul incedant.

BIBLIOGRAPHY

Primary Sources

(Anonymous works are listed alphabetically by title beginning
with item 67)

1. Abelard, Peter. *Historia calamitatum.* Ed. Jacques Monfrin. Paris, 1959.
2. ———. *Introductio ad theologiam.* PL 178.979-1114.
3. ———. *Planctus.* Ed. Guido M. Dreves. In *Analecta hymnica medii aevi.* 55 vols. Leipzig, 1886–1922. XLVIII, 223-32.
4. ———. *Planctus.* Ed. Giuseppe Vecchi. Modena, 1951.
5. ———. *Theologia christiana.* PL 178.1123-1330.
6. Adelhard of Bath. *De eodem et diverso.* Ed. Hans Willner. *Beiträge zur Geschichte der Philosophie des Mittelalters* 4:1 (1903).
7. Alain de Lille. *Anticlaudianus.* Ed. Robert Bossuat. Paris, 1955.
8. ———. *De planctu naturae.* Ed. Thomas Wright. In *Anglo-Latin Satirical Poets of the Twelfth Century.* 2 vols. London, 1872. II, 429-522.
9. ———. *Summa "Quoniam homines."* Ed. P. Glorieux. *Archives d'histoire doctrinale et littéraire du moyen âge* 28 (1953), pp. 113-359.
10. ———. *Tractatus de virtutibus et vitiis.* Ed. Odon Lottin. In *Psychologie et morale aux xiie et xiiie siècles.* 6 vols. Gembloux, 1948–60. VI, 27-92.
11. ———. *Textes inédites.* Ed. Marie-Thérèse d'Alverny. Paris, 1965.
12. Albericus of London. ("Mythographus tertius"), *Poetria.* Ed. G. H. Bode. In *Scriptores rerum mythicarum.* 2 vols. Celle, 1834. I, 150-239.
13. ———. Prologue to the *Poetria.* Ed. F. Jacobs and F. Ukert. *Beiträge zur altern Literatur der Herzogl. öffentlichen Bibliothek zu Gotha.* 3 vols. Leipzig, 1835. I:ii, pp. 202-04.
14. Andreas Capellanus. *De amore.* Ed. E. Trojel. Copenhagen, 1892.
15. Apuleius. *De philosophia libri.* Ed. Paul Thomas. Leipzig, 1908.
16. Arnulf of Orleans. *Allegoriae super Metamorphosin.* Ed. Fausto Ghisalberti, "Arnolfo d'Orléans, un cultore di Ovidio nel secolo XII," *Memorie del Reale Istituto Lombardo di Scienze e Lettere. Classe di Lettere* 24:4 (1932), pp. 194-229.
17. ———. *Glosule super Lucanum.* Ed. Berthe M. Marti. Rome, 1958. (American Academy in Rome, *Papers and Monographs,* Vol. 18.)

18. Bernardus Silvestris. Commentary on Martianus Capella. MS, Cambridge, University Library, Mm. 1.18, ff. 1r-28r.

19. ———. *Commentum super sex libros Eneidos Virgilii.* Ed. Wilhelm Riedel. Greifswald, 1924.

20. ———. *De mundi universitate.* Ed. C. S. Barach and J. Wrobel. Innsbruck, 1876.

21. ———. *Experimentarius.* Ed. Mirella Brini-Savorelli. *Rivista critica di storia della filosofia* 14 (1959), pp. 283-342.

22. ———. *Mathematicus.* Ed. Barthélemy Hauréau. Paris, 1895.

23. ———. *Mathematicus.* PL. 171.1365-80.

24. Boethius. *De consolatione philosophiae.* Ed. Ludwig Bieler. Turnhout, 1957. (*Corpus christianorum,* Vol. 94.)

25. ———. *The Consolation of Philosophy.* Tr. Richard Green. New York, 1962.

26. ———. *De institutione arithmetica.* Ed. G. Friedlein. Leipzig, 1867.

27. ———. *De Trinitate.* Ed. H. F. Stewart and E. K. Rand. In *Boethius: The Theological Tractates and the Consolation of Philosophy.* New York, 1918, pp. 2-31. (Loeb Classical Library.)

28. ———. *In Porphyrium dialogi.* PL 64.9-158.

29. Calcidius. *Commentarius in Timaeum Platonis.* Ed. J. H. Waszink. London, 1962. (*Corpus Platonicum Medii Aevi. Plato latinus,* Vol. IV.)

30. Chrétien de Troyes. *Erec et Enide.* Ed. Mario Roques. Paris, 1966.

31. Conrad of Hirsau. *Dialogus super auctores.* Ed. R.B.C. Huygens. Brussels, 1955. (*Collection Latomus,* Vol. 17.)

32. "Dionysius the Areopagite." *Hierarchia coelestis.* Tr. Johannes Scotus Eriugena. PL 122.1035-70.

33. Dominicus Gundissalinus (Gundisalvus). *De processione mundi.* Ed. Georg Bülow. *Beiträge zur Geschichte der Philosophie des Mittelalters* 24:3 (1925).

34. *Eneas.* Ed. J. J. Salverda de Grave. 2 vols. Paris, 1925–29.

35. Fulgentius. *Opera.* Ed. Rudolph Helm. Leipzig, 1898.

36. Garnier de Rochefort. *Sermones.* PL 205.559-828.

37. Gauthier de St. Victor. *Contra quatuor labyrinthos Franciae.* Ed. P. Glorieux. *Archives d'histoire doctrinale et littéraire du moyen âge* 27 (1952), pp. 187-335.

38. Geoffroi de Vinsauf. *Poetria nova.* Ed. Edmond Faral. In *Les arts poétiques* (see below, no. 114), pp. 194-262.

39. Guillaume de Conches. *De philosophia mundi.* PL 172.39-102.

40. ———. Glosses on Boethius, *De consolatione philosophiae.* MS. London, B.M. Egerton 628, ff. 165r-195r.

274

41. ———. *Glosae super Platonem*. Ed. Edouard Jeauneau. Paris, 1965.

42. Guillaume de Lorris, Jean de Meun. *Le Roman de la Rose*. Ed. Felix Lecoy. 3 vols. Paris, 1965–70.

43. Guillaume de St. Thierry. *De erroribus Guillelmi de Conchis*. PL 180.333-40.

44. ———. *Disputatio altera adversus Abaelardum*. PL 180.283-328.

45. Henri d'Andeli. *La Bataille des vii ars*. Ed. and tr. L. J. Paetow. Berkeley, 1914. (Memoirs of the University of California, 4, No. 1.)

46. Hugh of St. Victor. *Opera*. PL 175-77.

47. ———. *Didascalicon*. Ed. Charles H. Buttimer. Washington, 1939. (Catholic University of America, Studies in Medieval and Renaissance Latin, Vol. 10.)

48. ———. *The Didascalicon of Hugh of St. Victor*. Tr. Jerome Taylor. New York, 1961.

49. Jean de Hanville. *Architrenius*. Ed. Thomas Wright. *Anglo-Latin Satirical Poets* (see above, no. 8). I, 240-391.

50. Jean de Meun. See above, no. 42.

51. John of Garland. *Integumenta Ovidii*. Ed. Fausto Ghisalberti. Messina and Milan, 1933.

52. John of Salisbury. *Metalogicon*. Ed. C.C.J. Webb. Oxford, 1929.

53. ———. *Policraticus*. Ed. C.C.J. Webb. 2 vols. Oxford, 1909.

54. Johannes Scotus Eriugena. *Annotationes in Marcianum*. Ed. Cora E. Lutz. Cambridge, Mass., 1939.

55. Macrobius. *Opera*. Ed. James Willis. 2 vols. Leipzig, 1963.

56. ———. *Macrobius' Commentary on the Dream of Scipio*. Tr. W. H. Stahl. New York, 1952.

57. ———. *The Saturnalia of Macrobius*. Tr. P. V. Davies. New York, 1969.

58. Marie de France. *Lais*. Ed. Jean Rychner. Paris, 1966.

59. Martianus Capella. *De nuptiis Philologiae et Mercurii*. Ed. Adolph Dick. Leipzig, 1925.

60. Matthew of Vendome. *Ars versificatoria*. Ed. Edmond Faral, *Les arts poétiques* (see below, no. 114), pp. 106-93.

61. Pseudo-Quintilian. *Declamationes XIX Maiores*. Ed. G. Lehnert. Leipzig, 1905.

62. Remigius of Auxerre. *Commentum in Martianum Capellam, Libri I-II*. Ed. Cora E. Lutz. Leiden, 1962.

63. Servius. *In Vergilii carmina commentarii*. Ed. Georg Thilo and Hermann Hagen. 3 vols. Leipzig, 1884.

64. Thierry of Chartres. Commentary on Boethius, *De Trinitate*. Ed. N. M. Häring. *Archives d'histoire doctrinale et littéraire du moyen âge* 31 (1956), pp. 257-325.

65. ———. *De sex dierum operibus*. Ed. N. M. Häring. In "The Creation and Creator" (see below, no. 136), pp. 184-200.

66. ———. *Prologus in Eptateuchon*. Ed. Edouard Jeauneau. *Medieval Studies* 16 (1954), 171-75.

67. "Accessus ad auctores." Ed. R.B.C. Huygens. *Latomus* 12 (1953), pp. 296-311, 460-86.

68. *Altercatio Phyllidis et Florae*. Ed. A. Bömer. *Zeitschrift für deutsches Altertum* 56 (1918), pp. 224-39.

69. *Asclepius*, in Apuleius, *De philosophia libri*. Ed. Paul Thomas. Leipzig, 1908, pp. 36-81.

70. *De mundi coelestis terrestrisque constitutione liber*. PL 90.881-910.

71. *Liber Hermetis Mercurii Triplicis de vi rerum principiis*. Ed. Theodore Silverstein. *Archives d'histoire doctrinale et littéraire du moyen âge* 30 (1955), pp. 217-302.

72. *Metamorphosis Goliae episcopi*. Ed. Thomas Wright. *Latin Poems commonly attributed to Walter Mapes*. London, 1841, pp. 21-30.

73. ———. Ed. R.B.C. Huygens. "Mitteilungen aus Handschriften." *Studi medievali* 3 (1962), pp. 764-72.

74. *Ordo artium*. Ed. Ludwig Gompf. *Mittellateinische Jahrbuch* 3 (1966), pp. 94-128.

75. "Parce continuis." Ed. F.J.E. Raby, "*Amor* and *Amicitia*: a Medieval Poem." *Speculum* 40 (1965), 599-610.

76. ———. Ed. Peter Dronke. *Medieval Latin and the Rise of European Love-Lyric* (see below, no. 111). II, 341-52.

77. ———. Ed. Brian Stock. "*Parce continuis*: Some Textual and Interpretative Notes." *Medieval Studies* 31 (1969), 164-73.

Secondary Sources

78. Adler, Alfred. "Eneas and Lavine: *Puer et Puella Senes*." *Romanische Forschungen* 71 (1959), pp. 73-91.

79. ———. "The *Roman de Thebes*, a 'Consolatio Philosophiae.'" *Romanische Forschungen* 72 (1960), pp. 257-76.

80. Alfonsi, Luigi. "Storia interiore e storia cosmica nella 'Consolatio' boeziana." *Convivium* 23 (1955), 513-21.

81. d'Alverny, Marie-Thérèse. "Alain de Lille et la *Theologia*." In *L'homme devant Dieu: Mélanges offerts au Père Henri de Lubac*. 3 vols. Paris, 1964. II, 111-28.

82. ———. "Le cosmos symbolique du xiie siècle." *Archives d'histoire doctrinale et littéraire du moyen âge* 28 (1953), pp. 31-81.

83. ———. "La Sagesse et ses sept filles." *Mélanges F. Grat.* 2 vols. Paris, 1946. I, 245-78. See also above, no. 11.

84. Baron, Roger. *Études sur Hugues de St.-Victor.* Paris, 1963.

85. ———. *Science et sagesse chez Hugues de St.-Victor.* Paris, 1957.

86. ———. "La situation de l'homme d'après Hugues de St.-Victor." In *L'homme et son destin: Actes du Premier Congrès International de Philosophie Médiévale,* 1958. Paris and Louvain, 1960, pp. 431-36.

87. Battaglia, Salvatore. "La tradizione di Ovidio nel Medioevo." *Filologia romanza* 6 (1959), pp. 185-224.

88. Bennett, J.A.W. *The Parlement of Foules.* Oxford, 1957.

89. Bezzola, Reto R. *Les origines et la formation de la littérature courtoise en occident.* 3 vols. in 4. Paris, 1944–63. (*Bibliothèque de l'École des Hautes Études,* fascs. 286, 313, 319, 320.)

90. Bliemetzrieder, Franz. *Adelhard von Bath.* Munich, 1935.

91. Bolgar, R. R. *The Classical Heritage and Its Beneficiaries,* Cambridge, 1954.

92. Brandt, W. J. *The Shape of Medieval History.* New Haven, 1966.

93. de Bruyne, Edgar. *Études d'esthétique médiévale.* 3 vols. Bruges, 1946. (Rijksuniversiteit te Gent, *Werken Uitgegeven door de Faculteit van de Wijsbegeerte en Letteren,* Afl. 97-99.)

94. Chenu, M. D. "La décadence de l'allégorization." In *L'homme devant Dieu* (see above, no. 81), II, 129-35.

95. ———. *Introduction à l'étude de S. Thomas d'Aquin.* Paris and Montreal, 1950.

96. ———. "Involucrum: le mythe selon les théologiens médiévaux." *Archives d'histoire doctrinale et littéraire du moyen âge* 30 (1955), pp. 75-79.

97. ———. *La théologie au douzième siècle.* Paris, 1957.

97a. ———. *Nature, Man and Society in the Twelfth Century.* Tr. Jerome Taylor and L. K. Little. Chicago, 1968. (Selected chapters from *La théologie au douzième siècle.*)

98. Cilento, Vincenzo. *Medioevo monastico e scolastico.* Milan, 1961.

99. Ciotti, Andrea. "Alano e Dante." *Convivium* 28 (1960), 257-88.

100. Clagett, Marshall; Post, Gaines; Reynolds, Robert. Eds. *Twelfth-Century Europe and the Foundations of Modern Society.* Madison, 1961.

101. Clerval, J. A. *Les écoles de Chartres au moyen âge.* Chartres, 1895.

102. Courcelle, Pierre. "Étude critique sur les commentaires de la Consolation de Boèce (ixe-xve siècles)." *Archives d'histoire doctrinale et littéraire du moyen âge* 12 (1939), pp. 5-140.

103. Courcelle, Pierre. *Les lettres grecques en occident. De Macrobe à Cassiodore.* Paris, 1943. (*Bibliothèque des Écoles Français d'Athènes et de Rome*, fasc. 159.)

104. Curtius, E. R. *European Literature and the Latin Middle Ages.* Tr. Willard Trask, New York, 1953.

105. Damon, Phillip. "The Preconium Augustini of Godfrey of St. Victor." *Medieval Studies* 22 (1960), 92-107.

106. Delhaye, Philippe. " 'Grammatica' et 'ethica' au xiiᵉ siècle." *Recherches de théologie ancienne et médiévale* 25 (1958), pp. 59-110.

107. ———. *Le Microcosmos de Godefroy de St.-Victor: Étude théologique.* Lille, 1951.

108. Donovan, Mortimer J. "Priscian and the Obscurity of the Ancients." *Speculum* 36 (1961), 75-80.

109. Dronke, Peter. "L'amor che move il sole e l'altre stelle." *Studi medievali* 6 (1965), pp. 389-422.

110. ———. "Boethius, Alanus and Dante." *Romanische Forschungen* 78 (1968), pp. 119-25.

111. ———. *Medieval Latin and the Rise of European Love-Lyric.* 2 vols. Oxford, 1965.

112. ———. *The Medieval Lyric.* London, 1968.

113. ———. "The Return of Euridice." *Classica et Medievalia* 23 (1962), pp. 198-212.

114. Faral, Edmond. *Les arts poétiques du xiiᵉ et du xiiiᵉ siècles.* Paris, 1923. (*Bibliothèque de l'École des Hautes Études*, fasc. 238.)

115. ———. "Le manuscrit 511 du 'Hunterian Museum' de Glasgow." *Studi medievali* 9 (1936), pp. 18-119.

116. ———. *Recherches sur les sources latines des contes et romans courtois.* Paris, 1913.

117. Fleming, John V. The *Roman de la Rose.* Princeton, 1969.

118. Frappier, Jean. *Chrétien de Troyes.* Paris, 1957.

119. ———. "Vues sur les conceptions courtoises dans les littératures d'oc et d'oïl au xiiᵉ siècle." *Cahiers de civilization médiévale* 2 (1959), pp. 135-56.

120. Freccero, John. "Dante's Firm Foot and the Journey without a Guide." *Harvard Theological Review* 52 (1959), 246-81.

121. ———. "Dante's Pilgrim in a Gyre." *Publications of the Modern Language Association* 76 (1961), pp. 168-81.

122. ———. "The Final Image: *Paradiso* xxxiii.144." *Modern Language Notes* 79 (1964), 14-27.

123. Gandillac, Maurice de. "Le platonisme au xiiᵉ et au xiiiᵉ siècles." In *Association Guillaume Budé. Congrès de Tours et de Poitiers*, 1953. Paris, 1954, pp. 266-85.

124. Garin, Eugenio. *Medioevo e Rinascimento*. Bari, 1954.
125. ———. *Studi sul platonismo medievale*. Florence, 1958.
126. Gilson, Étienne. "La cosmogonie de Bernardus Silvestris." *Archives d'histoire doctrinale et littéraire du moyen âge* 3 (1928), pp. 5-24.
127. ———. *Heloise and Abelard*. Tr. L. K. Shook. Ann Arbor, 1960.
128. ———. "Le platonisme de Bernard de Chartres." *Revue néoscolastique* 25 (1923), pp. 5-19.
129. Green, Richard H. "Alan of Lille's *Anticlaudianus*: Ascensus mentis ad Deum." *Annuale medievale* 8 (1967), pp. 3-16.
130. ———. "Alan of Lille's *De planctu naturae*." *Speculum* 31 (1956), 649-74.
131. Gregory, Tullio. *Anima mundi. La filosofia di Guglielmo di Conches e la Scuola di Chartres*. Florence, 1955.
132. ———. *Platonismo medievale: studi e ricerche*. Rome, 1958.
133. Grillo, Peter R. "The Courtly Background of the Roman d'Eneas." *Neuphilologische Mitteilungen* 69 (1968), pp. 688-702.
134. Gunn, A.M.F. *The Mirror of Love: A Reinterpretation of the Romance of the Rose*. Lubbock, Texas, 1952.
135. Györy, Jean. "Le cosmos, un songe." *Annales Universitatis Scientiarum Budapestensis: Sectio Philologica* 4 (1963), pp. 87-110.
136. Haller, Robert H. "The *Altercatio Phyllidis et Florae* as an Ovidian Satire." *Medieval Studies* 30 (1968), 123-34.
137. Häring, N. M. "The Creation and Creator of the World according to Thierry of Chartres and Clarenbaldus of Arras." *Archives d'histoire doctrinale et littéraire du moyen âge* 30 (1955), pp. 137-216.
138. Haskins, Charles H. *The Renaissance of the Twelfth Century*. Cambridge, Mass., 1927.
139. ———. *Studies in the History of Medieval Science*. Cambridge, Mass., 1927.
140. Hatinguais, Jacqueline. "Points de vue sur la volonté et le jugement dans l'oeuvre d'un humaniste chartrain." In *L'homme et son destin* (see above, no. 86), pp. 417-29.
141. Hill, Thomas D. "La Vieille's Digression on Free Love." *Romance Notes* 8 (1966), 113-15.
142. Huizinga, Johan. "Über die Verknupfung des Poetischen mit dem Theologischen bei Alanus de Insulis." In *Mededeelingen der Koninklijke Akademie van Wetenschappen*. Amsterdam 74B, no. 6, 1932. (Reprinted in Huizinga's *Verzamelde Werken*, Amsterdam, 1949, IV.)
143. Huygens, R.B.C. "Guillaume de Tyr étudiant." *Latomus* 21 (1962), pp. 811-29.

144. Javelet, Robert. "Image de Dieu et nature au xiie siècle." *La filoso-fia della natura nel Medioevo: Atti del Terzo Congresso Internazionale di Filosofia Medievale 1964.* Milan, 1966, pp. 286-96.

145. Jeauneau, Edouard. "Macrobe, source du platonisme chartrain." *Studi medievali* 1 (1960), pp. 3-24.

146. ———. "Notes sur l'École de Chartres." *Studi medievali* 5 (1964), pp. 821-65.

147. ———. "L'usage de la notion d'integumentum à travers les gloses de Guillaume de Conches." *Archives d'histoire doctrinale et littéraire du moyen âge* 32 (1957), pp. 35-100. See also above, no. 41.

148. Jolivet, Jean. "Éléments du concept de nature chez Abélard." *La filosofia della natura nel Medioevo* (see above, no. 144), pp. 297-304.

149. Kelly, Douglas. "Courtly Love in Perspective: The Hierarchy of Love in Andreas Capellanus." *Traditio* 24 (1968), 119-47.

150. Klibansky, Raymond. "Plato's Parmenides in the Middle Ages." *Medieval and Renaissance Studies* 1 (1941–43), pp. 281-330.

151. Krayer, Rudolf. *Frauenlob und die Natur-Allegorese: Motivge-schichtliche Unterschungen.* Heidelberg, 1960. (*Germanische Bibliothek*, Reihe 3.)

152. Langlois, C.-V. *La conaissance de la nature et du monde au moyen âge.* Paris, 1911.

153. Laurie, Helen R. " 'Eneas' and the Doctrine of Courtly Love." *Modern Language Review* 64 (1969), 283-94.

154. Leclercq, Jean. *The Love of Letters and the Desire for God.* Tr. Catherine Misrahi. New York, 1961.

155. Le Goff, Jacques. *Les intellectuels au moyen âge.* Paris, 1957.

156. Leonardi, Claudio. "Nota introduttiva per un'indagine sulla fortuna di Marziano Capella nel Medioevo." *Bulletino dell' Istituto Storico Italiano per il Medioevo* 67 (1955), pp. 265-88.

157. Lewis, C. S. *The Allegory of Love.* Oxford, 1936.

158. ———. *The Discarded Image.* Cambridge, 1964.

159. Liebeschütz, Hans. "Kosmologische Motive in der Bildungswelt der Fruhscholastik." *Vorträge der Bibliothek Warburg*, 1923-24 (1926), pp. 87-144.

160. ———. *Medieval Humanism in the Life and Writings of John of Salisbury.* London, 1951.

161. Lubac, Henri de. *Exégèse médiévale.* 2 vols. in 4. Paris, 1959–64.

162. MacKinney, Loren. *Bishop Fulbert and Education at the School of Chartres.* Notre Dame, Indiana, 1958.

163. Marco, M. de. "Un nuovo codice del commento di Bernardo Silvestre all'Eneide." *Aevum* 28 (1954), pp. 178-83.

164. Mâle, Emile. *Religious Art in France: XIII Century*. Tr. Dora Nussey. London, 1913.

165. McKeon, Richard. "Medicine and Philosophy in the Eleventh and Twelfth Centuries: The Problem of Elements." *The Thomist* 24 (1961), 211-56.

166. ———. "Poetry and Philosophy in the Twelfth Century: The Renaissance of Rhetoric." *Modern Philology* 43 (1945-46), 217-34. (Reprinted in *Critics and Criticism, Ancient and Modern*. Ed. R. S. Crane. Chicago, 1952, pp. 297-318.)

167. Munari, Franco. "Tradition und Originalität in der lateinischen Dichtung des XII Jahrhunderts." *Romanische Forschungen* 69 (1957), pp. 305-31.

168. Muscatine, Charles. *Chaucer and the French Tradition*. Berkeley, 1956.

169. Nuchelmans, Gabriel. "Philologie et son mariage avec Mercure jusqu'à la fin du xiie siècle." *Latomus* 16 (1957), pp. 84-100.

170. Padoan, Giorgio. "Tradizione e fortuna del commento all' *Eneide* di Bernardo Silvestre." *Italia medioevale e umanistica* 3 (1960), pp. 227-40.

171. Paetow, L. J. *The Arts Course in Medieval Universities*. Urbana, 1910. (University of Illinois Studies 3, No. 7.)

172. Paré, G. M.; Brunet, A.; and Tremblay, P. *La Renaissance du douzième siècle. Les écoles et l'ensignement*. Paris and Ottawa, 1933.

173. Parent, J. M. *La doctrine de la création dans l'École de Chartres*. Paris and Ottawa, 1938.

174. Pollman, Leo. *Chrétien von Troyes und der Conte del Graal*. Tübingen, 1965. (*Beihefte zur Zeitschrift für romanische Philologie*, Hft. 110.)

175. ———. *Das Epos in den romanischen Literaturen*. Stuttgart, 1966.

176. Poole, R. L. "The Masters of the Schools at Paris and Chartres in John of Salisbury's Time." *English Historical Review* 35 (1920), 321-42.

177. Quain, E. A. "The Medieval Accessus ad auctores." *Traditio* 3 (1945), 215-64.

178. Raby, F.J.E. *Secular Latin Poetry*. 2nd edn. 2 vols. Oxford, 1957. See also above, no. 75.

179. Rathbone, Eleanor. "Master Alberic of London, 'Mythographus Tertius Vaticanus.'" *Medieval and Renaissance Studies* 1 (1941–43), pp. 35-38.

180. Raynaud de Lage, Guy. *Alain de Lille, poète du xiie siècle*. Paris and Montreal, 1951.

181. Robertson, D. W. "Marie de France, *Lais*, Prologue, 13-16." *Modern Language Notes* 64 (1949), 336-38.

182. ———. *A Preface to Chaucer*. Princeton, 1962.

183. Salmon, Paul. "Über den Beitrag des grammatischen Unterrichts zur Poetik des Mittelalters." *Archiv für das Studium der neueren Sprachen* 199 (1963), pp. 65-84.

184. Silverstein, Theodore. "Andreas, Plato and the Arabs: Remarks on Some Recent Accounts of Courtly Love." *Modern Philology* 47 (1949-50), 117-26.

185. ———. "The Fabulous Cosmogony of Bernardus Silvestris." *Modern Philology* 46 (1948-49), 92-116.

186. ———. "Guillaume de Conches and Nemesius of Emessa: On the Sources of the 'New Science' of the Twelfth Century." In *Harry Austryn Wolfson Jubilee Volumes*, 3 vols. Jerusalem, 1965. II, 719-34. See also above, no. 71.

187. Skimina, Stanislaus. "De Bernardo Silvestre Vergilii interprete." In *Commentationes Vergilianae*. Cracow, 1930, pp. 206-37.

188. Smalley, Beryl. *The Study of the Bible in the Middle Ages*, 2nd edn. Oxford, 1952.

189. Southern, R. W. *The Making of the Middle Ages*. New Haven, 1953.

190. ———. *Medieval Humanism and Other Studies*. Oxford, 1970.

191. Spicq, C. *Esquisse d'une histoire de l'exégèse latine au moyen âge*. Paris, 1943.

192. Spitzer, Leo, "The Prologue to the *Lais* of Marie de France and Medieval Poetics." *Modern Philology* 41 (1943-44), 96-102.

193. Stahl, W. H. "To a Better Understanding of Martianus Capella." *Speculum* 40 (1965), 102-15.

194. Stock, Brian. See above, no. 77.

195. Strecker, Karl. "Kritisches zu mittellateinischen Texten." *Zeitschrift für deutsches Altertum* 63 (1926), pp. 103-27.

196. ———. "Die Metamorphosis Goliae und das Streitgedicht Phyllis und Flora." *Zeitschrift für deutsches Altertum* 50 (1927), p. 180.

197. Tavani, Giuseppe. "Il dibattito sul chierico e il cavaliere nella tradizione mediolatina e volgare." *Romanistisches Jahrbuch* 15 (1964), pp. 51-84.

198. Thorndike, Lynn. *A History of Magic and Experimental Science*. 8 vols. New York, 1923–58.

199. Tuve, Rosemond, *Allegorical Imagery: Some Medieval Books and Their Posterity*. Princeton, 1966.

200. Van Winden, J.C.M. *Calcidius on Matter: His Doctrine and Sources*. Leiden, 1959.

201. Vernet, André. "Une épitaphe inédite de Thierry de Chartres." *Recueil de Travaux offert à M. Clovis Brunel.* 2 vols. Paris, 1955. II, 660-70.

202. Vinaver, Eugene. "From Epic to Romance." *Bulletin of the John Rylands Library, Manchester* 46 (1963-64), 476-503.

203. Viscardi, Antonio. "Le origine della letteratura cortese." *Zeitschrift für romanische Philologie* 78 (1962), pp. 269-91.

204. Von den Steinen, Wolfram. "Les sujets d'inspiration chez les poètes latins du xiie siècle." *Cahiers de civilization médiévale* 9 (1966), pp. 165-75, 363-83.

205. Von Simson, Otto. *The Gothic Cathedral.* 2nd edn. New York, 1962.

206. Wedel, Theodore. *The Medieval Attitude toward Astrology.* New Haven, 1920. (Yale Studies in English, No. 60.)

207. Wetherbee, Winthrop. "The Function of Poetry in the *De planctu naturae* of Alain de Lille." *Traditio* 25 (1969), 87-126.

208. ———. "The Literal and the Allegorical: Jean de Meun and the *De planctu naturae*." *Medieval Studies* 33 (1971), 264-91.

209. Wittig, Joseph S. "The Aeneas-Dido Allusion in Chrétien's *Erec et Enide*." *Comparative Literature* 22 (1970), 237-53.

210. Yates, Frances. *Giordano Bruno and the Hermetic Tradition.* London, 1964.

211. Zumthor, Paul. *Langue et techniques poétiques à l'époque romane.* Paris, 1963.

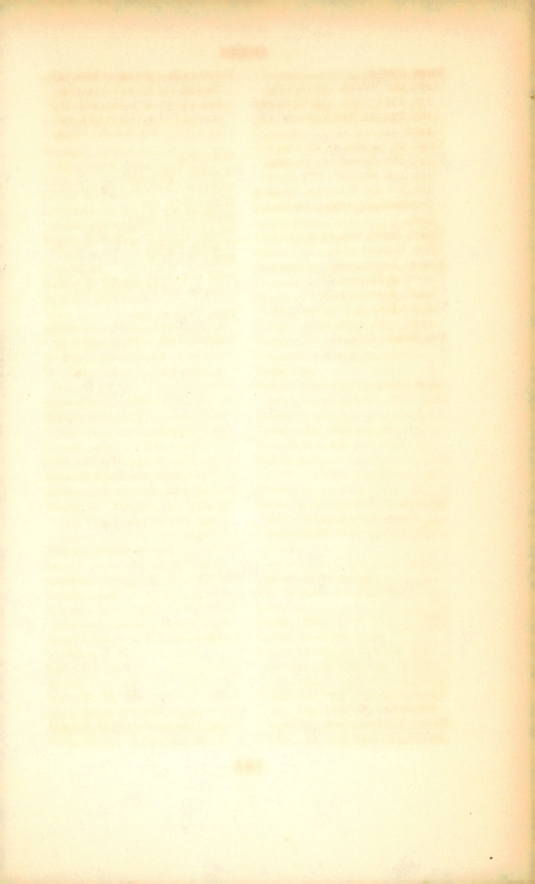